GW00733364

CHANAKYA'S VIEW

By the same author
Adi Shankaracharya: Hinduism's Greatest Thinker

CHANAKYA'S VIEW:
Understanding India in Transition

Pavan K. Varma

First published by Westland Publications Private Limited in 2019
Ist Floor, A Block, East Wing, Plot No. 40, SP Info City, Dr MGR Salai,
Perungudi, Kandanchavadi, Chennai 600096

Westland and the Westland logo are the trademarks of Westland Publications Private
Limited, or its affiliates.

Copyright © Pavan K. Varma, 2019

ISBN: 9789388689526
10 9 8 7 6 5 4 3 2 1

All rights reserved
Typeset by Ram Das Lal, New Delhi, NCR
Printed at Thomson Press (India) Ltd

No part of this book may be reproduced, or stored in a retrieval system, or transmitted
in any form or by any means, electronic, mechanical, photocopying, recording, or
otherwise, without express written permission of the publisher.

In tribute to Chanakya, one of the greatest strategist and thinkers the world has seen, and whose intellectual vision must continue to inspire us.

CONTENTS

POLITICS

VIEWPOINT

DIPLOMACY

ACKNOWLEDGEMENTS

These columns have been written over a period of six years. During this phase, I have, in tandem with my party, the JD (U), been on many sides of the political fence. However, it has been my attempt to write on issues as objectively as possible, and to speak truth to power as my conscience dictates. In this journey, I have benefitted greatly from interactions with many people, too numerous to recount, but all important in their own way, to whom I would like to record my deep gratitude.

I am grateful to *The Asian Age* and *Deccan Chronicle* which, through my fortnightly columns, provided me a valuable platform to express my views. In spite of often exceptionally pressing other engagements, I have written these columns without a single break. My deep gratitude is due to my editor, Kaushik Mitter, who has walked the journey with me in the writing of these columns.

I am indebted to my publisher, Westland, for publishing this book, and for the help and support its remarkable team of dedicated professionals provided in its making. In particular, I would like to record my genuine indebtedness to my editor, Sudha Sadhanand, who not only unfailingly gave valuable advice and suggestions, but also ensured, often through persuasive disciplining tactics, my compliance in meeting deadlines.

ACKNOWLEDGEMENTS

My personal secretary, Manish Tiwari, was always available to hold my hand, and provide valuable research and organisational inputs. A big thank you to him.

Finally, like for all my other books, this book too would not have been possible but for the unstinting support of my family, and above all, my wife, Renuka. Her support, patience, advice and encouragement is something I can never be too grateful for.

INTRODUCTION

*I*ndia is a young nation, but an ancient civilisation. The antiquity of our civilisation, its continuity, diversity, assimilation, and peaks of refinement, will always remain the background to the discourse of our young Republic. There are lessons from the past for everything that is unfolding today. Our present and our past are interlinked, as is inevitable in a nation that is the fruition of such a long civilisational journey.

Chanakya was a towering icon of our past. He lived some 2,300 years ago, in the fourth century BCE, and some two millennium before Machiavelli, and wrote one of the world's most incisive treatises on statecraft, the *Arthashastra*. In addition, in the course of one lifetime, he groomed a king, deposed another, helped to throw out the mighty Greeks, united a fractious territory, put his nominee on the throne of Magadha, and helped consolidate a great empire—the Maurya empire—extending from the western passes adjoining Afghanistan to the Bay of Bengal, and southern India, arguably the first true empire in India's history.

Why do we need to remember Chanakya when we ruminate on some of the developments of our modern democracy? To answer this question, we must understand the qualities that made Chanakya the beacon in whose arc light we need to judge our actions even today. First and foremost, Chanakya had the ability to speak truth to power, unerringly, without fear or favour, and with courage of conviction. This trait is absolutely essential for our nation, for unless there is the freedom to express contrarian points of view, democracy itself will shrivel. Secondly, he had a clear understanding of human behaviour, which he was willing to articulate without being a prisoner of ideological inflexibility, and without devaluing idealism itself. Thirdly, he believed in the importance of leadership that is capable of clear decision-making, but benefitting too from what critics have to say. Fourthly, he never lost sight of the fact that all politics must work for the overall good of the people. If this central tenet is ignored, no Constitution, however high-minded, is worthwhile. Fifthly, he considered economic prosperity the backbone of a nation's strength. If the treasury is empty, all promises are mere slogans and all pretensions to power are so much hot air. Sixthly, he believed in analysing systems. According to him, this required an open mind, and a true understanding of alternative opinions before a final decision is taken. Seventhly, he believed that systems must be just, and those who threaten the rule of law must be adequately punished. And finally, he laid great stress on a harmonious society, which is the real strength of a nation, for if a country is at war with itself, it can never be strong enough to face an external enemy.

Chanakya's legacy, of clear thinking while welcoming debate and discussion, is an inherent part of our cumulative civilisational heritage too. Debate, or civilised *samvad* and *shastrartha*, not diktat or blind fanaticism, has been the hallmark of our profound inheritance. This becomes clear from the foundational texts of Hinduism. The Upanishads were a lofty dialogue, between a guru and pupil. The Bhagavad Gita was a dialogue between Arjuna and Lord Krishna. The *Brahma Sutras* welcomed an opponent's point of view. Thousands of years ago, our sages emphasised the importance of an eclectic vision. *Ekam satya vipraha bahuda vadanti:* there in one truth, the wise call it by different names, was a verity pronounced by the Upanishads. It was our seers who benevolently proclaimed: *Anno bhadra kratvoyantu vishwatah:* let noble thoughts come to us from all corners of the world. Again, it was our saints who said: *Udar charitanam, vasudhaiva kutumbukam:* for the broad-minded, the entire world is their family.

In the *Arthashastra,* Chanakya puts down points of views opposed to his line of thought. In fact, the strength of his lucid convictions was based on the acceptance of the fact that there could be different ways of looking at the same issue. This openness is what characterised the debates of Adi Shankaracharya too, arguably Hinduism's greatest thinker. In the eighth century CE, he had a shastrartha with another highly learned scholar, Mandana Mishra. The two were resolutely opposed to each other's philosophical point of view. Shankara believed in the *jnana marga,* or the path of knowledge. Mandana believed in *karmakanda,* or the path of action. Yet, they could sit down in a civilised manner and debate their differences with complete respect for each other. Much later, in the medieval period, the great Mughal emperor, Akbar, could convene a gathering of thinkers with varying points of view to facilitate debate in his forum, the *Dīn-i Ilāhī.* During our freedom struggle too, iconic leaders like Jawaharlal Nehru, Sardar Patel and Netaji Subhas Chandra Bose—to name just a few—could fearlessly disagree with each other and with the father of the nation, Mahatma Gandhi.

The collection of columns in this book, written for *The Asian Age* and *Deccan Chronicle,* and other newspapers nationwide, under the title 'Chanakya's View', draw their inspiration from the world view of this great strategist and visionary, and the combined eclectic heritage of which both he and we are a part. They have been penned in the best traditions of *vimarsha,* or reflection, and *atma chintan,* or self-introspection, that has been our remarkable tradition. It is not necessary for the reader to agree with the point of view espoused. But, it is important for the reader to understand that for any issue, there can be different points of view. This freedom of expression is not only guaranteed to us by our Constitution, but by our history.

Indeed, the very nature of India demands that we eschew the straitjacket of imposed uniformity, and revel in the nuances of arguments, variations in assessments, the sophistication of informed debate, and the imperative need of a multi-dimensional lens that provides a wide-angle to the complexities of every situation. This is, quite simply put, because India is multi-dimensional. As a nation in transition, it has something of everything, a kaleidoscope of many shades and colours, a vibrantly plural, multicultural and composite society, not a monochromatic uniformity that only encourages one strand of thought. We have the very rich, and we have the very poor. The very rich are a handful, the very poor too numerous. In between we have a very large, pan-Indian middle-class. There is great diversity, manifested in our many languages, culinary choices, sartorial variations, topographical contrasts, and regional identities. We are the cradle too of four of the world's great religions—Hinduism, Buddhism, Jainism and Sikhism. The adherents of another great religion, Islam, are also part of us, and in very great numbers, making India a country with the third largest number of Muslims in the world. People of different faiths, and all these competing diversities co-exist in a vast and heaving aspirational struggle for upward mobility. This nation is on the move in one of the greatest transitions witnessed by any country.

There are great challenges ahead in this transition. We have the largest number of the abjectly poor in the world. We may be producing among the largest number of doctors and engineers, but we still have the largest number of people who cannot read or write. Around a small island of great affluence, hunger still stalks our land. In fact, there are more malnutritioned children in India than even in sub-Saharan Africa. There is a shortage of the very basics even in the midst of economic progress. Vast swathes of our population do not have access to assured electricity or potable water. Essential services like a good education and basic health care are scarce. Manufacturing has yet to reach its optimum level, and the agricultural sector languishes with one of the lowest rates of growth. We may be among the youngest nations in the world—sixty-five per cent of our population is below the age of thirty-five—but this demographic dividend counts for little if we cannot ensure that the army of the 'educated' young who join the workforce every day are employable and will get jobs.

In addition, we face major concerns on the security front. India is located in one of the most hostile nuclear regions of the world. We have two implacably hostile neighbours—China and Pakistan. Pakistan consistently follows a policy of explosive aggression and tactical appeasement against us, and uses terrorism as a State policy to further its goals.

Apart from external terrorism, we have homegrown terrorism, of which the Naxals are the most visible face. China's policy is clear-cut in seeking to contain India even if it continues to engage with us. We have 4,057 kilometres of a disputed Line of Actual Control (LAC) with China; a 778 kilometre Line of Control (LoC) with Pakistan; a total of 15,106 kilometres of international borders with seven countries; and, a 7,516-kilometre-long vulnerable coastline. Given these facts, our foreign policy, Intelligence and defence establishments have an onerous responsibility, and our approach to security cannot afford to be sloppy. It is essential for us to have a strategic doctrine that can anticipate, preempt, plan and strike, as the occasion demands, without being reactive, ad-hoc, unplanned and lacking in focus.

Indeed, diplomacy, defence and security were areas of very special concern for Chanakya. That is why he articulated the four tools of *sama*, *dama*, *danda*, *bheda*—reconciliation, inducement, deterrent action, and subversion—and the lesser known asana, or the strategic art of deliberately sitting on the fence. Each tactic had a special use. The need for us to ponder over his unsentimental legacy in this specific field, and to have a thoroughly revamped and effective security doctrine, and the infrastructure required to support it, is self-evident.

The collection of writings in this book—written over different periods of time over the last few years—are a contemplation, a meditation, on our large and diverse nation in transition, and the challenges that it faces and must deal with. It is divided into different sections to facilitate coherent reading, and collectively represents a point of view, which is—from my point of view—in the best traditions of an argumentative democracy, where ideas proliferate, and the freedom of expression is guaranteed. While most of the columns deal with issues, some also focus on personalities, simply because these personalities are also part of the larger canvas of ideas that constitute our great nation.

It is my hope that this book will ignite discussion and deliberation in a bipartisan spirit, keeping the overall good of our motherland in mind, for the interests of the nation must come first and last. If it succeeds in provoking vimarsha and *charcha*—reflection and debate—then I would be amply rewarded. If Chanakya was alive today, he would, I am sure, have welcomed this reflection and debate too.

PAVAN K. VARMA
New Delhi, May 2019

THIS IS NOT INDIA

A BALANCE SHEET FOR THE
INDIA OF TODAY

*W*inston Churchill once famously said that to say that India is a nation is to say the equator is one! For people like him, who projected the deliberately misguided hubris that the British created India and that but for their continued presence, India would not survive, the completion of sixty-nine years of the Republic is a fitting riposte. Our young Republic has not only survived, but has proved long ago that its survival is beyond doubt. We may be a young republic, but we are an ancient culture. When nationhood is underpinned by a strong and verifiable civilisational unity, the result is usually invincible.

Nation-building is a long and arduous process. That is why milestones of success should be followed by a stretch of introspection. There is much that we have achieved, but much more also needs to be done. As a vigilant nation, we should, even in such moments of legitimate celebration, draw up balance sheets that audit successes against failures, hits versus misses, achievement versus inadequacy.

The list of our successes is impressive. Unlike most countries that gained independence in the last century, we began as a democracy and have managed to remain the largest democracy in the world.

Given the incorrigibly hierarchical and unequal social system we inherited—and still grapple with—this is no mean achievement and has provided a new sense of empowerment to the hitherto marginalised. We have also reinforced the territorial unity and integrity of the State. It may surprise many that since 1947, although there have been many insurgencies against the Republic, not a single one has succeeded. Our scientists and doctors and engineers have done us proud. Our armed forces have enabled us to hold our head high. And, in many sectors of the economy, we have made real breakthroughs, such as the green and white revolutions and the major expansion of the IT sector.

As against these achievements—and many more can be listed—there still remain very major areas of concern. The first is rampant inequality. India may be the world's largest democracy, but we still have the largest number of the abjectly poor in the world. We also still have the largest number of those who cannot read or write, and even worse, more malnutritioned children than sub-Saharan Africa. It is true that over the last several decades, large numbers have been redeemed from below the poverty line, but those condemned to unspeakable poverty are still far too many to sustain the claim that India is a rising economic superpower.

The pervasive persistence of poverty has institutional reasons. Agriculture still employs over sixty per cent of our people. But, after the initial green revolution, the agricultural sector has largely languished. This is reflected in the lopsided nature of our GDP basket, where the service sector—employing the least number of people—contributes the most, with manufacturing a distant second and agriculture at the very bottom. If agricultural productivity and incomes do not rise, the vast majority of our people will remain locked in a cycle of poverty, especially since labour-intensive manufacturing industries that can provide jobs outside agriculture have also grown far below expectation.

4

The standards of public health and education need urgent attention. Government deliverables in these two areas are abysmal. The public school system is in shambles, leading to a mushrooming of sub-standard private schools and an overall structure where, apart from some minuscule pockets of excellence, the young are being educated with far below-average levels of skills and training. Jobs are woefully scarce, and those that are there are faced with an army of the 'educated' young who, given their skill levels, are essentially unemployable.

Our democracy is vibrant but in need of urgent reform. The biggest malaise is the continued nexus between unaccounted money and politics. Indeed, this is the *beej*, the very seed of corruption in the country. For decades now, the Election Commission has proposed a series of reforms—and more powers to proceed against offenders—but the political class has sat on these proposals and done nothing. The recent attempt to allow anonymous donors to contribute to political parties through bonds is hardly the answer to the need for foundational reform in this vital area, where every rupee collected by a party must be accounted for.

New dangers have also emerged. The first is the emergence of ultra-Right forces of exclusion that are threatening the plural and composite fabric of our nation. There is every reason to be proud of being a Hindu, but there is no reason to assert that India is exclusively a Hindu nation. Such an assertion deliberately ignores the fact that many faiths have always lived and prospered in India, and while appeasement of any one is wrong, each of the great religions that exist in our country need to be given respect. Allied to this religious aggression is a virulent form of ultra-nationalism that looks upon all dissent as anti-national and is willing to resort to violence to enforce such a brittle point of view. In fact, the impunity with which certain groups, like the Karni Sena, have taken the law in their own hands—even stoning a bus full of school children in Gurugram—cannot happen without the complicity at some level of the state authorities. The resultant social instability that such forces are creating militates directly against our economic ambitions, because internal peace and harmony are essential, not only for India to be an attractive global investment destination but also for the development agenda that we hope to implement.

This balance sheet between the plusses and minuses can be much longer. But, as we celebrate the completion of sixty-nine years as a Republic, there is enough reason to celebrate, just as there is enough cause to introspect. Nations that endure and prosper cannot become victims of only euphoria. They must be also willing to see what is wrong, even as they pay tribute to so much in our history as a young nation, that is right.

(This article was originally published on 28 January 2018)

THE REPUBLIC OF 'HURT'

When we adopted our Constitution in 1950 and became a Republic, our heart was in the right place. But somewhere, this 'heart' has transmuted itself to 'hurt'. Anyone and everyone has assumed that they have the right to be hurt about what anyone or everyone is doing! If not vigilant, we are fast becoming the Republic of Hurt Feelings, simply on the assumption that what an individual or a group does not like entitles them, under the misuse of the freedoms guaranteed by the Constitution, to protest in any manner that they chose to.

The latest case in this saga of hurt is the song of Priya Prakash Varrier. I must confess that when I saw the clipping of the song from the forthcoming Malayalam film, *Oru Adaar Love*, I was absolutely charmed. It was, to my mind, a captivating enactment of adolescent love, and had just the right mix of sensuality and innocence that anyone who has gone through love or infatuation at that age will vouch for.

The folk song was written as far back as 1978 by a Muslim, P.M.A. Jabbar, and was first sung by another Muslim, Thalassery Rafeeq, in praise of the Prophet and his wife Beevi Khadija. But now, some Muslim organisations have protested that the song 'hurt'

7

their religious sentiments. Where was their 'hurt' for the last three decades, and what has made them suddenly voice it today? What is worse, in order to harass the makers of the film and Priya Varrier, the hurt brigade filed multiple criminal proceedings in Telangana and Maharashtra, but none in Kerala itself! We have to be eternally grateful to the Supreme Court that, on a petition filed by Priya, it has stayed all criminal action or FIRs or private complaints against her, and the film's director and the producer.

Those who claimed that their religious sentiments were hurt by the song, were in reality, a fringe group who believe that on the basis of their own narrowness of thinking and their ossified religious fanaticism, they can use the law with impunity to browbeat creativity and freedom of expression, and make the State hostage to their ridiculous machinations. The SC has given a befitting riposte to their nefarious designs.

But, to become 'hurt' is not only the monopoly of one group of people or religion. You will find the hurt brigade on every side of the national spectrum. Actress Sunny Leone was to participate in a New Year's Eve event on 31 December last year in Bengaluru. But the Karnataka Rakshana Vedike Yuva Sene (KARAVE) announced that an invitation to her would be an 'assault' on the city's culture. The secretary of the KARAVE said that he would have no objections if she attended the programme wearing a sari 'as per Indian culture'. But if she wore anything else, the members of his organisation would commit suicide. For days, they took out rallies and burnt effigies of Leone. Reportedly, the Karnataka police refused to provide the requisite security to the event or the organisers. Finally, the hurt brigade succeeded. The event was cancelled.

The kind of 'morality' outrage that was witnessed in Bengaluru is on display in many parts of the country, including most visibly in UP on 14 February, Valentine's Day. Now, I am not a great votary of

Valentine's Day, nor am I against it. At one level, it's a 'cute' Western import—like so many other things in our lives—and at another, a bit of mindless mimicry. But that is not the question here. For hoodlums to chase young couples because their being together on this occasion is against 'Indian culture' is so absurd that I don't know whether to laugh or cry. Have these lumpen protesters heard of Vatsyayana and know in which period he lived? Are they aware of the Radha–Krishna love lore, and ever read Jayadeva's beautifully erotic rendering of it in the *Gitagovinda*? Do the names of great poets like Chandidasa, Vidyapati, Bihari, Keshavdasa, Mira, Andal sound familiar to them, and are they even remotely informed about the sensual lyricism with which they describe the dalliance between Radha and Krishna? What do they know about the legendary stories of romance between Sohni–Mahiwal, and Laila–Majnu? The 'hurt' of the moral brigade is mostly indirectly proportional to their abysmal ignorance of Indian culture. And, when they strut about using violence and abuse to protect it, they are not protecting 'Indian culture' but reinforcing a Victorian morality that was used by our colonial masters to condemn Indian culture.

The other day, I finally found time to see the film *Padmavat*. I could not for the life of me understand why the Karni Sena was so hysterically hurt about this film. In fact, the film bent backwards to glorify the legacy of Rajput traditions and culture, and there was nothing whatsoever to be hurt about its contents. But no matter. Most of those of this Sena who resorted to threats and violence and abuse to vent their hurt had, amazingly enough, not even seen the film. For months, they held the release of the film hostage to their misplaced sense of hurt, and it was only, once again, when the SC firmly intervened that sanity prevailed.

In a mature democratic Republic, there is room for citizens to have their own opinion and the right to express it. This right is protected by the Constitution. But neither the Constitution nor basic civility gives the right to some to be perennially hurt whenever they so please and believe that they can either manipulate the law to harass those that don't agree with them, or worse, take the law into their own hands to express their 'hurt'. The lawless community of hurt people in our country is proliferating at an alarming pace, and there seems to be no boundaries on what can hurt whom: what one wears, or eats, or drinks, or does to prove one's patriotism. At this rate, what will really be hurt is the freedom of choice and expression that our Republic guarantees to every citizen, and which elected governments, either at the Centre or in the States, are duty bound to protect, not encourage.

(This article was originally published on 25 February 2018)

JINNAH AT ALIGARH
MUSLIM UNIVERSITY

*T*here are two entirely separate issues for consideration in the ongoing unrest at the Aligarh Muslim University (AMU) regarding the portrait of Muhammad Ali Jinnah hanging since 1938 in the student union's office. First, should a portrait of a man who actively worked for the Partition of India, created Pakistan and stoked hatred between Hindus and Muslims be hung in the university? And second, if not, what is the best way to have an earlier wrong rectified?

I say these are separate issues because if you don't make the distinction, you are likely to fall like a ripe apple in the lap of the Hindu Yuva Vahini (HYV) goons who protested against Jinnah's portrait. In fact, Samajwadi Party (SP) MP Praveen Nishad, who just won the Gorakhpur by-elections, did exactly that. Protesting the behaviour of HYV members, he began, on TV, to praise Jinnah, comparing him to Gandhi and Nehru. This was music to the musclemen of the HYV. It was precisely the reaction they wanted. It fulfilled their principal agenda to establish that they were 'nationalists', and those opposing them were anti-national followers of Jinnah, quite deserving to be banished—as they often say to all those who oppose them—to Pakistan.

11

Whether AMU should have a portrait of Jinnah can be debated without unnecessarily glorifying the founder of Pakistan. Some people can argue that this portrait was installed in 1938, when Jinnah was given a life membership of the university's student union. This was prior to his becoming a prominent pawn in the British game of divide and rule, and the proponent of Pakistan. It is also true that until the communal fires were ignited by Jinnah and his ilk, the gentleman was a prominent name among those fighting for India's Independence—a fact acknowledged then by no less a person than Mahatma Gandhi. In fact, even in the midst of the current turmoil in AMU, a BJP minister in UP, Swami Prasad Maurya lauded Jinnah, saying that his contribution to the freedom struggle cannot be ignored. History, even when it deals with people whom we now denigrate, cannot be entirely erased. There is, for instance, a prominent building in Mumbai still called Jinnah House, and a portrait of the Quaid-e-Azam hangs even now in the hallowed precincts of the Mumbai High Court, in recognition of his being one of the leading lawyers of his times. If this is the case, why remove a portrait metaphorically gathering dust since 1938 in AMU?

Equally, however, there can be good reasons for AMU to consider whether the portrait needs to be removed. Whatever Jinnah's earlier contributions may have been, he is, for most Indians—even if not for all historians—the main villain in the movement for the partition of India. In achieving this goal, he spewed communal venom and happily colluded with the British. He is not by any stretch of imagination someone who deserves a place of respect for Indians. As distinguished poet Javed Akhtar tweeted: 'it is a matter of shame that AMU still honours him with a portrait.'

There can, thus, be two ways to look at what the HYV protestors were demanding. But there are no two ways in strongly condemning the manner in which they acted. Consider the facts. On 1 May,

BJP MP Satish Gautam wrote to the vice-chairman of the AMU, asking why a portrait of Jinnah was adorning the walls of AMU. The letter itself cannot be faulted, but what followed certainly can. The very next day, hoodlums of the HYV—an organisation which was allegedly founded by Yogi Adityanath, the chief minister of UP—barged into the AMU campus and clashed with university students, leading to forty-one people being injured—some seriously—of which twenty-eight were students and thirteen policemen. By most accounts, these goons were armed, including with lethal weapons. Most shockingly, eyewitnesses say that the police stood as mute spectators as these thugs ran amuck.

Whatever the merits of the case with regard to the Jinnah portrait, who has given the HYV the licence to take the law into its own hands? Why have its members suddenly made an issue of a portrait installed since 1938? Is the timing entirely coincidental, or is it part of a larger agenda to stoke communal hatred and division? And, even if their cause has legitimacy, why could they not wait until the university provided a reply to the letter sent by BJP MP Satish Gautam? Why has not a single FIR been registered by the police against those who perpetrated this violence? Why has Yogi Adityanath not strongly condemned this hooliganism by members of his own organisation? Has he forgotten that he is now the chief minister of a state, not an activist of an ultra-Right-wing organisation of self-anointed protectors of Hinduism? And, was it a coincidence that the violence was unleashed inside the campus just moments before former Vice President Hamid Ansari was to visit the university?

These are exceptionally important questions. Jinnah may have been 'an enemy of the nation', as deputy chief minister of UP, Keshav Prasad Maurya, indignantly proclaimed. But so are members of organisations like the HYV, if they believe that they have the ordained right to usurp the law and resort to violence against anybody who disagrees with them. There are reports that HYV worthies have stormed into churches in Gorakhpur and elsewhere and disrupted services. In Gurugram in Haryana, Muslims offering namaz this last Friday were stopped by Hindutva outfits that went around the city shouting slogans like 'Jai Shri Ram' and 'Bangladesh *wapas jao*' (Go back to Bangladesh). Jinnah died long ago. But are we seeing the spirit of communal divisiveness that he represented being reincarnated in the behaviour of Right-wing goons in the name of Hinduism, even as authorities mandated to uphold law and order remain mute spectators? What kind of anarchy is this, and where will it lead to? That is the central issue in what is unfolding now at AMU.

(This piece was originally published on 6 May 2018)

THE SHAMEFUL MENACE OF COW LYNCHINGS

I sometimes feel that what is categorically unacceptable is becoming, more and more, par for the course in our Republic. When it first happened, cattle lynching made the news. Now, it seems to happen with such a frequency that the initial shock has dissipated. The event is reported, commented upon, mostly perfunctorily, and life goes on. If we believe that India, apart from being the world's largest democracy, is also one of the oldest and most refined civilisations, such a level of insensitivity questions our credentials on both counts.

Last week, in Godda district of Jharkhand, two men were beaten to death with sticks and stones over alleged cattle theft. Their half-naked bodies were strung out on bamboo poles and paraded through the village by a cheering mob. Both were Muslims. The father of one of the victims said that his son was a bona fide cattle trader. Such incidents have not happened for the first time in Jharkhand. In March 2016, two cattle traders were killed on suspicion and their bodies hung from a tree. In June 2017, Muslims were again the target of cow vigilante violence, and beaten to death.

There have been many other shameful incidents. In UP, in September 2015, Akhlaq Khan was lynched to death by a mob on the suspicion of eating beef. His son was also attacked and beaten to near pulp. In Rajasthan, in April 2017, Pehlu Khan, a dairy farmer, was attacked on the road as he was transporting cattle for sale by a mob of over 200 cow vigilantes. He was lynched to death, even as he kept making the plea that he was innocent. Six others with him were also brutally beaten. Shockingly, in the first instance, the state government charged the victims for 'cruelty to animals!'

The targets of such attacks are not only Muslims. The nation can never forget the visual footage of four Dalits being stripped, tied to a car, flogged and beaten with rods, in Una, Gujarat, in July 2016. They were attacked in this inhuman and vicious manner only on the suspicion that they were peddling beef. The truth is that it is people from this community who are expected to dispose of cattle carcasses and skins when cows die. Such an 'unclean' task is assumed to be their responsibility; but it is precisely for doing what their tormentors would consider below their social status to do, that they were so ruthlessly beaten up, and that too on the unfounded suspicion that they were eating or selling beef.

Why have such incidents continued to proliferate? In August 2016, following the uproar over the Una incident, Prime Minister Modi finally broke his silence and said that cow vigilantism made him angry, and he condemned such actions. That was a welcome indictment. But subsequent incidents beg the question whether the ultra-Right Hindutva followers of the BJP listen to the PM. Statistics reveal that there has been a ninety-seven per cent upsurge in cases of cattle lynching since the BJP came to power in 2014. Surely, this cannot be a coincidence. Studies also reveal that eighty-six per cent of those attacked are Muslims, but as Una so dramatically revealed, Dalits too are fair game. What is even more shocking is that fifty-two per cent of such attacks take place on the basis of rumours. The perpetrators of this dastardly behaviour seem to believe that they have the silent support of the authorities and can get away by taking the law into their own hands. In fact, Christophe Jaffrelot, the noted sociologist argues, that the State has in a certain way 'outsourced' its own bias to such vigilantes, thereby both achieving what it desires and yet claiming to be uninvolved in what is happening.

The question is, what can be done to erase this blot on our civilisational values, and—for those who believe that such gruesome violence is justified in the name of Hinduism—the great legacy of Hinduism itself? In April 2017, the Supreme Court asked six states—Rajasthan, Gujarat, Jharkhand, Maharashtra, UP and Karnataka—to respond to what they propose to do to prevent cow vigilantism. Significantly, five of these six states are ruled by BJP governments. It would be interesting to know what these states have promised to do in response to the court's directive, and even more significantly, why is what they have promised to do not having the desired effect on the ground. In September 2017, the SC instructed that each state should appoint in each district a nodal police officer to take strict action against cow vigilantism. Again, it should be put in the public domain how many states have acted upon this directive: if not, why not, and if so, with what efficacy? In the spirit of the SC directive, it must be revealed how many culprits have been caught, proceeded against under the law, and awarded exemplary punishment.

It is time also to know how many organised vigilante groups are currently in existence. Has the Central government attempted to identify such groups? Have state governments done likewise? According to some estimates, the National Capital Region (NCR) alone has around 200 such groups. Surely, given the impunity with which many members of such groups flaunt their intentions, it will not be difficult for a committed police force backed by the requisite political will to identify the leaders among such criminals, bring them within the ambit of the law, and take preventive action before the next incident of lynching takes place.

The fact of the matter is the requisite political will is lacking. Too many of these perpetrators believe that somewhere, they have the indulgence of their political masters. Far more damagingly, many believe that they are acting in this barbaric manner to 'protect' Hinduism. There can be no bigger disservice to the grandeur of Hinduism than this kind of illiterate claim. Many states have legitimate laws against cow slaughter, and they need to be respected. But no country can have another set of rules for those who believe that they are a law unto themselves, in the belief that they have the benign indulgence of those elected to uphold the law.

(This piece was originally published on 17 June 2018)

NATIONAL SECURITY: NOT
A HOLY COW

*F*rankly, I am stumped. It has become near impossible now to know what is the definition of patriotism, who is a nationalist, who is not, what qualifies one to be called a patriot and what damns one to be labelled an anti-national. In the increasing shrillness—and ignorance—of political abuse, it has become futile to attempt to argue, debate, discuss, ask, listen, question, praise or critique. Each such attempt is immediately put in a slot, where the lid is shut on the message, and the entire focus becomes to vilify the messenger.

This quality of national discourse is nothing short of a disaster for a civilisation-State like India. The foundations of our civilisation, going back to the dawn of time, were based on *moulik soch*, the power of original thought. Our freedom struggle, too, was founded on a highly cerebral basis, where even people on the same side had the freedom to differ, and the opportunity to interrogate and debate. What has happened over the years that, today, the bona fides of anybody who does not immediately conform to one or the other brittle polarities of political discourse, are questioned? In fact, discourse itself is suspect. If you have any doubts in the matter, just watch some of the 'debates' on our leading TV channels.

I want to raise this issue especially in the context of national security. Undoubtedly, this is a sensitive subject. In a situation of war or a declared national crisis, the democratically elected government of the day is fully entitled to take such decisions as it deems appropriate, and all political parties, irrespective of other differences, must unite in solidarity to support such action.

It was in this spirit that the JD (U) was one of the first parties to express support for the surgical strike that took place in September 2016 against Pakistan army/terrorist bases in POK. We placed on record our deep appreciation for the valour, courage and daring of our brave armed forces. And, we did not ask for any proof about whether the surgical strike took place. Such a stand was based on the express recognition of the fact that the government of the day, based on inputs that it receives which are confidential, is best placed to act in the national interest, and it is not appropriate to raise questions merely on the basis of political partisanship in these matters. It is significant that the JD (U) took this measured and responsible position even when, at that time, it was in the Opposition and not a member of the ruling coalition, the NDA.

It was expected of the government that, having announced that a surgical strike had been carried out and congratulated our armed forces for their bravery and courage, it would not seek to derive any political dividends from an act in the national interest, which, by definition, is above political acrimony. It was regrettable too that some political leaders and parties sought proof whether the strike took place. In the face of such gratuitous and misplaced provocation, the correct response of the government should have been not to over-react, and reiterate the points highlighted by the Directorate General of Military Operations or DGMO and other senior army officers on what had been achieved.

But some twenty months after the surgical strike, the government has countenanced the release of an 'edited' video of the surgical strike. What was the need for this? Would not such evidence, when none was sought to be provided, endanger national security? On whose authorisation was such an 'edited' video prepared? How did it get 'leaked?' Is the government planning to take action against those who could have 'leaked' such sensitive footage, and if not, why not? If at all the government felt that such evidence could now be shared publicly, why did the Ministry of Defence not release the video officially and take ownership of the material? And, finally, how is it that even the 'leak' happened selectively, with some media outlets claiming huge credit for 'breaking' this video, while others were not so favoured?

A second question concerns what the government is planning to do in the future to stem Pakistan's continued and increased ceasefire violations. To attempt to draw attention to this matter has nothing to do with the validity of the surgical strikes, which is a finished chapter, and is no longer a matter of doubt or debate. But almost two years after the strike, it is a matter of concern that there has been an exponential increase in the number of ceasefire violations by Pakistan. In the whole of 2017, there were, as per government figures, 110 violations. In the first four months of 2018, there have already been, again as per government figures, 300 ceasefire violations. This has led to loss of lives—martyrdom of our armed forces and deaths of innocent civilians—apart from great damage to property. In fact, Pakistan army shelling continued unabated even during the unilateral ceasefire declared by our government during the period of Ramzan.

Is asking the government what it proposes to do to handle the current situation on the border, wrong? Or, is such a debate part of the fabric of democracy, where all citizens and all responsible political parties are stakeholders in national security and can raise issues about the depredations against our country, without being told that they are anti-national, can go to Pakistan, are denigrating our armed forces and strengthening anti-Indian elements in Pakistan? On the contrary, the fact that in a democracy like ours such a debate is possible, even desirable, is precisely what makes India different from Pakistan.

The time has come for our country to find the right middle ground between unwarranted cynicism and unnecessary hype where national security is concerned. To ask the right questions, even about national security, is the job of the political Opposition. To answer, without questioning the motivations of the interrogator, is the duty of the government. This is how mature democracies work. But, if we are not careful, democracy will soon be replaced by demagoguery in the name of a contrived hyper-nationalism that does little justice to our credentials as a civilisation-State.

(This piece was originally published on 1 July 2018)

SWACHH BHARAT: ARE WE A NATION OF HARMONIOUS SCHIZOPHRENICS?

Sometimes I wonder: are we a nation of harmonious schizophrenics? A nation and a people who have the infinite capacity to constantly and simultaneously live on two planes of experience and consciousness, and not know the difference? I ask this question in the context of the nationwide campaign of 'Swachh Bharat'. Launched with great fanfare in 2014, it was PM Modi's flagship programme to make India a cleaner country.

In terms of intent, the idea cannot be faulted. We are as a people incorrigibly impervious to the filth we coexist with. It is almost as though we don't notice it as we go about our everyday lives. A pious Hindu will take a dip in the holy waters of the Ganga totally unaffected by the filth and garbage on and around the bathing ghat, and the polluted state of the river itself. His concern is the religious ritual and the rewards it could yield; anything outside this personal zone of priority remains perpetually out of focus. The practice of religion sanctions this self-centredness: a Hindu will be obsessed with the ritual purity of his person, but not notice the filth around him.

It is precisely for this reason that most often the greatest amount of filth is seen around our most sacred temples. When Mahatma

Gandhi visited the famous Kashi Vishvanath temple in Varanasi, he was 'deeply pained' by what he saw. In his autobiography, he describes the approach through a narrow and filthy lane, swarming with flies, and rotten and stinking flowers inside the temple. The same absence of cleanliness can be seen, for instance, at the Jagannath temple in Puri. Garbage is strewn all around. I have personally seen huge cockroaches on the ornate garlands around the deities. Swarms of flies feast off the prasad. None of this seems to distract or deter the devotees.

How much has this state of affairs changed today? No doubt the vast amounts of money spent on advertising the Swachh Bharat slogan has created some awareness about the need for a cleaner India, but has this really helped to create one? Just last week, a bench of the Supreme Court—no less—exasperatedly asked who is responsible for the increasing mound of undisposed garbage in Delhi and the lack of a policy for waste management. Delhi generates more than 10,000 tons of garbage every day. Of this, only a fraction is treated, and the rest dumped in landfills. According to reports, the Ghazipur landfill in the capital is more than fifty metres high and could soon dwarf the Qutub Minar! The position of Bhalswa and Okhla landfills is equally perilous. The apex court asked with anguish why the solid waste management rules framed by the Centre in 2016 had not been implemented. In September last year, the court had asked the government to 'show strong desire and commitment' to deal with the problem of waste disposal, after two people died when the Ghazipur landfill had collapsed. When for eight months the government did not come up with any strategy to tackle such appalling conditions, the court was compelled to issue orders to fix erring authorities.

If this is the mess in the capital of India, one can only imagine what the situation in other cities must be. Mumbai, the financial capital, has seen—like always—a spectacular municipal collapse after the monsoons arrived this year. The drainage system completely failed, with sewage and garbage floating around in rivers of filth in the main highways of the city. Air pollution levels in all our cities are perennially at hazardous levels, affecting the young and the elderly in a manner that could enduringly affect their health. The Yamuna is unbelievingly toxic; the Ganga is far from clean; and natural lakes and water bodies in the high-tech capital of Bengaluru froth with chemical pollutants.

It is true that progress has been made in the construction of toilets. In January 2018, the government claimed that six crore toilets have been built across rural areas, and three lakh villages and 300 districts have been declared as Open Defecation Areas (ODA). This is encouraging news. But without devaluing such an achievement, I think an independent agency needs to do an audit to see how many of these toilets are actually functioning. There is a reason for this scepticism. In April this year, the CAG report for 2016–17 stated that not a single toilet was constructed in Delhi under the Swachh Bharat Central government plan and that, in fact, the forty crores allocated for this remains unused!

Keeping all this in mind, I find it both amusing and a matter of concern that the NITI Aayog has only now come up with an 'action plan' to further the goal of Swachh Bharat. This delayed reaction is in response to a recently released World Health Organisation (WHO) report that bluntly states that fourteen of the fifteen most polluted cities are in India. The action plan speaks of institutional measures to reduce air pollution through the increasing use of electric vehicles, prevention of burning of crop residue, shutting down of polluting power plants, incentivising waste processing and taxing landfill sites, mandating compulsory mechanical dust-removal measures in cities, etc.

But the real question is that surely such an action plan should have been the first step after the PM's clarion call for a Swachh

Bharat? If institutional measures—apart from the construction of toilets—were not taken for the last four years, and are only now being formulated, is this not a rather strange way to implement the laudable goal of Swachh Bharat? The fact of the matter is that radical steps of a systemic nature needed to be planned, funded for, monitored and implemented, to make India physically cleaner. A slogan, however well intentioned, can never be a substitute.

(This piece was originally published on 15 July 2018)

RUMINATIONS ON THE 'LUTYEN'S ELITE'

*R*ecently, I gave an interview to the online digital news portal, *The Print*, wherein I said that the Lutyens' elites are like marooned islands, rootless, adrift and identified largely by English, English and English. This led to a great many comments in support of what I said, and against it. I think, therefore, that I need to elaborate a little more on what I meant.

First, the phrase 'Lutyen's elites' does not necessarily connote a defined territorial space. It is, far more, an attitude, a sense of entitlement and an assumption of superiority based largely on inheritance, an old boy's privileged network, and the tendency to judge people only on the basis of the fluency and accent with which they speak English. Secondly—and it is important to state this—it is not as if there is no talent in this so-called elite. There are, among it, people of intellectual eminence who, even if most comfortable only in English, and largely confined only to a small and incestuous circle where only this language is spoken and understood, are concerned contributors to the good of the country. Thirdly, this is not a diatribe against English per se. English has, for historical reasons, become a language spoken by a great many people in the world. It is an indispensable tool to interface with a globalising world. Moreover, as a language, it has a beauty and dexterity of its own. Languages by themselves are not guilty of cultural domination, their usage is.

The problem arises when English becomes a cause for social exclusion. The Lutyen's elite actually believes that it has the right to preside over this linguistic apartheid and treat the rest of India as victims or aspirants. The ability to speak this language as pucca sahibs do then becomes the sole touchstone for entry into the charmed circle of the ruling elite, the only criterion for social acceptance. Those who speak it with the right inflexion are 'People Like Us'. Those who cannot are the others, the 'natives', bereft of the qualifying social and educational background. In my earlier avatar as a diplomat, I once had a boss who represented the worst traits of the Lutyen's elite. If he had a visitor from the Hindi or Urdu media, he used to call me on the intercom and say: 'I say, old chap, I have some HMT and UMT wallahs with me. Can you please handle them?' HMT stood for 'Hindi Medium Type', and UMT stood for 'Urdu Medium Type'. Incidentally, he also pronounced Urdu as 'Ardu'.

Fortunately, the number of these relics of the past is dwindling. Those who still remain, live on mostly as caricatures, isolated in their linguistic insularity and adrift from their cultural and linguistic roots. They are oblivious to the emergence of another India, where English is important, but where the concerns and priorities and talents are not entirely defined by how it is spoken. And yet, it would be a mistake to believe that the empowerment of the new has completely effaced the deference to the old. When I was posted as the Director of the Nehru Centre in London, Sunil Kumar, a young student of the London School of Economics, came to see me. His family comes from Bihar, but he has been educated in England, and his parents now live in California. He narrated to me what happened to him on a visit to Delhi: 'I thought I'd have a coffee at a trendy coffee-shop chain next door. I was wearing a kurta over my jeans, and the hostess at the door spoke to me in Hindi: *"Kahan ja rahe ho? Idhar* coffee *bohat mehngi hai,"* (Where do you think you're going? The coffee is very expensive here). I asked her, in Hindi, how expensive it was. She said: *"Baavan* rupees *ka ek* cup," (Fifty-two rupees a cup). I then asked her in English: "How much is baavan?" She paused, and noticing the way I spoke English, and noticing too that I was Anglicised enough not even to know the Hindi numerical, her whole demeanour changed. Replacing her dour expression with a smile, she welcomed me in.'

This incident happened some years ago. But, even today, not too much has changed, and the Lutyen's elite knows that. The most unfortunate impact of the disproportionate importance given to English is the relative devaluation of our own languages. Badly spoken English is being accepted—even lauded—as the new pan-Indian lingua franca, even as the old elite condescendingly laughs at it and considers it an endorsement of its own superiority. For a nation that has an inestimably rich linguistic heritage—with at least two dozen languages that have evolved over centuries with a rich corpus of literature and sophisticated scripts of their own, this is nothing short of a tragedy. It was this linguistic shoddiness in English that once prompted Atal Bihari Vajpayee to quip that the British finally left India not because of the freedom movement, but because they could not bear any more the massacre of the English language!

But India is changing. The Lutyen's elite is the only segment that has not internalised this sufficiently, or understood that their claim to effortless social standing, access to the best educational institutions and the best jobs is under challenge. Its members continue to speak Hindi in a chi-chi style to servants; they define modernity only in Western terms; they consider any talk of the refinements of ancient India as somehow 'unsecular'; they insist on eating even a chappati and tandoori chicken with a knife and fork; even if their 'mother tongue' is Hindi, they want it linguistically pauperised to suit their own ignorance of it; they consider even formal Indian attire as unacceptable in the 'gentleman's' clubs left behind by the British; and they have a general disdain for anyone not from their own background. Frankly, they are marooned in a shrinking island, and if they don't change, will soon become irrelevant.

(This piece was originally published on 29 July 2018)

INTOLERANCE: BANNING OF WENDY DONIGER'S BOOK

*O*utrage is an easily ignited emotion but only rarely has long-term staying power. Some situations require not the melodrama of outrage, but the far more difficult response of serious and sustained concern. The decision of a publishing house to withdraw all copies of Chicago University Professor Wendy Doniger's book, *The Hindus: An Alternative History,* and to reduce all unsold copies of the work to pulp, requires precisely such a response. The publisher took this decision as a result of a movement by an organisation called the Shiksha Bachao Andolan (Save Education Movement), which felt that Doniger was insulting to the Hindus and the Hindu faith.

It is true, of course, that no one has the right to wilfully or maliciously hurt religious sentiment. But all of us have the right to question what constitutes hurt. Hurt cannot be defined on the basis of somebody's self-righteous assertion that only I know what Hinduism is. It cannot be defined by the inflexible dogmas of those reflexively intolerant to anything that remotely looks like a critique or is in variance with their narrow interpretations. Nor can it be defined on the basis of somebody's inadequate knowledge, or worse, ignorance masquerading as piety.

Hinduism has a glorious legacy of the most remarkable eclecticism. The Upanishads and the Vedas clearly bring out its lofty dialogic nature and the tradition of debate and questioning that it has always nurtured. A religion with no one Church, no one text and no one Pope, Hinduism is a way of life and has never been a brittle collation of rigid dogmas to be ritualistically followed unthinkingly. The great philosopher Shankaracharya, who revived Hinduism in the eighth century CE, could lyrically question the very world view of practised Hinduism. In his immortal *Nirvana Shatakam*, he says with divine abandon:

Na me raga dvesha, na me lobha moha,
Mado naiva me naiva matsarya bhava,
Na dharmo na chartho na kamo na moksha,
Chidananda rupah, Shivoham, Shivoham.

(Dharma, Artha, Kama and even Moksha don't matter. All that matters is Bliss and Awareness—Chidananda Rupa, and once you access that, you become the ultimate in many other religions, Shiva himself!)

There are six systems—not one—in Hindu metaphysics. There is the Charvaka school, which is openly atheistic and ridicules the very notion of god. There is a powerful Tantric school of worship, secretive and replete with many practices that would be considered by the conventional as decidedly unorthodox. The Hindu pantheon has thousands of divinities, even stones and trees, while, at another level, the Upanishads say, *Neti, Neti:* Not this, Not this, refusing to give any attribute to divinity because that would circumscribe its seamless canvas. Ramanuja and Shankaracharya fought a prolonged intellectual battle over what constitutes divinity, the attributable Saguana concept or the attribute-less Nirguna one. Our sages at the dawn of time propounded the profound maxim: *Ekam satya vipraha bahuda vadanti:* There is one truth, the wise call it by different names. The same eclecticism is reflected in another of Hinduism's great guidelines: *Anno bhadra kratvoyantu vishwatah*—Let noble thoughts come to us from all corners of the world. In the Jagannath temple in Puri, there are occasions when devotees have the freedom to roundly abuse Lord Krishna for not responding to their prayers. They do it because they believe He belongs to them, and they have a right to this intimacy. Our Bhakti movement saints and our Bauls have sung about the Almighty in the most unconventional ways. It must require a great deal of uninformed audacity on the part of the members of Shiksha Bachao Andolan to assert that they alone know what this great religion stands for.

One grouse of the Andolan is that Doniger has a 'sexual approach' to Hinduism. This puritanism in the context of Hinduism is so illiterate that it is offensive. It was the British during the colonial period who were scandalised at the philosophical acceptance of Kama in Hinduism. *They* accused Hindus of unacceptable carnality and 'unspeakable things', with a view to asserting the superiority of Christianity. The Hindus always knew that Kama, or the pursuit of the physical as part of a balanced life, is one of the four *purusharthas* or goals of Hinduism, and that the sensual is equally a reflection of the divine. Educated Indians during—and alas after—colonialism internalised the British critique and set out to foolishly sanitise their religion of all categories that they thought would not win Western approbation. Such 'reformers' need to remember that in Hinduism, it is Krishna, not Rama, who is seen as the *purna* avatar, the complete divinity. Ram was Maryada Purushottam. He is said to have thirteen of the sixteen attributes that constitute complete divinity. Krishna has all sixteen, and the three extra ones He has are of the sringara rasa, the sensual mood. The exquisitely erotic poetry of Jayadeva, Bihari, Chandidasa, Govindadasa and many others about Radha and Krishna wonderfully evoke this mood. Most of our gods have female consorts. They are not complete without them. Our mythology is full of the grand celebration of the sensual, even as it also fully accepts the *absence* of the physical as a path to the divine. That is why in the temples of Konarak and Khajuraho, while the panels at the base have explicitly erotic imagery, the panels in the middle show our gods with their consorts, and the *shikhar* or pinnacle has only the trinity: Brahma, Vishnu, Mahadeva or Shiva.

The cause for real concern is that fundamentalist organisations are seriously positioning themselves to hijack Hinduism to suit their narrow, uninformed and bigoted notions. If liberal India succumbs so easily to this onslaught, it would embolden others. All kinds of lumpen elements would sit on a pedestal and lecture us on what constitutes 'correct' religious practice and belief. The moral police would be out in full force and resort to vandalism and violence with impunity. Is this the kind of India we want?

(This piece was originally published on 16 February 2014)

ARE HINDUS THREATENED IN INDIA?

year has passed since the Bharatiya Janata Party government came to power. Many people believe it is too early to pass a judgement. Others say that expectations have been firmly belied. BJP spokespersons list many achievements. Their opponents proclaim that this is merely propaganda: no segment of society is happy, not the farmers, not the poor, not the middle class and not even the corporates. The truth probably lies somewhere between these two extremes.

But as I have argued before, the real danger is the attempt of some ultra Right elements to institutionalise the art of ideological brainwashing. One of their favourite themes is that Hindus are somehow 'threatened' in India. On 6 January 2015, BJP MP Sakshi Maharaj issued a peremptory command to all Hindu women to produce at least four children, 'to protect the Hindu religion,' which, he said, would otherwise be swamped by those who have 'four wives and 40 children.' On 13 January, a BJP leader from West Bengal, Shyamal Goswami, said that Hindu women should have five children each. A week later, Vasudevanand Saraswati, the Shankaracharya of Badrikashram, merrily doubled the demand: every Hindu woman should have ten children, he thundered at the Magh Mela at Allahabad

35

(now Prayagraj). Not forty '*pillas*' (puppies) but four children should be the reproductive duty of every Hindu woman, reiterated Sadhvi Prachi on 13 February.

What we are witnessing is a new campaign of demographic scaremongering. At one level, this insensitively reduces Hindu women to subordinate child-producing machines at the beck and call of every irrational demagogue. At another level, the entire campaign has no real co-relation to facts. The categorisation of our population according to religion is done every decade by the Registrar General and Census Commissioner of India. The last census, which provided these figures, was that of 2001. (The 2011 census figures have not been released yet.) According to the 2001 census, Hindus constitute 80.5 per cent of our population and Muslims 13.4 per cent. The corresponding figures in 1991 were 82.6 per cent and 11.4 per cent. It is quite clear, therefore, that Hindus continue to constitute the overwhelming majority and are under no threat of 'extinction' as the rabble-rousers seek to project.

Moreover, even with these overwhelming figures for Hindus, their actual numbers could actually be higher since there were several methodological errors that need to be factored in. Firstly, in 1991, Muslim majority Jammu and Kashmir was not included in the detailed census because it was categorised as a 'disturbed region'. Since in several districts of Jammu and Kashmir, the Total Fertility Rate (TFR)—a measure of the number of children born to a woman if she were to live to the end of her child-bearing years—has actually dipped to below-replacement levels, the rate of the rise of the Muslim population, as reflected in the final census figures, was exaggerated. Secondly, for the first time, the census questionnaire took cognisance separately of Buddhists, Jains, Adivasis and others, who were in the past docketed as Hindus. According to the census, India has eight million Buddhists, four million Jains, six million Adivasis and others. If these eighteen million were added to the total tally of Hindus, as was done in the past, the percentage of Hindus would be higher.

Several sangh parivar websites cite polygamy and aversion to birth control as the reasons for the alleged rise of the Muslim population. Narendra Modi himself publicly and derisively labelled Muslims as 'Hum paanch, hamare pachees' people in 2002. However, whatever the popular stereotype, the truth is quite at variance. According to the 1961 census, polygamy is practised most by the Adivasis (15.2 per cent), the Buddhists (7.9 per cent), Jains (6.7 per cent), and the Hindus (5.8 per cent) come next. The figure for the Muslims is the lowest (5.7 per cent). Although these figures are dated, they do indicate that polygamy, while permissible, is not widely practised by most Muslims. Besides, according to empirical data, there are 936 women for every 1,000 Muslim men. If, in these circumstances, each Muslim male was to marry four women, seventy-five per cent of Muslim men would remain unmarried!

On family planning, the fact is that population growth is falling in almost all countries with large Muslim populations. In Turkey, for instance, sixty-three per cent of all reproductive couples use contraception. In more conservative Indonesia, the comparable figure is forty-eight per cent. Misguided religious evangelism has rarely prevented people from making rational choices about themselves. Family planning was once frowned upon in Catholic conservative Italy and Spain, but in both these countries, the TFR is as low as 1.2 per cent. Even in India, Muslims in more prosperous and educated Kerala have one of the lowest TFRs at 1.6 per cent.

The fundamental truth is that poverty breeds. Countries where people are abysmally poor and deprived of education and healthcare, and where women empowerment is low, population growth rates are higher. This has nothing to do with religion or geography and applies equally to Hindus and Muslims. Those couples who choose to restrict their families to two children don't have fewer 'religious' cells in their brain. They are merely able to make more informed choices about their well-being as a consequence of socio-economic empowerment.

Hindus are, and will remain, the overwhelming majority in India. The ratio between Hindus and Muslims has remained relatively stable over the decades. The figures for the 2011 census are awaited and one wonders why their release is so delayed. As more Muslims benefit from economic development and as more Muslim women get empowered, the Muslim population growth rate will inevitably fall further, just as in the case of Hindus. The fear psychosis being created has no basis in facts but is entirely based on perpetuating false stereotypes with the aim of stoking religious hatred for electoral gains. The pity is that the BJP leadership is largely silent on these matters.

(This piece was originally published on 24 May 2015)

ARE VVIPs SPECIAL KIND
OF RELIGIOUS DEVOTEES?

On Tuesday, 14 July, Justice Lodha pronounced his judgement on the guilty in the IPL scam. That very morning, twenty-nine people died in a stampede at Rajahmundry in Andhra Pradesh. Lakhs of devotees had gathered there for the Godavari Maha Pushkaram, a religious festival that takes place every 144 years. The tragedy occurred at the same ghat that had been cordoned off for the benefit of Chief Minister Chandrababu Naidu, who took a dip in the Godavari in isolated splendour along with a puja that lasted for an hour. While he possibly obtained divine blessings for his political ambitions and future moksha, the crowds swelled. When ordinary devotees were finally allowed in, twenty-nine people, mostly elderly women, lay dead, their bodies mutilated. Another twenty-five were seriously injured. The chief minister, having completed his puja, had left. Our television channels took note of this tragedy, but their main obsession was what punishment had been meted out to Gurunath and to Kundra and others in the IPL scam.

Life is cheap in our country. Dozens of people die needlessly, but we take it in our stride. It is true that planning had gone into preparing for the Maha Pushkaram. According to reports, some 1,600 crores had been spent on preparations, against a sanctioned amount of 336 crores. But it is also true that arrangements were still not fully complete even on the eve of the event. Fund allocations for facilities were being sanctioned even a day before the auspicious occasion. Eyewitnesses have confirmed that the police force was inadequate and the crowd management poor. Moreover, why was the administration taken by surprise by the large numbers who came for the holy dip? The last Maha Pushkaram had taken place in 1871, 144 years ago. The fact that around five crore devotees would come during the ten-day auspicious period up to 25 July for such a rare event was known to most people. The state itself had given the event maximum publicity.

Deaths due to stampedes, or poor management and arrangements, are not new in our country. The lives lost at Prayag during the Mahakumbh, at Datia in Madhya Pradesh in 2006 and again in 2013, and during the Sabarimala pilgrimage, should have loomed large before the planners. But obviously, these were remote memories, both for the administrators and for their boss, the chief minister.

Do VVIPs have a special hotline to the Almighty? Even as per an enlightened reading of Hindu scriptures, their true dharma should be less their own salvation and more the welfare of their *praja*, subjects or people. How could Naidu, as he went about his hour-long puja and leisurely holy dip, remain oblivious to the unbearable pressures building up beyond the VVIP cordoned off area? Could he not hear, as he solemnly chanted his prayers, the anguished cries of the mass of people compressed against the barricade, about to collapse under the sheer weight of human pressure?

There is little doubt that the special arrangements made for the puja of the chief minister had a direct correlation to the unspeakable tragedy that unfolded immediately after he left. Like a river in spate held back against a fragile dam, devotees spilled out, as much to reach the ghat as to escape the inhumanly cramped space in which they were forced to be confined. It is equally a no-brainer that while the chief minister and his entourage was present, the main focus of the police and administrative machinery was to take care of his needs, not that of the lakhs of ordinary citizens.

Many years ago, I was Press Secretary to President Shankar Dayal Sharma, who was an intensely religious person, and there is nothing per se wrong in that. A day after his swearing in, he flew in the IAF Boeing earmarked for the President, to Puttaparthi to seek the blessings of Sai Baba. From there, his jet took off to Tirupati for another round of worship. I was present with him at both places. At Tirupati, notwithstanding the large throng of devotees at the holy site, the temple was cordoned off. I recall too that once when he was in Mumbai, he decided to visit the Siddhi Vinayak temple on his way to the airport. It was a working day, and his journey was in the middle of the day. The entire city was paralysed.

Faith plays a very important part in the lives of most Indians. This is not surprising given the fact that four of the world's great religions—Hinduism, Buddhism, Jainism, Sikhism—were born here; we also have the second-largest number of Muslims in the world; and Christians, who are a small percentage of the population, are still larger in number in India than the combined population of Hungary and Greece. But while faith must have its own place, why should those who follow it be treated like cannon fodder by the powerful? Which religion ordains that those who are VVIPs have a special right to prayer and worship, even if this costs dozens of lives? Long years ago, Chanakya made a seminal point in the *Arthashastra*: 'In the interests of the prosperity of the country, a king should be diligent in foreseeing the possibility of calamities, try to avert them before they arise, (and) overcome those which happen.' In the same text, he also wrote: 'It is the people who constitute a kingdom; like a barren cow, a kingdom without (empowered) people yields nothing.'

It is time that Chandrababu Naidu, and all our VVIPs, understand this. An impartial and thorough enquiry should be ordered into what happened at Rajahmundry. And, even as I write this, my prayers are with all the common devotees in their lakhs, who have gathered at the Rath Yatra in Puri. Finally, however important cricket is, perhaps our media could, on that fateful day, have given a little more attention to those who died on the banks of the Godavari.

(This piece was originally published on 19 July 2015)

WHO IS ANTI-NATIONAL?

*I*n the context of the growing allegation of the BJP's role in nurturing intolerance, I was surprised the other day when a well-known anchor asked me on a live TV show whether I prefer economic growth to the agitation on tolerance. My answer was that to posit the two as binary polarities is Fascist. I did not choose my response casually or on the spur of the moment. It was Hitler who progressively suppressed individual freedoms on the altar of economic growth. In fact, it was his argument that any voices that distract from the State's professed march towards economic prosperity are anti-national and need to be suppressed. It was an expedient form of xenophobic nationalism that neither ensured economic prosperity nor individual freedoms, plunging Germany towards one of the most shameful chapters in human history.

I strongly believe that India is nowhere close to becoming a Fascist State. But still, it is important to learn the right lessons from history. Undoubtedly, a democracy should have effective economic governance, but it should also allow the freedom to dissent and debate. The equation is not either–or. To critique the ruling party or to disagree with its policies cannot be construed, in a democracy, as an anti-national act. Nor should a subversive and mala fide motivation be ascribed to every act of disagreement. Unfortunately, this is precisely what is happening today. Anyone who criticises this government is either accused of having a political animus or is considered anti-national or is seen through the prism of his/her religion or is dismissed as part of the regressive forces that are trying to sully the name of India internationally. This is, to say the least, both undemocratic and rather silly.

There is little doubt that ever since the BJP government came to power in May 2014, the level of tolerance has seen a steady erosion. The brutal killings of respected scholars and thinkers like Kalburgi, Dabholkar and Pansare, and the lynching of Akhlaq in Dadri, are only examples of a new breed of Right-wing Hindu evangelism that self-righteously believes that any opposing opinion or critical voice has no right to exist. Every time such an incident of intolerance occurs, there is a predictable lack of firm disapproval from the BJP leadership, and the silence of an otherwise eloquent prime minister is particularly deafening. This only further emboldens and encourages such elements. The net result is an increasingly brittle nation perpetually in danger of fracturing into violence.

The BJP's defence of recalling the acts of intolerance in the past is disingenuous. The prime minister, in one of his rallies in Bihar, mentioned the gruesome pogrom against the Sikhs in 1984 as a means to corner those who are protesting the growing intolerance of today. His opponents fell to the bait of recalling the genocide in Gujarat in 2002. This form of competitive communalism is hardly the sign of a mature nation. All acts of intolerance in the past are emphatically condemnable. But, what happened in the past, on either side of the political spectrum, cannot become a reason to condone what is happening today.

Moreover, automatically and arrogantly dismissing the returning of awards by a host of eminent writers, scholars, scientists and artists cutting across regions and languages, as an act of political partisanship—as the BJP is doing—is extremely short-sighted. Many of these intellectuals have not been averse to the BJP, and not all are pro-Congress. Collectively, they reflect not so much a political animus as a genuine cry of anguish at the verifiable erosion of the space for dialogue and dissent. Nor is the artifice of blaming only the state governments credible. Of course, law and order is the responsibility of state governments, and the government of Akhilesh Yadav, for instance, must bear some of the responsibility for the Dadri lynching. But it is equally a fact that the lumpen religious fanatics emboldened by the BJP and the RSS represent a pan-Indian phenomenon. States must try to prevent them from taking the law in their own hands, but the BJP, too, must do more to rein them in.

As a proud Hindu, for me the most distressing thing is that these fanatics claim to act and speak for Hindus. The militant, intolerant and illiterate Hinduism that such forces represent is a blot on the refined, eclectic, tolerant and sophisticated philosophical foundations of Hinduism. Hinduism was and will remain, in its true sense, a dialogic religion. This can be seen in the Upanishads, where even a shishya or pupil had the right to question the Guru. Those who are seeking to reduce the grand legacy of Hinduism to intolerant hate and violence would do well to remember that Shankaracharya, arguably one of the world's greatest philosophers, revived Hinduism in the eighth century AD not by lynching or killing his opponents or throwing ink on their faces but by a series of shastrarths or cerebrally persuasive arguments conducted across the length and breadth of Bharat.

When those who rule stop listening to the *aawam* or the people, one can be sure that *burre din* or bad days are ahead. When those in power begin to dismiss anything that they don't like as partisan, motivated, unrepresentative and irrelevant, one can be sure that the spirit of democracy is in danger. When those who run governments begin to believe that the nation should only mirror what they believe is right, the plural and composite fabric of India is in danger. The debate on intolerance will not go away just because the government can organise counter-demonstrations by its loyalists. The debate will cease when they begin to understand that in a country like India, good governance and religious and social harmony are essentially two sides of the same coin.

(This piece was originally published on 8 November 2015)

THE THEKEDARS OF ISLAM

S heikh ul Islam Faqeehul Asar Hasrat Mufti Taqi Usmani is a Hanafi Muslim scholar from Pakistan, who also served as a judge in that country's Federal Shariat court. The esteemed gentleman has recently come out with a fatwa that Muslim women should not post pictures of themselves or their family on social media, including specifically, Facebook.

Our own Darul Uloom Deoband, which claims to be the highest Islamic seminary in India, came out earlier this month with a fatwa that is even more bizarre. It banned Muslim women from plucking, trimming and shaping their eyebrows! The same seminary, which has a separate wing to issue fatwas—Darul Iftaa—had earlier issued directives that say that Muslim women cannot hold jobs, either in the government or in the private sector, nor can they become judges.

Other Islamic seminaries, and so-called Islamic clerics, have not been lagging behind in their misplaced activism. A maulvi in Midnapore (West Bengal) issued a fatwa on what Sania Mirza should wear or not wear. The Majlis Bachao Tehreek has issued a fatwa against exiled Bangladeshi writer, Taslima Nasreen, offering unlimited financial rewards to anyone who can kill her.

The venom that suffuses such fatwas should not be underestimated.

47

In Bihar, on 30 July this year, the day Nitish Kumar won the trust vote with the support of the BJP after breaking ties with the RJD and the Congress, the only Muslim minister in his new cabinet, Khursheed, alias Firoz Ahmed, chanted the slogan 'Jai Shri Ram' outside the Bihar Assembly. A fatwa was immediately issued by Maulvi Sohail Quasmi of the seminary Imarat Shariah, pronouncing that the minister's marriage must be annulled for his act of 'error'. Firoz Ahmed protested at first, even saying that he would not be cowed down by such threats, but later succumbed to the pressure and apologised.

Apart from the Islamic seminaries, we have organisations like the All India Muslim Law Board. The Board was set up in 1973 to protect and interpret Muslim personal law, and projects itself as the leading body to articulate Muslim opinion in India. However, it has hardly covered itself in glory for the opinions it has held. For instance, the Board objected to the law on the Right of Children to Free and Compulsory Education (2009), on the ground that it will infringe on the madrasa system of education. Are madrasas private properties of the Board, beyond the purview of law and reform? The Board also supported child marriage. Its members prevented Salman Rushdie from participating in the Jaipur Literature Festival in 2012, even when this participation was only to be in the form of a video conference.

The Board has been the most retrogressive to Muslim women rights on the question of triple talaq. It actually said that while the practice was not without blemish, it must still be regarded as valid. Fortunately, the Supreme Court intervened in the matter in August this year and pronounced it illegal. Even worse, the Board justified the practice of Nikah Halala, wherein a divorced Muslim woman must actually sleep with another man before she can remarry her first husband. A report carried out by *India Today* revealed that 'Islamic scholars' were actually charging a hefty fee for one night stands with divorced Muslim women so as to sanction their wish to remarry their first husband.

The fact of the matter is that Muslim clerics, and organisations like the All India Muslim Personal Law Board, represent the worst form of medieval patriarchy and appear to be completely impervious to the rights of Muslim women sanctioned within the Quran. They have thus far exercised a monopoly on what constitutes 'correct' Muslim behaviour, and are stubbornly unwilling to accept that their views are outdated, iniquitous, and insensitive to notions of gender equality, to the much-needed reform within the Muslim community, and to the concept of a modern and progressive society. It is not surprising that of the fifty-odd people who constitute the Board, women are in a complete minority, not more than four as per the Board's own website.

The truth is that there is a great deal of evidence of fundamentalism and an ostrich-like aversion to change among the self-anointed guardians for the welfare of Muslims. Such guardians, who issue all kinds of ridiculous fatwas at the drop of a hat, need to be challenged, not the least by liberal Muslim opinion itself, of which, unfortunately, we don't see too much evidence. Politicians too must stop pandering to such medieval interpretations of Muslim personal law, merely for vote-bank politics, as happened in the Shah Bano case in 1985.

There is another important reason to consider. As my good friend, commentator and journalist Shahid Siddiqui says, one cannot counter Hindu fundamentalism by pandering to Muslim fundamentalism. Both are wrong, and both need to be condemned and opposed. In one sense, both extremes feed off each other. When Muslim clerics issue fatwas merely because a Muslim has the temerity to acknowledge Lord Rama, Hindu fundamentalists go to the other extreme and paint all Muslims as being anti-Hindu. This grossly distorts the debate and the possibility of a meeting ground—which most Hindus and Muslims would be more than happy to share—between people of different faiths, who together make up the vibrant Ganga-Jamuni tehzeeb or culture of our composite and plural national fabric.

Besides, the time has come to ask: do these ultra conservative *thekedars* (meaning, contractors) of Muslims actually represent the real wishes of the community? In 2003, *Outlook* magazine carried out a survey in which the bulk of the respondents (forty per cent) replied in the negative when asked: do you consider those fighting the Babri Masjid case as true spokespersons for the Muslim community?

Many Muslims may, perhaps, have reason today to suffer from a siege mentality. We need to oppose those forces that have created this mentality, but equally, Muslims too must show the courage to embrace liberal opinion and challenge the stranglehold of those who claim, in such primitive ways, to speak for them.

(This piece was originally published on 22 October 2017)

THE DEMISE OF 'SHASTRARTHA' OR CIVILISED DISCOURSE IN INDIA

*T*here is something seriously wrong in the quality of our public discourse. A certain coarseness has pervasively invaded it that does little credit to our claim of being one of the oldest and most refined civilisations. People talk at each other, not to each other. Abuse, slander, malice, innuendo and below-the-belt diatribes flourish. There is a brittleness in public life that recognises only absolute black and white, cutting out all shades of grey, or doubt, or the possibility of another equally valid point of view. In short, the great art of civilised dialogue appears to be mostly dead in the world's largest democracy.

How has this come to pass? It is not something that has always been our tradition. In fact, far from it. In the eighth century CE, the great Adi Shankaracharya had emphatic differences with another scholar of great eminence, Mandana Mishra. To resolve these, they agreed to have a *shastrartha*, a discourse or a dialogue. The points of divergence were fundamental. The Jagad Guru believed in the jnana marga, or the path of knowledge as the way to salvation. Mandana Mishra was a follower of the Purva Mimamsa school of Hinduism, that believed in *karma kanda*, the practice of rituals as prescribed by the Vedas, as the path to redemption. But, in spite of this divide, they were willing to have a civilised dialogue. Shankara even agreed to Mandana Mishra's wife, Ubhaya Bharati, to be the umpire in the debate, which continued in a civilised way for weeks, with the whole of Bharat—even in the days of no TV and social media—following its progress by word of mouth. Mandana Mishra lost the debate, and became the Jagad Guru's most prominent follower, as did his wife.

The Upanishads were a dialogue between a guru and a disciple. The *Bhagavad Gita* was, in many senses, a dialogue too, between Lord Krishna and Arjuna. The *Brahma Sutra,* which—along with the Upanishads and the Gita—comprises the three foundational texts of Hinduism, is not a dialogue per se, but the extensive commentaries or *bhashyas* written on it are. The commentaries—including the seminal one written by Shankara—invariably include the viewpoint of the 'opponent', or the one who is in disagreement. This disagreement is not disdainfully dismissed but sought to be countered by reason and argument.

This dialogic aspect of our civilisational history is not confined only to ancient India. The great Mughal ruler, Akbar, began a series of debates under the awning of his dialogic forum, Dīn-i Ilāhī. In this platform, the proponents of Islam had to face the viewpoints of those of other faiths, with the ultimate aim of finding a meeting point of synthesis that would combine the best in all faiths. More recently, our freedom movement is a shining example of the primacy of civilised dialogue. The letters that Nehru and Gandhi wrote to each other show on how many vital issues the two were in disagreement; but, while these were voiced without inhibition, they were always civil. This is also seen in the letters between Nehru and Netaji Subhash Chandra Bose. Here, the ideological points of divergence were even more pronounced, but both argued their case with great respect for the other. After Independence, there was a phase when some of the finest debates took place in parliament, where speakers with firmly entrenched views were willing to listen with respect to the opposing argument. In fact, there is the famous incident when Prime Minister Nehru, after listening to a young Atal Bihari Vajpayee's scathing indictment of his policies, went to congratulate Vajpayee, and even predicted that he had the material to become the prime minister one day.

What has happened to this civility, this generosity of spirit, this ability to listen to the other with respect, even if you are emphatically in disagreement? The kind of debased vocabulary of people in public life we get to hear today is nothing short of shameful. There is no notion of linguistic restraint. The only aim is to score an immediate hit at the opponent, irrespective of the language and the veracity of facts. Are our leaders suffering from a terminal sense of insecurity that becomes disgustingly accentuated every time an election is imminent? Or, is this kind of discourse par for the course? Is political acrimony—even rivalry—so great that it removes all barriers to public civility? Is there lack of political supervision, or even worse, is there is complicity on the part of those who are in a position to counsel their subordinates to speak in a more dignified manner? The worst aspect of this situation is that one undignified jibe provokes another of the same ilk, until the entire national discourse is hijacked by linguistic anarchy.

The malaise is contagious. When our political leaders are culpable in taking discourse to its lowest common denominator, TV channels do the same. Or, perhaps it is the TV 'discussions' that influence the public discourse. There are very few TV channels where one can watch a civilised discussion. Most have fallen prey to shouting matches, with panellists outdoing each other in the simultaneous display of lung power, with the full encouragement of the anchor. Social media, while certainly democratising public debate, has also legitimised abuse. The press of a button on your mobile phone can send into cyberspace filthy expletives and innuendoes, and trigger hate campaigns with troll armies amplifying this garbage.

There are honourable exceptions to this narrative who need to be lauded. Nitish Kumar is one such person, and I don't need to say this because I belong to the same party. Not once have I heard him using undignified language, and that sets the template for those who are his spokespersons too.

Such examples need to be replicated. All of us need to reflect on what can be done, before we go further down the drain of the endless name-calling that goes about in the name of public debate. At a personal level, I, along with some others, have set up a public platform called 'Shastrartha', whose sole aim is to further, through public programmes, the dying art of civilised dialogue.

(This piece was originally published on 2 December 2018)

BAJRANG DAL AUR VHP KO GUSSA KYON AATA HAI?

I rarely go to a cinema hall to see a film, but I made an exception for *PK*. On the last day of 2014, my wife and I went to a nearby PVR and saw the new Aamir Khan release, and thoroughly enjoyed it.

The film is an unabashed satire on the ritualism, superstitions and prejudices that proliferate under the awning of religion. It also makes a hard-hitting attack on religious charlatans, the so-called mullahs, sadhvis, sants, gurus and mahants who make a living feeding off the insecurities and fear of ordinary people. The film does not attack religion per se. In fact, it pays deep respect to religion in a spiritual sense where the journey is a personal and direct one between the devotee and the Almighty. Its attack is focused on the false intermediaries who obtain much ill-begotten wealth in their ungodly misuse of religion.

As I left the hall, I asked myself why this film made the cadres of the Bajrang Dal and the Vishwa Hindu Parishad (VHP) so angry. For days, they went on a vandalising streak, breaking public and private property and burning posters of the film. At one level, I understood the real reason for their hysterical anger. Religion is a powerful instrument of control. In its name, people have shed their own blood and that of others. In its name, people have perpetuated the greatest cruelties and acts of discrimination. In its name, riots have taken place and even genocides. The Bajrang Dal and the VHP believe in using religion to whip up hatred in order to ignite religious divides between people. Their aim is to further religious polarisation for short-term electoral dividends. They arrogate to themselves the pedestal to speak for all Hindus, but not for altruistic reasons. Their goal is to use Hinduism to sever the bridges of brotherhood, love and community with those of other faiths. In other words, for them, Hinduism is an instrument of control. *PK* questions the raison d'etre of those who seek to control religion; it questions the basis of self-professed intermediaries; it questions the very need of such middlemen who use religion for their own self-interest. It is but natural, therefore, that the Bajrang Dal and VHP are very annoyed by *PK*'s message.

But the real problem is also that the protesters are exceptionally ignorant about the phenomenal grandeur of thought of Hinduism. At the philosophical level, Hindu metaphysics sees the Almighty as the omnipresent, omnipotent, omniscient, indivisible Brahman, which is beyond physical form, and indeed, beyond definition because any definition would circumscribe the absolutism of this attribute-less entity (Neti, neti, not this, not this). The powerful Nirguna and Advaita traditions of Hindu philosophy have espoused this unqualified non-duality of godhood for centuries. If the Almighty itself is beyond form and definition, who are these people who claim to speak on its behalf for their own selfish reasons?

At another level, Hinduism has always sustained within itself a tradition of self-critique, of corrosive honesty and candour which has allowed it to reinvent itself time and again. The most evocative and influential votary of this tradition was Shankaracharya himself, who in the eighth century was responsible for the revival of Hinduism after it had gone into decline as a result of a surfeit of ritual and superstition and the (consequent) appeal of Buddhism. In the *Bhaja Govindam*, Shankaracharya has this telling shloka: *'Jatuli mundi, lunchchit keshah, kashayambar bahu krit veshah, pashyanappi na pashyati mudho, hayudar nimitam bahu krit vesha'* (Matted locks, shaven head or hair set loose, saffron robes are very deceptive; frauds they are unable to see, fools, they become monks to make a living). In the *Nirvana Shatakam*, Shankaracharya again hits out at blind ritualism: *'Na punyam, na paapam, na saukhyam na dukhkham, na mantro na teertham, na vedo na yagna,'* (No virtues, no sin, no happiness no sorrow, no mantra, no pilgrimage, no Vedas no sacrifice). The important point is that Hinduism allows for this critique. Unlike the Semitic religions, Hinduism has no one God, no one text, no one Church and no one Pope. It allows its followers the freedom to dissent while being within the larger tradition of sanatan dharma. That is why Hinduism can include even the Charvaka school, which argues that god need not exist, and also accommodate the unorthodox Tantric tradition.

But even in Islam, the Sufi tradition has done a good job of lampooning the superstitions and rituals of the mullahs. Ghalib, who internalised Sufi mysticism best, writes famously: *'Kahan maikhane ka darwaza Ghalib, aur kahan vaiyaz; bas itna jaante thhe kal woh jaata tha jab hum nikle'* (The tavern door and the preacher are truly poles apart; all I know is I saw him enter as I left to depart!) What is satire at one plane became the reiteration of a transcendent vision of the Absolute at another, and no one could state it as beautifully as Ghalib: *'Hum muvahid hain, hamara kesh hai tark-e-rasoom; millatein jab mit gayeen, azza-e-iman ho gayeen'* (God is one, that is our faith; all rituals we abjure; 'Tis only when the symbols vanish, that belief is pure). This innate suspicion of the orthodox religious establishment was the leitmotif of the powerful Bhakti movement too. Guru Nanak, Kabir, Tuka Ram, Meera—and many more—shunned the hypocrisy of organised religion and advocated the ecstasy of direct communion with the Almighty.

The vandalising crew of the Bajrang Dal and the VHP venting their ire on *PK* thus represent the semi-literate, lumpen evangelism of those who do not know their own religion and are bent on imposing their limited thinking on the intrinsic grandeur of Hinduism. The worry is that they are actually acting upon a cynically crafted plan to foment religious hatred to divide the country for the sake of votes. The entire nation must be vigilant to their designs.

(This piece was originally published on 4 January 2015)

A SPIRITUAL HINDU

I am proud to be a Hindu, but I am deeply concerned at some things that are happening in the name of Hinduism. The Hinduism that I subscribe to had sages who had the courage to say millennia ago that tolerance and inclusion are the essence of the spiritual vision. Centuries before Christ was born, at a time when people, for lack of other exposure, believed that only what they believed was right, our sages pronounced *Ekam satya vipraha bahuda vadanti* There is one truth, the wise call it by different names. Around the same time, when most other people believed that only their world had legitimacy, our sages had the courage to say: *Udar charitanam vasudhaiva kutumbukam*: For the broad-minded, the entire world is their family. Those who laid the foundations of our religious world view could confidently say, at a time when most other social groupings were insecurely insular, that: *Anno bhadra kratvoyantu vishwatah*—Let noble thoughts come to us from all corners of the world.

Unfortunately, this great religion is being hijacked today, but not by outsiders. It is being undermined by a small group of Hindus who believe that they alone know what Hinduism is. Unlike our sages who said that the one truth can be interpreted by the wise in many ways, their approach is to say that we alone have a monopoly on truth. Unlike our founding fathers who wished to embrace the entire world as their family, these 'Hindus' believe in singling out for exclusion anyone who does not agree with them. And, unlike our wise ancestors who invited noble thoughts to flow from all directions, these fanatics have a closed mind to any other opinion.

This tragic coup is unfolding before our eyes, and the majority of Hindus are watching mutely. One reason for this sorry state of affairs is that these self-anointed guardians of our religion are violent people. They do not believe in persuasion, discussion, dialogue, debate, shastrarth or argumentation. Nor do they believe in the rule of law. They believe that they have the right to silence those who oppose them through physical violence and brute force. And, the level of their violence directly corresponds to the level of their ignorance. What is worse is that they believe that they can get away by breaking the law, because those who are supposed to be the guardians of the law are actually on their side.

The most ugly and frightening symptom of this devaluation of Hinduism is the emergence of vigilante squads consisting of lumpen groups who now roam around this ancient land, beating up and killing people on the basis of mere suspicion. They have no sanction or remit or locus standi or authority to do so except their own illiterate hubris and the belief that they can get away with it because the authorities will not take action against them.

This last part is a very worrisome development because it undermines not only the rule of law that is the very basis of an organised, democratic society but the Constitution and the Republic itself. It is for this reason that the Supreme Court issued notices on 7 April to six states, seeking to know within three weeks why groups calling themselves 'gaurakshaks' or protectors of the cow, should not be banned like other outlawed outfits for taking the law into their own hands. The six states are UP, Rajasthan, Gujarat, Haryana,

Maharashtra and Karnataka. The highest Court has also asked these states to explain what administrative measures they have taken to prevent such vigilantism. It is not a coincidence that of the six states, five are BJP ruled.

Many Hindus hold the cow in reverence. That sentiment should be respected. In many states, there are laws banning cow slaughter. Those laws should not be infringed. But enforcing the law is the jurisdiction of those authorised to do so. If citizens believe that they can, in the name of religious belief, take the law into their own hands, we are looking at a state of anarchy. Enough has already happened to justify the Supreme Court's directive. Mohammad Akhlaq was lynched in UP on the suspicion of eating beef; Dalits were flogged in public in Gujarat on the suspicion that they were cattle thieves; Majloom Ansari and Inayatullah Khan, who were on their way to a cattle fair, were hung from a tree in Jharkhand; Zaid Ahmed Bhat was burnt alive on a highway in Udhampur in Jammu and Kashmir on the suspicion that he was smuggling cattle; a young twenty-five year old was thrashed to death by cow vigilantes in Ahmedabad; another twenty-nine year old was lynched by a mob in Udupi for ferrying cattle in a van; and now, we have the latest incident of Pehlu Khan beaten to death by gaurakshaks in Rajasthan.

This manner of taking the law into one's own hands presents a very strange version of the slogan, 'Sabka Saath, Sabka Vikas.' Prime Minister Narendra Modi said that the majority of those masquerading as gaurakshaks were just 'anti-social' elements. But that view does not seem to be shared by those implementing the law in the states in which his party is in power. The deeply worrisome thing is that one act of hijacking the law emboldens the next. We now hear of Yuva Hindu Vahini workers halting church services in Gorakhpur. Some days ago, members of the Karni Rajput Sena attacked filmmaker Sanjay Leela Bhansali and vandalised the sets of his film on Padmavati, at the Jaigarh Fort in Rajasthan. We also hear reports of excesses being committed against couples and young boys and girls by vigilantes acting under the sanction of 'anti-Romeo' squads.

Hinduism does not sanction this kind of violence. Nor can Hinduism, which upholds dharma, countenance this kind of wilful abrogation of the law of the land. Those claiming to act on behalf of Hindus are, therefore, shaming the vast majority of Hindus. All those who live the genuine Hindu experience must work together to stop them.

(This piece was originally published on 9 April 2017)

POLITICS

THE REMARKABLE VICTORY OF
NARENDRA MODI: 2019

*T*he 'Modi tsunami' of 2019, where for the first time since 1971 a party has come back to power with an absolute majority larger than what it had before, has opened up a new paradigm of politics. The contours of this change need to be understood, especially by Opposition parties, for only then can they internalise the magnitude of the change that confronts them. If they choose not to see, or understand, the new political landscape, they do so only at their own peril.

There are two principal takeaways from this election. The first takeaway is that the politics of entitlement, and of dynastic politics, has received a major challenge. The political battlefield is littered with fallen dynasts. The most visible setback is to the Congress, the principal Opposition party, where Rahul Gandhi is at the helm, solely because he is a member of the Gandhi family. Rahul lost his own election from the family sinecure of Amethi. His party has been decimated, increasing its paltry tally of forty-four in the last elections by a meagre eight seats. The Congress party is in urgent need of surgical introspection, and needs a new leadership, a new narrative, a new operational strategy, and a new cadre.

The fate of other dynasts is equally pitiable. Akhilesh Yadav, who runs the Samajwadi Party only because he is the son of Mulayam Singh Yadav, performed terribly in UP. His wife lost the elections, as did other members of his family. Ajit Singh, son of Chaudhary Charan Singh, lost too in UP, as did his son, Jayant Singh. Tejaswi Yadav in Bihar, at the helm of the Rashtriya Janata Dal (RJD) only because he is the anointed son of Lalu Prasad Yadav, could not win a single seat in Bihar. In Haryana, the scions of the famous political clans of the state—the Chautalas, Hoodas, and Bhajan Lal—bit the dust. Naveen Patnaik, who came to power in Odisha as the son of the stalwart Biju Patnaik, managed to retain a majority of the seats both for the Lok Sabha and in the state Assembly, but not without facing serious inroads from the BJP. True, some dynasts survived. Jagan Reddy, son of former state chief minister, the late Y.S. Rajasekhara Reddy, swept Andhra Pradesh. In Tamil Nadu too, Stalin, son of the late M. Karunanidhi, the towering satrap of Tamil politics, did extremely well. At the individual level too, many newly-elected MPS are the progeny of influential politicians. However, the hitherto unchallenged thesis that progenies have an ordained right to inherit the political mantle from their influential parents, has suffered a definitive setback.

A second takeaway is that old equations of caste arithmetic have been overwhelmed by the political chemistry of the 'new politics'. In UP, the conventional expectation was that a gathbandan (alliance) of Yadavs, Dalits, Jats and Muslims, would be invincible, purely in terms of the numerical aggregation of caste. The alliance was decimated. In Bihar, the RJD had thought that it could pose a formidable challenge because of the time-tested coalition of Muslims and Yadavs. That coalition too was decimated. Leaders mired in old political equations could not understand that members of their 'captive' flock could transcend caste fealties and take an independent view of who they would wish to vote for. The vertical prism of caste blinded many 'old school' leaders that horizontal aspirations would escape the silos to which conventionally they had been confined. The result is that henceforth the 'two plus two equals four' calculations of parties that refuse to see beyond caste and creed will need a serious rethink, and while caste will not entirely go away in the calculation of all political parties, its pivotal importance—as it used to be in the past—has suffered serious erosion.

What were the strengths of the Modi 'tsu-namo', that it largely swept aside entrenched dynasties and caste citadels? Certainly, the most important single element is leadership. This election was Narendra Modi's election. People voted for him, and in his name. That was because he combined—whether you like him or not—eloquence, charisma, energy, vision, will, decisiveness, and above all, a cultural rootedness that spoke in the idiom ordinary people could identify with. There was just no one in the Opposition who came even close to challenging his appeal.

The crafting of a definitive narrative was also important. That narrative consisted of identifiable elements. First, it focused on the tangibles that were delivered in the last five years touching the quality of lives of the poor—toilets, housing, electricity, direct cash transfers, gas cylinders, health schemes, roads and other infrastructure projects. Second, it tapped into a widespread angst among ordinary Hindus that—starting from the Shah Bano case of 1985—there has been a deliberate attempt to forsake the secular principle of respect for all religions and adopt a policy of appeasement of the minorities—read Muslims—for only 'vote-bank' politics. Third, following the Balakot attack, it evoked nationalism, and the paramount importance of the security of the nation against external threats. And, lastly, it raised the hopes of the young by the slogan 'New India'. This was especially relevant since India is one of the youngest nations of the world, with some sixty-five per cent of the people below the age of thirty-five. The young are impatient, aspirational and tired of the formulas of the past. Even though the concept of 'New India' was never spelt out in great detail, the idea was appealing, for it brought into play the possibilities of new avenues, new opportunities, and a new vision for transforming the country. These elements of the narrative were projected and disseminated by a highly motivated, disciplined, and huge cadre—for which the credit must go to party president, Amit Shah.

A mandate so huge also bestows great responsibilities and raises very large expectations. It is hoped that the NDA government will rise to the occasion. In particular, it must work to create an India of social harmony, where there is the fullest respect for all faiths, and discordant voices of hate and divisiveness are kept in check. The dictum of the great strategist Chanakya must always be remembered: a nation is only as strong as the harmony it fosters within.

(This piece was originally published on 2 June 2019)

THE CULPABILITY OF PAKISTAN

*M*oments of crisis require national unity underpinned with statesmanship. The dastardly attack by a suicide bomber on the CRPF convoy that claimed forty lives of our braves, is such a moment. Such a brazen attack that took so many lives is unprecedented. The Jaish-e-Mohammad, based in Pakistan has proclaimed that it is responsible for the attack. Since the Jaish operates unhindered from Pakistan, the culpability of Pakistan is established. Pakistan's Prime Minister Imran Khan's speech, in which he had asked India to give proof of Pakistan's complicity, is a fine example of deceit. Pakistan knows it is culpable. The question is, what should India do?

First, it is only to be expected that there is a strong popular feeling that Pakistan should be punished for what it has done. Such a response is legitimate. However, our response must not be impulsive or impetuous. It needs to be carefully planned and calibrated, with the right degree of surprise. Jingoism, war-mongering and bravado must be avoided. Options must be strategically weighed and consequences carefully anticipated. We are, after all, dealing with a face-off between two nuclear powers. Decision making requires maturity and statesmanship, which should not be equated with pusillanimity.

A major responsibility lies with the political leadership. It is a little surprising, therefore, that in his first reaction, our prime minister has said that our armed forces have been given a free hand. Presumably, this means that at the ground level, our armed forces can take such decisions that are needed to protect our borders and repel, and even punish, predators. However, the political executive cannot wash its hands off national strategy.

Secondly, we must do whatever is feasible to strengthen and reinforce the effectiveness of our armed forces and para-military personnel. They must now be provided state-of-the-art weaponry, surveillance technologies, interceptor devices, drones and perimeter security of armed installations. The proxy war that Pakistan is waging against us is not going to end soon. Only a well-equipped force can counter it. Any shortfall in fulfilling our armed forces' legitimate operational requirements must be met on a war footing. At the same time, we must take immediate measures to strengthen our Intelligence gathering abilities, including through a covert presence in Pakistan.

Thirdly, we need to redouble our efforts to isolate Pakistan internationally on its nexus with terrorism. Such efforts need to go beyond 'dossier-diplomacy', wherein we continue to provide more evidence of Pakistan's complicity, when the world already knows that Pakistan is complicit. After all, Osama bin Laden was finally traced to a safe house in Pakistan. That the Jaish and the Lashkar-e-Taiba are global terrorist organisations, operating freely from Pakistan, is well known. Our aim now must be to persuade key countries to go beyond their verbal condemnation of terrorism to specific action against Pakistan.

Sometimes, I think we are too complacent about having put Pakistan on the back-foot diplomatically. The fact of the matter is that China is still Pakistan's all-weather friend; countries like Saudi Arabia are still willing to pump billions of dollars to shore up that terrorist State; and even the USA needs Pakistan to further its strategic interests in Afghanistan. It is important for our foreign office to take a realistic view of the situation, even as we use our leverage and persuasion to convince the world that action against Pakistan where it hurts is necessary.

Fourthly, we need to do a rigorous analysis of what went wrong in Pulwama. Was there an Intelligence failure? Was there a lack of coordination? Did we fail in showing requisite anticipation? Were Standard Operation Procedures (SOPs) not followed where the movement of large convoys is concerned? To ask such questions is not an anti-national act. In fact, it is patriotism that pushes a nation to learn from mistakes, if any, so that such terrorist attacks do not take place in the future. Such post-facto reviews have taken place in the past as well, such as after Kargil. To nullify efforts to learn from the past by resorting to sterile jingoism is to do a great national disservice.

Fifthly, attacks against Kashmiri students and citizens from the Valley in other parts of India must forthwith cease. The need of the hour is national unity. Jammu and Kashmir is an integral part of India. By attacking people from that state, we are only playing into the hands of the terrorist masterminds from across the border that want India to be divided. Those indulging in this anti-national violence must be immediately punished. I would urge our prime minister to make a statement condemning this senseless behaviour, and assuring every citizen of Jammu and Kashmir full security. In this context, the deplorable statement of Meghalaya Governor Tathagatha Roy, advocating the boycott of Kashmir and Kashmiris, merits his removal from this high Constitutional post.

Ultimately, the biggest riposte to Pakistan's nefarious designs is a happy and prosperous Jammu and Kashmir within the Union of India. If by withdrawing security and other government facilities to the members of the discredited Hurriyat, we have signalled that they are no longer desirable interlocutors, then we must find other credible interlocutors. Home-grown terrorists in the Valley indoctrinated by Pakistan, must be dealt with firmly. But, to proceed on the assumption that all Kashmiris are terrorists would be disastrous. The commencement of a dialogue and a healing process to counter the increasing radicalisation in Kashmir, especially among the youth, is not an easy task. But, it cannot be abdicated.

In any vibrant democracy where elections are around the corner, sober but resolute thinking often becomes a victim to the immediate benefits of rhetoric and bluster. We must not allow this to happen. We have suffered a grievous tragedy. Pakistan must be punished for its transparent complicity in perpetrating it. But how this is done requires dispassionate planning, away from the arc lights of public approbation. The Indian State must rise to the occasion, weighing all options carefully without losing sight of larger goals. Even as some nations support our cause, or appear to support it, this will be, in the final analysis, our battle. The great Chanakya put it succinctly: Nations respect those nations that respect themselves.

(This piece was originally published on 24 February 2019)

BALAKOT: A PARADIGM SHIFT

*I*n my view, the fundamental aspect about the air strike at the Jaish training camp in Balakot is that it signifies a paradigm shift in our security doctrine. In a pre-dawn attack on 26 February, twelve of our Mirage-2000 fighter jets crossed the Line Of Control (LOC) and used precision-guided SPICE-2000 bombs to hit terrorist targets deep within Pakistan territory.

Why do I call this a paradigm shift? Because since 1971, we have never in self-defence crossed the LOC. We did not do it after 26/11. We did not do it even after Kargil, when there was a verifiable armed intrusion into our territory by Pakistan. The intruders were on vantage points. To evict them we would have to send to certain death hundreds of our young officers and soldiers. In view of this, our obvious response should have been to cross the LOC, seal it, and starve the intruders by lack of supplies. But we did not do this. Instead, our policymakers went about the Chancelleries of the world collecting certificates of good behaviour and restraint.

This time, post-Pulwama, we showed the national resolve, in self-defence, to move from credible deterrence to—what is called in military terms—compellance, demonstrating to the enemy nation that when provoked beyond a point, we are willing to retaliate by entering its territory and taking out its terrorist bases. It seems almost certain that Pakistan was taken by surprise. It must have concluded, that like in the past, India will not go beyond the rhetoric of a 'befitting reply'. The Balakot attack thus created—to use another military term—'psychological dislocation' in the enemy camp and demolished its complacency with regard to India's lack of retaliatory options.

This, indeed, is the principal takeaway of Balakot. The controversy about what damage was caused by our air-strike is entirely irrelevant. The controversy was created in the first place by irresponsible statements by members of the BJP, giving different figures of the number of casualties. They were not authorised to do so. The only statement that matters is what was said by the armed forces in their press briefing. Anything else could be said only by an authorised representative of the government on the authority of the Cabinet Committee on Security (CCS).

It would be unfortunate if a conscious attempt is made to politicise the Balakot attack. Nitish Kumar made a categorical statement that matters of national security are, by definition, national in nature and not a subject of partisan politics. No politicisation does not mean that no questions can be asked about Balakot or Pulwama. In a democracy, people have the freedom to ask, and the right to know. To conflate any such query or desire mechanically with anti-nationalism is, in fact, politicisation. What needs to be eschewed is seeking votes over the valour and sacrifice of our brave soldiers. In this context, the statement of Yeddyurappa, BJP leader in Karnataka, wherein he said that as a result of Balakot, the BJP would win many more seats in that state, is highly regrettable.

Pulwama also is subject to interrogation. Could the attack have been prevented? Such questions are inevitable in a democracy and should be welcomed to prevent another attack of this nature from happening. To say that anyone asking such questions is unpatriotic is also politicisation through the instrument of ultra-nationalism.

Will Balakot impact voting choices in the coming parliamentary elections? It could, and it may not. If people believe that the current government has shown unprecedented spunk in responding to Pakistan's nexus with terrorism, it will reap the credit as well. If post-Balakot there is a verifiable impact on Pakistan's sponsorship of terrorism, that credit too will come to the current ruling party. If, however, terrorism from across the border continues unabated, and cross-border infiltrations claiming the lives of our soldiers and civilians increase, the government and the ruling party will have to accept the downside too. The security situation on our borders with Pakistan, and in the Valley, is dynamic. Much can happen between now and the dates of polling.

Besides, it is not as if voter choices hinge inflexibly on any one factor. National security is one variable, but a voter is motivated by several others, including local issues, the economic situation especially with regard to jobs and agrarian distress, party affiliations, and the regional calculus of power. To posit national security as a single polarity against many other variables would be silly. It is not an either–or situation. The bottom-line is that if the ruling party is seen to be competent in containing or responding to the threat from across the border, security issues will have some bearing on voter sentiment. To what extent, remains to be seen.

The task is far more difficult for the Opposition. Nationalism is an electorally inflammable issue. Even if it is not desirable to use it for partisan political gain, the ruling party will seek to benefit from it. The Opposition must devise the fine line between being supportive to national imperatives and asking the right questions at the right time in the right measure, to the ruling party. Its best bet would be to seek accountability from the government, whenever there are good reasons to do so, on the success of the battle against terrorism emanating from across the border.

Pulwama was a tragedy. To the extent possible, such tragedies must not happen again. Balakot was an action waiting to happen. The decision to implement it must go to the credit of the government. But any attempt to sensationalise it or make it sound like the definitive answer to Pakistan's terrorism, as was done with the surgical strike, could be counter productive. This is the challenge for the ruling party.

(This piece was originally published on 10 March 2019)

THE 'STEEL FRAME' IS IN DANGER

Sardar Patel is credited with creating the 'steel frame' of India, which was an all-India bureaucratic structure. Such a structure, which included what are called all-India services, such as the Indian Administrative Service (IAS), and the Indian Police Service (IPS), was expected to be impartial, beyond partisan politics, and guided by a code of conduct that ensured neutrality and administrative effectiveness. Governments may come, and governments may go, but the steel frame was the bi-partisan executive continuity of the business of government. It was conceived as the executive bedrock, immune to political pressure, continuing in perpetuity, even if political parties, and the governments formed by them, lost or won at the hustings.

But Sardar Patel probably did not visualise what happened recently in Kolkata, where a senior IPS officer was 'shielded' by the state government, led by the feisty Mamata Banerjee, from being arrested by a team of the Central Bureau of Investigation (CBI). It was a classic case of the Central government being at loggerheads with the state government in an all-out political slugfest, where the collateral damage was clearly the erosion of some of the fundamental premises on which the 'steel frame' of India was built.

The crux of the problem is that in conceiving the civil services, in the manner that they exist today, Sardar Patel had accepted that officers will be supervised at the dual level of both the Centre and the state. When they are posted as part of the Central government, they will follow the directive of the controlling authority in Delhi, and when they are posted in states, they will be substantially under the authority of the state government.

In the case of Rajiv Kumar, the police officer in the eye of the Kolkata storm, he is, as the Police Commissioner of Kolkata, answerable to Chief Minister Mamata Banerjee, but his cadre controlling authority is the central Ministry of Home Affairs. There is, as envisaged, an overlap with regard to who he reports to in his current avatar, and who is responsible for his overall conduct in terms of his being a member of an all-India service. It is this duality that enabled Mamata Banerjee to prevent his 'surrender' to the CBI. And, it is this duality too that has now prompted the Union Home Ministry to take action against Rajiv Kumar, and other police officers serving in West Bengal, including the Director-General of Police, under several rules of the All India Services (AIS), 1968. This action could include removing the 'delinquent officers' from the empanelment list, which would bar them from serving at the Centre, and withdrawing medals or decoration conferred on them for meritorious services.

The Central government also took this matter to the Supreme Court. In a judicial directive that plays a fine balancing act between the prerogatives of the CBI, the central investigating agency, and the state government, the Court directed that Rajiv Kumar could be questioned for his alleged non-cooperation against the guilty in the chit fund scam, but he could not be arrested, and that the interrogation would be in a 'neutral' place—which was neither Delhi nor Kolkata, but Shillong. The Court's directive was hailed as a victory by both the opposing sides—the BJP and Mamata Banerjee. But this is far from being the end of the story.

The crux of the matter is not an immediate solution to this incident, but the far more serious issue of Centre-state relations where officers of the all-India services are concerned. The steel frame devised by Sardar Patel was premised on a cooperative interface between the Central and state governments. But if that cooperation ceases, the entire system is likely to be jeopardised. If, for instance, state governments begin to doubt the bona fides of the Central government with regard to action against all-India officers and refuses to cooperate in the implementation of existing service procedures, the consequences can be very serious. Officers of the all-India services serving in their states could, with the backing of the state chief minister, ignore the directives of the Central government in its capacity as the cadre-controlling authority. Since state governments are often ruled by political parties who are in opposition to the party at the Centre, such political confrontations could proliferate, and there could be many more Rajiv Kumars caught in the ensuing political battles. One very deleterious consequence could be the further politicisation of the bureaucracy, with officers on deputation to the Centre or serving in the states, deciding to jettison their mandatory political neutrality in favour of open partisanship with political parties, either at the Centre or in the states.

In the case of the IPS, the situation is further complicated because 'police' and 'public order' are in the State list under the Constitution, and not in the Concurrent list. This could further bolster the claim of ruling parties in the states to resist any 'encroachment' of their jurisdiction by the Central government. What happens then in crimes that are not restricted only to one state, and have inter-state implications? The chit fund scam is a case in point. It has a footprint across several states. This massive Ponzi scheme has defrauded some seventeen lakh investors to the tune of 3,500 crores. Investigations have to carried out in states, but the designated investigating agency is a Central one, the CBI. The victims are crying out for justice, but the investigation has become a football being kicked around as political parties at the Centre and the state fight out their political battles.

The fact of the matter is that the steel frame, like many other institutions in the federal polity that is our Republic, rests on the foundation of trust between the Centre and the states. If the trust deficit becomes too wide, institutions of this nature will fall through the gap. In the political cacophony of the world's largest democracy, and the pressures that build up as political differences become more acrimonious with general elections approaching, we need to be very careful about what the collateral damage is to the time-tested institutions that have always safeguarded our nation.

(This piece was originally published on 10 February 2019)

SCRUTINISING EVMs

*I*s it possible that a press conference in London by a seemingly deranged man about the working of EVMs in India, can hijack all media debate for days on end in the world's largest democracy? One would think not, but this is precisely what happened last week. On 20 January, a gentleman called Syed Shuja, who says he has 'political asylum' in the US, invited the media, and representatives of all political parties in India, to witness what he described as a 'hackathon', where he would demonstrate that all elections conducted through EVMs were rigged. No political party turned up to give credence to this preposterous claim. But, Kapil Sibal, a senior leader of the Congress party did.

Kapil Sibal later clarified that he was in London on a personal visit and that he attended this event in his personal capacity. This is possible, and Sibal has every right to entertain himself in any way he wishes. But what is absurd is to give credence to Shuja. This is the mistake the Congress party made. In trying to defend the presence of Sibal at this joke of an event, it ended up giving credibility to this crackpot.

Who is Shuja? He is a self-declared EVM hacker, with what appears to be a completely cock-and-bull story about his past. According to the Indian Journalists Association (IJA), which had organised this press conference, he was given political asylum by the USA in March 2018. However, the name in the documents released by the IJA is of one Syed Hyder Ahmed; the date of birth of Shuja does not match with the documents; Shuja's claim that he worked with the Electronics Corporation of India Ltd (ECIL), has been rubbished by the ECIL. In an official letter to the Election Commission (EC), the ECIL has categorically stated that no such person worked with it or was associated with the design and development of EVMs.

Shuja's claim is that eleven of his teammates were murdered in a guest house in Hyderabad in the presence of BJP MLA, G. Kishan Reddy. Reddy emphatically denied the allegation. Moreover, the Foreign Press Association (FPA) in London, to which the IJA is affiliated, has squarely distanced itself from the rantings of Shuja. Deborah Bonetti, the Director of the FPA, said in a tweet that Shuja, 'provided no proof for the very extreme allegations' he made and that he should not have been given a platform. She further said that the FPA 'strongly disassociates itself with any claims made by the speaker.' Even Ashish Ray, the head of the IJA, admitted that Shuja could not 'substantiate his allegations, and left a roomful of scribes highly sceptical if not annoyed.'

If this is the level of Shuja's credibility, why did our media—and many of our leading politicians—give so much space and time to what he said? The answer is unfortunate but simple. The world's largest democracy spent less time in demolishing the outrageous allegations of an obvious lunatic, and more to the presence of Kapil Sibal at the event. As a consequence, Shuja's ridiculous claims got largely unanalysed publicity and made Indians, as a whole, look rather foolish in the eyes of the international community. For days there was nothing else to discuss on many TV channels except what this madman had said. What should have been disdainfully dismissed with a flick of a finger by any mature democracy, became the subject of mainstream discussion till days after the IJA press conference in London.

What is worse is that the central point that Shuja made, entirely on baseless grounds, that EVMs can be—and have been hacked—became a subject matter of a full-fledged debate in our great land. Kapil Sibal, who must be feeling a little sheepish about being the only political leader who was present at the Shuja circus, sought to defend himself by saying that the claims of this self-styled cyber expert 'were very serious and must be probed.' Congress spokespersons followed suit. A man whose allegations were rubbished by the very organisation that organised his presser, transformed into the mascot of 'reforming' the Indian democratic system, making it a classic case of making a dubious messenger into a giant messiah!

It is utter nonsense to postulate that EVM machines are capable of mass hacking. Shuja's claim that the 2014 parliamentary elections were rigged through a manipulation of the EVM machines is laughable. So is Shuja's assertion that the historic win of the AAP party in the last Delhi state elections was rigged. The country has seen countless elections where EVMs have been used. Some have been won by the BJP, and some by the Congress. There is no pattern to even remotely suggest that electoral results in all these elections is part of some Machiavellian plan involving the systematic rigging of EVMs.

Yes, there could be scope for improving the functioning of EVMs. But this is a matter that the EC is more than competent to handle. Suggestions regarding Voter Verified Paper Trail Audits or VVPATs—or any other way to strengthen the impartiality and effectiveness of EVMs—are welcome. The correct thing is to discuss these matters within our own forums, and not give so much importance to ridiculous charges emanating from foreign soil. Responsible people, like S.Y. Qureshi, the former CEC, have publicly stated that EVMs are not susceptible to mass rigging. Do we listen to people like him or to Shuja? It seems that we need to remind ourselves that we are not a tin-pot democracy born yesterday, but that elections in India are the world's single largest organised human operation whose credibility—in spite of some shortcomings—has stood the test of time.

One last point: the demand that EVMs should be replaced by ballot papers, is truly misplaced. The greatest abuse of the electoral process took place when ballot papers were the only option, and in many parts of India, all that elections meant was which candidate had the greater muscle power to capture more ballot papers. If more can be done to remove any residual doubts regarding the working of EVMs, the EC should do so. But, to ask for a reversal to ballot papers would be by far a wrong step, and least of all because of the allegations of people like Shuja.

(This piece was originally published on 2 January 2019)

THE ELECTION COMMISSION
MUST PLAY ITS ROLE

*T*he Election Commission justifiably enjoys a great deal of respect. Over the years, it has established for itself a reputation of conducting elections in India—including that of the President and Vice President of India—with commendable efficiency and dedication. By and large, the impartiality of the EC has not come under a cloud, and its autonomy, as an institution, is not in doubt.

However, the effectiveness of the EC is in question today. This is not because of lack of good intent, but because the EC, for whatever reason, seems to be reticent in taking action in a dynamic and decisive manner when the Model Code of Conduct (MCC) in force, is violated.

What is the cause of this reticence? Does the EC lack sufficient deterrent powers, or does it not want to fully use these powers even when the provocation so demands? This is a fundamentally important question, since the parliamentary elections—the world's largest organised human exercise where the electorate is a staggering 900 million—is about to unfold, and it is imperative that people retain their faith that the supervision and conduct of these elections by the EC are done effectively and impartially.

The EC derives its powers from a categorical provision in the

Constitution. Article 324 vests it with the powers to 'conduct' elections. This is an all-powerful, omnibus clause. In pursuance of this clause, the EC puts out a Model Code of Conduct for all political parties and candidates. The MCC is not a wishy-washy document. For instance, it clearly says that 'No party *shall* include in any activity which may aggravate existing differences or create mutual hatred or cause tension between different castes and communities, religious or linguistic.' It also says, inter alia, that, 'There shall be no appeal to caste or communal feeling for securing votes.' These are unambiguous injunctions.

The Chief Election Commissioner is ensconced with full security of tenure. Clause 5 of Article 324 says, 'The CEC shall not be removed from his office except in the like manner and on the like grounds as a Judge of the Supreme Court (SC) and the conditions of service of the CEC shall not be varied to his disadvantage after his appointment.' This literally means that while in office, the CEC's tenure is near invincible, for—as in the case of an SC judge—he can only be removed when a resolution is passed by a two-thirds majority of both Houses of Parliament on the grounds of proved misbehaviour or incapacity. The CEC and the two Election Commissioners draw salaries and allowances at par with those of the judges of the SC.

Why then is the CEC, and his two colleagues, so diffident and restrained in acting against open violations of the political class? The MCC is a mandatory document. The powers of the EC are unfettered under the Constitution. And yet, what we see is the EC issuing at best a rap on the knuckles or an ineffectual reprimand when politicians flout the MCC. The most recent example is the EC's response to Yogi Adityanath's attempt to politicise the armed forces by using the phrase '*Modiji ki sena*' (Modi's army). Instead of taking suo motu deterrent action in the matter, the EC issued him a notice, and then merely said that he should 'exercise caution' and be 'more careful' in future references to the armed forces in his poll campaign speeches. When the process is so dilatory, and the deterrence is so mild, is it any wonder that in spite of the EC's notice to Yogi Adityanath for using such a phrase, a senior Cabinet minister in the government, Mukhtar Abbas Naqvi, used precisely this very phrase again.

Another example is that of Rajasthan governor Kalyan Singh. He was video-taped openly saying that he is a BJP supporter, and exhorting people to vote for Prime Minister Modi. This is a grave violation of his constitutional mandate to be apolitical. The EC took cognisance of this violation and sent its views to the President of India, who passed it on to the Home ministry for advice. Nothing further has been heard of the matter. A similar event happened during the Assembly election in Uttar Pradesh in 2012, when the CEC wrote to the President seeking intervention in a matter where two Cabinet ministers of the UPA government wilfully and repeatedly flouted the instructions of the EC. The President passed on the EC's letter to the Prime Minister's office (PMO). Given the fact that the two erring ministers belonged to the then prime minister's party, it was not surprising that he did very little about the matter.

The basic fact is that the world's largest democracy needs a makeover of the role of the EC. If the EC does not itself proactively take deterrent action in conducting the elections, its role is weakened and its instructions rendered ineffective. Frankly, our politicians—cutting across all parties—care little for epistles advising caution or expressing displeasure. They will behave as per the rules only when they believe that the EC can and will *punish* them for deliberate violation of the MCC. Such punishment could include suspension of campaigning for a defined period of time, or even countermanding of an election, or disqualification of a candidate. This fear of the law can be instilled by a powerful autonomous body deriving its powers from the Constitution, which the EC is.

It is not surprising that the ordinary citizen misses the likes of T.N. Seshan, who instilled fear in the political class in the interests of the impartial conduct of elections. Ultimately, the EC is as good as the incumbent at the helm, and it is for precisely this reason that the SC should take quick action on the matter pending before it on whether the CEC and the Election Commissioners should be appointed by a collegium, and not merely by choice of the ruling party in power. The manner in which the EC currently acts reminds me of a couplet by Ghalib:

Hamne maana ke taghaful na karo ge lekin
Khaaq ho jayenge hum unko asar hone tak

(I accept that you may not reject but yet I will be reduced to ashes by the time you react)

(This piece was originally published on 7 April 2019)

WHY IS INDIA THE WORLD'S LARGEST ARM'S IMPORTER?

The recent VVIP helicopter scam needs to be investigated thoroughly, but without losing sight of one basic fact: so long as India retains its place as the world's biggest importer of arms, and so long as what we need to buy runs into thousands of crores, the whiff of corruption will almost never leave the corridors of the Ministry of Defence.

Chanakya taught us the need to have clarity in thinking. He had the faculty to identify a problem with honesty, and then to work with courage and focus to resolve it. What is the problem with our defence deals? The problem is that due to institutional incompetence we have catapulted ourselves into becoming the world's biggest purchaser of arms but have neither prepared ourselves to deal with this situation nor taken stock of our indigenous defence production capabilities to get out of it.

We set up the Defence Research and Development Organisation (DRDO) as far back as 1958, but its performance has been, in a word, awful. Among its many spectacular failures is the production of the Light Combat Aircraft, which was commissioned over a decade ago but is running about half a decade behind schedule with a cost overrun of around 5,000 crores. Other projects allocated to DRDO, such as the Airborne Early Warning and Control System and the Naval Light Combat Aircraft, have also missed deadlines by several years. Our defence PSUs have been equally tardy. Hindustan Aeronautics Ltd (HAL) could not rectify simple design faults in the HPT-32, forcing our Air Force to import propeller-driven trainers. The Intermediate Jet Trainer (IJT) prototype is nowhere close to flying, and the Light Attack Helicopter and the multi-purpose civilian aircraft, Saras have forever been in the pipeline. DRDO, whose aim was to produce seventy per cent of our defence needs by 2005, is still lackadaisically hovering around thirty per cent—and much of what emerges from its factories are put together using 'screwdriver' technology.

To see a nation with global aspirations blundering so egregiously when it comes to meeting critical defence requirements is nothing short of scandalous. As a result of our woefully inadequate indigenous defence production, India has become the world's largest importer of arms. China, with a much larger arsenal and a much bigger defence budget, has dropped to fourth place because its internal defence production has been efficiently upgraded. Arms imports have come down dramatically. Russia and Ukraine are the only outside suppliers of China's weaponry, most of which is now produced at lesser cost at home. If India had pursued its indigenous arms production effectively, we would not require such huge defence purchases and could be even exporting arms and using that income for development.

Our procurement policy is also in deep disarray. Obviously, defence purchases must be corruption free, but for that, we have to put our own house in order, which we are nowhere close to doing. Equally, to ban every major foreign supplier on the basis of the first allegation of corruption is to display a 'morality paralysis' that is suicidal. When several firms compete to supply to the world's largest buyer, the easiest thing for the loser is to allege corruption. It is for the Raksha Mantri to show the guts not to be concerned only about his personal integrity, but also about the crucial security interests of the nation. A morality halo is one thing, but it cannot be at the cost of vital security interests. In his letter of March 2012 to the prime minister, former COAS General V.K. Singh had bluntly stated that the war-waging capability of the army has been 'seriously degraded' because of delays in critical procurements. Yet, little could be done to rectify matters since, in a classic case of cutting one's nose to spite one's face, most of the major firms who could supply what we needed had been banned by the ministry of Defence in the UPA government due to allegations of corruption.

The nation is thus faced with a double jeopardy: we cannot produce what we need internally, and we cannot import—in time, ethically and efficiently—what we must buy from abroad.

So, what do we need to do? Firstly, the DRDO and the defence PSUs need a major overhaul. The CAG should produce a major report on them so that projects past their sell-by dates are weeded out and a realistic review is made of what these organisations are capable of producing in the future. This report must be prepared in three months. Secondly, indigenous defence production should be opened to Public-Private Partnership (PPP). It makes no sense to extensively buy from private foreign manufacturers while keeping armaments out of the purview of our own private sector. A targeted indigenisation policy should be prepared wherein certain sectors of defence production are outsourced to, or earmarked for partnership with, private agencies, with a transparent process for selection and a strong accountability regime. Thirdly, raising the current cap of twenty-six per cent for FDI in defence production to forty-nine per cent is a good idea. In a situation where our own private sector is not allowed to set up armaments industries and we are the world's largest importer of arms, there can be no harm, at least in the mid-term, of allowing the world's leading arms manufacturers to set up arms manufacturing subsidiaries within the country to supply the country's defence needs, especially as we are already importing arms from them. Fourthly, we need to vastly improve our existing procurement policy, by setting up an integrated Defence Procurement Directorate with the representation of the CAG to vet procurement processes, so that it works ethically and to stringent timelines.

Chanakya believed in getting to the root of a problem in order to solve it. The absence of the reforms mentioned above is the root cause why skeletons tumble out every time we do major defence purchase deals. We must understand the real problem, not merely be mesmerised by the symptoms.

(This piece was originally published on 3 March 2013)

A NON-FUNCTIONING PARLIAMENT

*P*oliticians are supposed to have their finger on the pulse of the people, but they are hopelessly out of sync with what people feel with regard to the spectacle they make of themselves in parliament. The simple fact is that Indians are fed up of parliament looking like a circus gone berserk. They are tired of the indiscipline, ruckus, din, vandalism, hooliganism and sheer bad behaviour of their elected representatives, both in some state assemblies and in the *sansad*—the highest temple of democracy.

The ongoing session of parliament has not functioned for a single day. Within minutes of the House convening, MPs shout slogans, display placards, hurl invectives, and enter the well of the House, thereby forcing an adjournment. On some occasions, an attempt is made to convene the House a second time, but now mostly both the Lok Sabha and the Rajya Sabha are adjourned for the full day. The next day the same tasteless charade is repeated again. In its entire history, the House of Commons has not been adjourned for a single day. Soon we will be able to say with pride that there is not a single day when our parliament is not adjourned!

Does this behaviour further the cause of the protesting MPs/ political parties? I think not. There was a time when a spectacle in parliament leading to an adjournment made the news. No longer. Since adjournments—preceded by the predictably undecipherable din—happen so regularly, they have no news value, and only create another ripple of disgust in the ordinary citizen. In fact, the paralysis of parliamentary business is increasingly proving to be counter-productive: people are more annoyed at parliament's non-functioning than supportive of the reasons why it is not allowed to function. The agitating MPs would do far more for their cause if they allowed for a discussion, where they could present their point of view in a reasoned manner, and enable the entire country, through the media to hear it.

There is little to be gained in trying to establish culpability for this deplorable state of affairs. All parties are culpable. When the UPA government was in power, it blamed the BJP for the disruptions. This was not untrue. The BJP actually sought to give 'ideological' sanction to their parliamentary indiscipline. Arun Jaitley and Sushma Swaraj, Leaders of the Opposition in the Rajya Sabha and the Lok Sabha respectively, asserted that disruption of the House is a legitimate part of a parliamentary strategy. As a consequence, parliament did not function for days on end.

But now the shoe is on the other foot. The BJP occupies the treasury benches, and the Congress—along with its erstwhile UPA allies—is in the Opposition. No one in politics suffers from amnesia in these matters. So, the Opposition is now doing to the BJP what it did to them. The treasury benches protest, just as the UPA, when in power, used to. This undignified game goes on as part of a hopeless vicious circle, while the nation—and the world—watches the antics of the world's largest democracy.

What can be done? It is true that the primary responsibility to run the House lies with the treasury benches. The ruling party must interact with respect with the Opposition—both in the House and outside, or in forums in parliament created for this purpose—so that logjams are broken. A key role here is that of the Minister of Parliamentary Affairs. In the UPA years, Rajiv Shukla held this post. Pranab Mukherjee, then Leader of the House, used to tell Rajiv that his performance would be judged by the amount of time he spends in the Opposition benches, building bridges, and diluting friction. The same responsibility now lies with the leaders of the BJP, and it cannot be implemented with arrogance or disdain. But, equally, the Opposition cannot say that it is blameless. There is nothing the treasury benches can do if the Opposition is hell-bent on not allowing the House to run. That is the plain truth.

Can the Speaker of the Lok Sabha and the Chairman of the Rajya Sabha enforce discipline? Of course, they can. The presiding officers of the two Houses are invested with wide-ranging disciplinary powers. They decide when a member speaks and for how long; they decide what will not go on record; they can direct a member to withdraw from the House for a specific period; any member who flouts their orders can be named, and in such cases, may have to withdraw from the House; they can warn a member for flouting rules and suspend him; the marshals of the Houses work under them; and, within the House, their rulings in such matters, are unchallengeable. With such powers at hand, why do presiding officers not exercise them to maintain the discipline and decorum of the House? For too long now, blatantly unacceptable behaviour has been tolerated or condoned by presiding officers, and this lack of a resolute stand has undoubtedly contributed to the slide into parliamentary chaos over the last few years.

The basic fact is that the non-functioning of parliament must stop. Over 2.5 lakhs is spent per minute to run parliament. The current leg of the budget session is for twenty-three days, of which fourteen have so far been wasted. Important bills that affect the lives of ordinary citizens are pending, even as every day both Houses are adjourned. There is merit in the proposal that if parliament does not work due to lack of parliamentary decorum, members should not be paid their allowance for that day, and presiding officers should be impartial in enforcing this rule.

The nation expects reasoned debates of the highest calibre from its elected representatives—as, indeed, used to be the case in the past. The Opposition must establish the validity of its point of view through the dignity and substance of debate and not through slogan shouting. The treasury response should be likewise. To put it bluntly, the people of India have had enough of the unseemly shenanigan in parliament. The time has come for all political parties to get this message.

(This piece was originally published on 25 March 2018)

CREDIBLE RULES FOR INDIA'S DEMOCRACY

*W*hat has unfolded in Karnataka has made one thing abundantly clear: the world's largest democracy must establish some definitive and transparent rules, in order to retain its credibility. The prospect of no single party getting a clear majority on its own in many states, and even in the parliamentary elections due in 2019, looms large. If this happens, the grey zones, where the distinction between morality and legal interpretations blur as per convenience, must cease to exist. Each political player must know that in the event of a hung House, these are the rules of the game, and no amount of skulduggery can change how the democratic script will play out.

The shenanigans in Karnataka provide a perfect trigger for the Supreme Court to lay down these clear-cut rules. The highest court in the land has risen to the occasion in the past. There was the landmark judgement in the S.R. Bommai case in 1985, which made clear that a party that claims majority must do so on the floor of the House, and not in the drawing room of the Governor. This eliminated the subjective satisfaction of the Governor, or even the President of India, as the criteria for a political party to lay claim to a majority. Even earlier, parliament had passed the amendment to the tenth schedule of the Constitution, relating to defections, to prevent horse-trading and the blatant misuse of money power to buy legislators. In 2005, some more principles were laid down by the Supreme Court in the Rameshwar Prasad case.

But obviously, these are not enough. Frankly, however much the legal pundits may quibble, there is no categorical clarity on what course of action has legitimacy in a hung House. Does the Governor invite the single largest party first? Does he give priority to a pre-poll alliance? Or, does he choose a post-poll alliance? There are precedents to support either of these choices. When it has suited it, the Congress has supported the principle of priority being given to the single largest party. This was seen, most recently, in the elections in Goa, Tripura and Meghalaya, where it was the single largest party. On that occasion, the BJP argued that a post-poll alliance has the first right to be invited to form the government, because it was not the single largest party. Now, in Karnataka, the two parties are arguing precisely the opposite: the BJP asserts that the single largest party must be preferred, and the Congress is espousing the rights of the post-poll alliance.

Certain facts are clear. The BJP did well in the Karnataka elections, but not well enough. It emerged as the single largest party with 104 seats, but not a clear majority. In spite of the choreographed projections of euphoria on behalf of BJP spokespersons, the party must introspect why, after five years of the Siddaramiah government—and the mood of anti-incumbency it was expected to generate—it did not get a clear majority on its own. This question becomes all the more relevant since the BJP had pulled out all the stops to secure this majority. Prime Minister Modi held twenty-one rallies, and credit must be given to the indefatigable energy he invested to boost the BJP's prospects. Dozens of Central ministers were parked for days in Bengaluru. No stone was left unturned to influence the voters. And yet, the majority mark remained elusive.

This was in stark contrast to what happened in 2013, when after five years of BJP rule, the Congress led by Siddaramiah got a clear majority of 122 seats. Quite clearly, five years later, the BJP could not repeat this. Either there was not that degree of anti-incumbency sentiment against Siddarmiah, or the mood against the BJP was not that positive, or the efforts put in by Rahul Gandhi helming the Congress, was effective enough to ensure that the BJP did not do as well as it hoped to.

In all of this, what has certainly gone out of the democratic window is any notion of public morality. All concerns about corruption were finessed by caste calculations. Only this can explain the choice of Yeddyurappa, who had spent time in jail on corruption charges, as the BJP's chief ministerial candidate. His strength was not probity, but his alleged hold on the powerful Lingayat community. The tainted Bellary brothers were taken on board by the BJP merely on winnability considerations. Unfortunately, it is now accepted that the high constitutional office of the Governor will not necessarily be objective. A disgusted public has also accepted that when it comes to securing a majority, horse trading, involving mind-boggling amounts of money, will be the choice of political parties. 'Resort' politics, where legislators who are empowered to make laws that will affect our lives, are herded into stringently enforced insulation so that they can be prevented from being bribed, is accepted as the norm. It is also accepted that biased presiding officers of the Assembly, will do the needful to evade the provisions of the anti-defection law.

The bitter truth is that we are becoming a very sordid democracy. I don't think politicians will reform. That is why, the Supreme Court must intervene and lay down a new set of clear-cut guidelines, on how we can endeavour to run a more ethical democracy, and intervene again, proactively, to ensure that its rules are enforced. Otherwise, we will continue to have such situations where, in the pursuit of power, each party, throwing all principles to the wind, will quote whatever precedent or legality that suits it. This ambivalence must end.

As I finish writing this column, the floor test in the Karnataka Assembly has concluded. Amidst the unseemly drama, the Congress–JDS combine has proven its majority. The Karnataka elections are over. But, in the process, Indian democracy has, in more ways than one, emerged as the loser.

(This piece was originally published on 20 May 2018)

THE SUBVERSION OF DELHI
STATE GOVERNMENT

*A*most bizarre drama is unfolding in the capital of India. A government, elected with one of the most overwhelming mandates in recent history, is being deliberately paralysed by a nominated Lt Governor backed by a cynical Central government. The situation has now escalated into much more than a power struggle between the Lt Governor and the Chief Minister. It is also no longer merely a question of political one-upmanship. Nor is it only a symptom of the transient political adversities which are commonplace in the world's largest democracy. Bluntly put, the situation has now developed into one that has deeply serious consequences for the smooth and efficient functioning of the federal structure of India.

Let us look at the facts. First, it is true that Delhi does not have full statehood. To my mind, that in itself is an anomaly. In a state with more people than the combined population of countries like Hungary, Greece, Bhutan and Cyprus, it is dysfunctional that a popularly elected chief minister does not have full powers to implement the promises on which the electorate has elected him. Every successive chief minister, be he or she from the BJP or the Congress, has argued the case, on purely functional and democratic grounds, for full statehood for Delhi, and the former has probably been the most strident, even going so far as to make it a part of their manifesto in the parliamentary elections. But let us, for the moment, leave this apart.

Even as a Union Territory, what are the powers that the Constitution confers on the nominated, unelected Lt Governor? Article 239 AA, clause 4 lays down that he will function on the aid and advice of the council of ministers on all matters on which the Legislative Assembly has the power to make laws. According to Article 239 AA, clause (3) (a), the Legislative Assembly of Delhi has the powers to make laws on all matters mentioned in the State list or the Concurrent list of the Constitution, except land, public order and the police. Thus, these three exceptions are the only areas where, in a Union Territory, the Lt Governor has extra powers compared to that of governors in other states.

In conformity with this explicit legal situation, the mandate of the Lt Governor is to facilitate the functioning of the democratically elected government, and not amplify his restricted powers to obstruct the mandate of the people. It is precisely here that my good friend Najeeb Jung, for whom I have otherwise great affection, has erred rather inexcusably. To overrule the chief minister's choice for Chief Secretary, or to countermand other administrative appointments made by the Delhi government, is tantamount, in my view, to reducing the duly elected chief minister to a cypher.

The real issue is that, whatever the legal situation, there are certain conventions and precedents regarding the interaction between the president and the prime minister, and governors and chief ministers. These conventions provide an informal but institutionalised forum for quiet consultations and in-camera discussions, even on issues on which there are differences. The purpose is to never convey the impression that the Governor is seeking to browbeat a democratically elected leader. The importance of this convention, which also has constitutional guarantees, must prevail even if the governor is an appointee of a party which is different to or opposed to the democratically elected political party.

What we are seeing in Delhi is diametrically opposite. The impression is rapidly gaining ground that the Lt Governor is acting in a deliberately *adversarial* role to the mandate given by the people to his chief minister. In many ways, this development is, for Delhi, quite unprecedented. There have been in the past BJP chief ministers with Lt Governors appointed by the Congress, and Congress chief ministers under Lt Governors who are BJP appointees. But this kind of unseemly fracas has never happened in the past.

Moreover, it is evident that the government at the Centre is using the post of the Lt Governor to embarrass the AAP government. If this is not the case, what can explain the manner in which the Central government has amended Article 368 of the Constitution by a mere notification? The powers to amend the Constitution (as has been argued by eminent lawyers like K.T.S. Tulsi and others) lie exclusively with parliament. But, through its notification of 21 May, the Central government has unconstitutionally amended the Constitution by adding a fourth power to the three already given to the Lt Governor. This fourth power, termed as 'services', has been unilaterally added to clause 3 of Article 239 AA by the stroke of a 'notification'. This is, as Tulsi says, 'autocratic, dictatorial and undemocratic.'

The opposition by the Lt Governor to the deputation of some police officers from Bihar to the Anti Corruption Bureau (ACB) of the Delhi government is also quite inexplicable. The Delhi police may be under the Home ministry, and, therefore, by extension, under the Lt Governor, but the ACB is explicitly under the charge of the chief minister, and, to my understanding, this position has been categorically upheld by a very recent judgement of the High Court. Why should the Lt Governor then veto a move by the chief minister to strengthen a unit legitimately under him with the laudable purpose to rein in corruption?

To my mind, the NDA government at the Centre should be very, very careful in trying to use the Lt Governor to hobble or embarrass the democratically elected chief minister of Delhi. Who knows, tomorrow the shoe can be on the other foot, with a BJP chief minister and a Lt Governor with affiliations to another political party. Would the BJP like to be treated in the same manner in which they are treating Arvind Kejriwal?

What is happening in Delhi should alert all political parties on the perils of derailing democracy through the misuse of the office of the nominated Governor or Lt Governor. Certainly, the people of Delhi, who gave the AAP a massive mandate, will not accept this cynical game being played out at their cost. Perhaps, the time has come for Hon'ble President to intervene in his gentle but firm manner.

(This piece was originally published on 7 June 2015)

THE IC-814 HIJACKING:
DILETTANTISM IN SECURITY

*T*o what extent can issues of national security become hostage to partisan politics? This is the question that has come to the fore in the reactions to *Kashmir: The Vajpayee Years* by J.S. Dulat, former chief of the spy agency, RAW. Dulat was the RAW chief in 1999 when the hijacking of flight IC-814 took place. He has contended that there was a 'goof-up' in our handling of the crisis. The Congress party has seized upon this revelation to castigate the then leadership of the BJP-led NDA and, in particular, the 'policy paralysis' that resulted because of a difference of approach between Deputy Prime Minister Advani and Prime Minister Vajpayee. The BJP has reacted predictably, dismissing Dulat's book as a retired bureaucrat's attempt at catching the limelight, and wondering why an event that happened sixteen years ago should be discussed at all. The Congress, it says, is making political capital out of the new book when in reality it was party to the decision to do whatever is possible to save the lives of the passengers who were held hostage.

Indian Airlines flight IC-814 took off from Kathmandu for New Delhi on 24 December 1999 at 4:53 p.m. Within minutes, it was hijacked by five Pakistanis led by Ibrahim Athar, the brother of

Maulana Masood Azhar, one of the most violent and brutal leaders of the terrorist organisations, Harkat-ul-Ansar and Harkat-ul-Mujahideen. Delhi was informed of the hijacking at 4:56 p.m. At 7 p.m., the plane landed at Amritsar. Apparently, authorities at the airport had instructions not to let the plane take off, but it managed to do so and reached Lahore in Pakistan, where it was refuelled. At 10:30 p.m., the plane left for Lahore and the pilot was asked to fly to Kabul. However, since Kabul airport did not have night landing facilities, the plane landed at Dubai at 1:32 a.m. on 25 December. On the morning of 26 December, it took off from Dubai and landed shortly thereafter at Kandahar in Taliban-ruled Afghanistan. It remained there until the evening of 31 December when the hijacking ended with the release by the Government of India of three dangerous terrorists—Mushtaq Zargar, Omar Sheikh and the dreaded Masood Azhar—who were escorted to Kandahar in an Indian plane by Foreign Minister Jaswant Singh himself. The lives of all the passengers, save one, the young and newly married Rupin Katyal, whose throat was slit, were secured. The Taliban released the hijackers, who returned to Pakistan to continue the business of killing Indians.

It is important to recall these facts because, for an entire generation of the young, these are too old to recall. The question that has raised a lot of political heat is whether there was a 'goof-up' in the manner in which we handled the hijacking. To my mind, there is little doubt that after the hijacked plane fortuitously landed in Amritsar, our response was both weak and ineffective, thus allowing the plane to leave for Lahore. This inference is not meant to stoke partisan political responses. It is meant for us, as a nation, to take stock of our security responses, and to analyse what went wrong objectively, so that we are better prepared next time, God forbid, if there is a crisis of this nature.

It is easy, of course, to be judgemental in hindsight, but even a sympathetic observer like former Foreign Secretary and National Security Adviser, the late J.N. Dixit, who thought that generally the government acted as well as it could, felt that 'some conclusions are inescapable.' In his book, *India and Pakistan in War and Peace*, published in 2002, he writes:

There was a lack of coordination in terms of speed and time between the authorities at Delhi and Amritsar. The runaway was not blocked immediately after the landing of the plane at Amritsar. The NSG (National Security Guard) commandos did not scramble into their action/operation mode with sufficient speed. The hijackers had enough time to take off without facing any effective resistance.

Much of the above is vouched for by Dulat's account. The instructions from Delhi were neither unambiguous nor emphatic. The DGP of Punjab did not want to take any action on his own account. Confusion prevailed. The hijackers could not believe their unexpected good fortune. An argument has been made, and not without justification, that the safety of the hostages was a major constraining factor in delaying decisive action. However, the opposite is probably true. Preventing the plane from taking off again would have given time to negotiate with the hijackers. Besides, there was no guarantee that should the plane be allowed to leave, the safety of the hostages would be guaranteed. The strategically correct thing was to buy time and block the runaway immediately and make contact with the hijackers to negotiate the safe release of the passengers.

Any other country with effective and quick security responses would have capitalised on the incredible stroke of good luck that led the hijacked plane to land at an airport within its own boundaries. This is the plain truth, and to accept it with honesty should be seen not as a game of political one-upmanship, but to encourage an objective appraisal of what transpired so that the right lessons can be drawn for the future.

Dulat's account, belated as it is, should be best seen in this context. The reality is that irrespective of which political party is in power, our Intelligence and security preparedness are still far below par, and even now very little is being done to rectify this sorry state of affairs.

(This piece was originally published on 5 July 2015)

JUDICIAL APPOINTMENTS: NEED FOR INTROSPECTION

On 16 October this month, a five-member bench of the Supreme Court, presided over by Justice Jagdish Singh Khehar, struck down the National Judicial Appointments Act (NJAC) of 2014. By doing so, it restored the collegium system of appointing judges and turned down the attempt to broad-base the appointment process by including the Union Law minister, and two other 'eminent' persons, with veto powers for any two NJAC members to block an appointment they opposed.

It is true that the NJAC law was approved by parliament unanimously, and was subsequently ratified by twenty state assemblies. But it is also true that all laws are subject to judicial scrutiny, and the Supreme Court remains the highest court to examine if any law goes against the basic structure of the Constitution, and the separation of powers between the executive and the judiciary as guaranteed thereunder. Arun Jaitley has dubbed the powers conferred by the Constitution on the highest court of the land as 'the tyranny of the unelected.' This is, to say the least, unwarranted. Does he believe that the Supreme Court has legitimate powers to examine the constitutionality of laws only if the judges are elected? Or, is he trying to say that just because the Lok Sabha has directly elected members, a party with a majority can pass any law, and expect the highest court to blindly endorse it? Arun Jaitley must understand that a majority in the Lok Sabha is not a license to run amuck; the Constitution has prescribed certain checks and balances, and these must be respected.

However, while respecting the Supreme Court's decision, it is essential to point out that the judicial system itself is in need of urgent reform. Reportedly, there are close to 65,000 cases pending disposal in the Supreme Court. Some forty-four lakh cases are pending in our twenty-four high courts. And, about 2.6 crore cases are pending in the lower judiciary. Shockingly, while this is the enormity of pending cases, 406 posts out of a total approved strength of 1,017 posts of judges of the high court are, as per reports, lying vacant. The maximum number of pending cases—over ten lakh—are with the Allahabad High Court. But in this very court, there are eighty-five posts vacant out of an approved strength of 160 judges! In the Mumbai High Court, thirty-three of the ninety-four posts are vacant; in the Gujarat High Court, twenty-four out of fifty-two posts are vacant; in the Karnataka High Court, thirty-one out of sixty-two posts are vacant; and in the Punjab and Haryana High Court, thirty-three out of sixty-four posts are vacant.

Who suffers the most in this situation? It is the ordinary litigant, who waits for years before his/her case finds final disposal. Quite clearly, therefore, even if the Supreme Court believes that the collegium system is the best instrument for the appointment of judges, it must also accept responsibility for ensuring that the posts of judges do not remain vacant and the disposal of cases is expedited. The date when the post of a judge is falling vacant is known. The highest court needs to do much more to put in place a transparent, fair and time-bound system to prevent vacancies from lingering. For instance, why can't it be made incumbent on the registrars of the high courts in question to process vacancies at least six months in advance? And, why can't the chief justices of high courts be held accountable for recommending names in time for such vacancies?

In addition, there must be a much higher degree of supervision and monitoring of the judicial system by the higher judiciary. Article 235 of the Constitution gives high courts control over the subordinate judiciary, and this is a responsibility, which, given the manifestly tardy pace of judicial proceedings and the alarmingly high number of pending cases, the Supreme Court must ensure takes place. The Second Administrative Reforms Commission (ARC) and the then Planning Commission's approach paper on the Twelfth Five Year Plan makes useful suggestions in this regard, including the creation of a court audit and inspection team, the formulation of broad guidelines for the expeditious disposal of different kinds of cases, the preparation of a manual for summary trial proceedings, guidelines to prevent unwarranted adjournments, the amendment of the Criminal Procedure Code to fix a time limit for various stages of trial, and better monitoring of the functioning of the court system. Further, all courts in the country must, in the national interest, make public, every six months, figures of the number of cases disposed of and the number pending.

India is the only country in the world where judges appoint judges. If our Supreme Court believes that this unique distinction needs to be preserved, then it must also accept the responsibility to ensure that it works in an effective and transparent manner. Whatever the Constitutional issues involved, the real tyranny for the ordinary citizen is to have a system, meant ostensibly for his/her good, that does not function optimally. The Supreme Court must be aware that as important as it is to ensure the independence of the judiciary is the need to make an independent judiciary deliver, for justice delayed is justice denied.

(This piece was originally published on 25 October 2015)

WHY A FACELESS BUREAUCRAT, JAIDEV SINGH, MADE HISTORY

*M*ost people would not know that someone called Jaidev Singh recently did something that has never been done before in the history of democratic India. Jaidev Singh is a bureaucrat who is currently Principal Secretary, Legislative and Parliamentary Affairs, Government of Uttarakhand. On 10 May 2016, he not only entered the chamber of the Uttarakhand Vidhan Sabha, where bureaucrats are not allowed entry but sat on the sacrosanct Chair of the Speaker and conducted the proceedings of the Assembly. In achieving this remarkable feat he has, in my opinion, earned a place for himself in the *Guinness World Records*. He has also ensured that his name figures in any history written henceforth of the legislative functioning of the world's largest democracy.

Recent political developments in Uttarakhand hardly need recounting. Of relevance is the fact that nine members of the ruling Congress party in the state were sufficiently seduced by the charm of the BJP to become rebels. When the state budget was to be passed on 18 March 2016, these rebels, along with BJP legislators, sought to bring down the government by asking for a division of votes. The Speaker decided to proceed otherwise and declared the budget to have been passed by voice vote. The BJP and its nine newly acquired accessories protested to Governor K.K. Paul that the Harish Rawat government has lost its majority. The Governor directed the Rawat government to prove its majority on the floor of the House on 28 March 2016.

Up till this point, the script is clear, and Jaidev Singh would still probably be clueless about his remarkable tryst with destiny a few weeks later. As expected, the Speaker expelled the nine rebel MLAs under the anti-defection provisions of the Tenth Schedule of the Constitution. To my mind, he did the right thing. The Anti-defection law was brought in precisely to prevent situations like this, where a handful of MLAs decide to suddenly break away from a party to join the opposite camp, thereby toppling a legitimately elected government. The decision to defect has hardly anything to do with 'conscience'. It is mostly the consequence of cynically dangled allurements and unseemly and vulgar horse-trading.

The next series of events nudged Jaidev Singh's moment of history closer. With its nine devoted followers having been expelled by the Speaker, the task for the BJP of dislodging a democratically elected government through the back door became more difficult. Hence, a day before the scheduled floor test in the House, the BJP government in New Delhi decided to impose President's rule in the state. Now followed a series of appeals to the judiciary that made supposedly responsible legislators look like errant schoolboys. First, Harish Rawat appealed to the Uttarakhand High Court against the decision to impose President's rule. The court fixed 31 March as the new date for a floor test, but also said that the nine expelled MLAs could participate. Against this decision, a division bench of the High Court stayed the floor test and also stayed further hearings in this matter. Inevitably, the Supreme Court intervened on 21 April and directed the Rawat government to prove its majority on the floor of the House.

Against this, the Central government appealed afresh to the Supreme Court, and the SC directed that President's rule be restored in the state. Finally, the SC fixed 10 May 2016 for the floor test. It directed that for this to be held, President's rule would be lifted for two hours! The test would be conducted, our highest court pronounced, not by the Speaker. For the first time ever, a bureaucrat would sit in the Speaker's august Chair to decide who had the majority. Jaidev Singh's historic moment had come.

What is the takeaway from this sequence of events? Our Constitution defined a structured balance between the legislature, the judiciary and the executive. In working out this separation of powers, the assumption was that each of the three wings would effectively perform their respective roles. But our Constitution makers could never have foreseen what happened in Uttarakhand. The antics of our legislators, driven by their political masters, literally invited unprecedented judicial intervention. The judiciary, faced with a legislative crisis that refused to resolve itself, converted, in my humble opinion, that intervention to overreach. Article 212 of the Constitution explicitly rules out the jurisdiction of any court on how legislatures conduct their business. In effect, this means that the decision of the Speaker in the House in accordance with the powers conferred on him/her is explicitly beyond the jurisdiction of courts. But in this case, the courts did sit in judgement over the Speaker's actions taken under his legitimate powers within the House.

I believe other options were there. If the Hon'ble Court wanted to ensure fair voting in the House, it could ask for the entire proceedings to be video recorded or telecast live. But, to instruct the Speaker to vacate his Chair for the Secretary who reports to him is clearly unprecedented, and I am afraid about what this portends for the future. The SC would rightly never cede to any legislative authority its own judicial powers as defined in the Constitution. Would it allow the court to be presided over by an MP or a bureaucrat, and then allow the judgement to be sent in a sealed envelope to parliament to be opened? With great respect, how then could it expect the legislature to devalue its Presiding Officer and allow a bureaucrat to conduct the proceedings of the House?

In the heat and dust of rivalry, political parties forget that what they do in response to the imperatives of the immediate, becomes a precedent written in stone for the future. Jaidev Singh had his twenty-four hours of fame. My worry is that those twenty-four hours may continue to cast a dark shadow over the relations between the legislature and the judiciary for years to come.

(This piece was originally published on 5 June 2016)

THE ROLE OF GOVERNORS IN
THE CONSTITUTION

*W*hy is the Supreme Court's decision to reinstall the Congress government in Arunachal Pradesh, and to restore the status quo ante as prevailed on 15 December 2015, a milestone in the evolution of India's democracy? The judgement is of this nature because it lays down definite guidelines on the role and functioning of Governors, and the corollary issues of the Anti-defection law, and the use or misuse of Article 356 of the Constitution.

A Governor is appointed under Article 163 of the Constitution and is supposed to be a constitutional authority completely aloof from any political loyalties. In reality, however, Governors are appointed by the ruling party at the Centre, and are mostly people who are close to it, both in terms of ideology and past political activities. Some, among them, in fact act as the veritable agents of the ruling party that appointed them.

Pronouncing upon this pernicious unconstitutional practice, the five-member constitutional bench of the SC clarified categorically that a Governor is not an elected representative, but only an executive nominee whose tenure depends on the pleasure of the President, and whose powers flow from the advice of the Cabinet. Justice Khehar was emphatic in saying that, 'The Governor must remain aloof from any disagreement, discontent or dissension within parties. The activities within a party, confirming turbulence, or unrest within its ranks, are beyond the concern of the Governor. The Governor must keep clear of any political horse-trading, and even unsavoury political manipulations.'

Furthermore, the learned judges set red lines on a Governor's interference in the proceedings of a state legislature. 'As long as the democratic process in the Assembly functions through a government which has the support of the majority, there can be no interference at the behest of the Governor. The Governor must keep away from all that goes on within the House .... Interjects at the hands of the Governor, in the functioning of the state Legislature, not expressly assigned to him, however bona fide, would be extraneous and without any Constitutional sanction.'

The SC's stinging observations were prompted by the openly partisan conduct of Arunachal Governor Jyoti Rajkhowa. Apart from his alleged role from behind the scenes in engineering the defection of MLAs from the ruling Congress party, Rajkhowa committed four cardinal sins. Firstly, he unilaterally convened the Assembly on 16 December 2015, acting against the advice of the Cabinet to convene it on 14 January 2016. Secondly, he nullified the Order of the Speaker disqualifying the defecting Congress MLAs. Thirdly, he countenanced the Assembly being convened in a Community Hall of a hotel and allowed it to be presided by the Deputy Speaker who had already been disqualified by the Speaker under the Anti-defection Act. Fourthly, he even imposed an agenda on this ridiculous gathering, by insisting that the removal of the Speaker must be taken up as the first item of the proceedings.

Had the SC not put a check to this kind of behaviour, it would have legitimised a sordid and unethical script of political activism that was in evidence both in Arunachal and Uttarakhand. The modus operandi is to first break a handful of MLAs from the democratically elected ruling party through blatant horse-trading. Next, when the Speaker rightly disqualifies the defecting MLAs under the Anti-defection Act, to move a resolution for the removal of the Speaker. Finally, to make an obliging Governor recommend that 'the constitutional machinery has broken down,' justifying the imposition of President's rule under Article 356 of the Constitution. The Central government then acts upon this recommendation with alacrity, thereby removing a democratically elected government through the back door.

The age of 'Aya Rams and Gaya Rams' (denoting frequent floor-crossing) was largely eclipsed by the Anti-defection Law passed in 1985. This law was further strengthened in 2003. The era of large scale misuse of Article 356, for which all parties, including especially the Congress, must take the blame, is also largely over. The SC's judgement in the S.R. Bommai case in 1993 explicitly lays down that the only place to test the majority of a party is the floor of the House. It is equally clear that the SC can exercise judicial review over decisions to impose Article 356, and has, indeed, struck down such arbitrary decisions in the past. Even the President has, in at least two landmark cases, rejected the recommendation for President's rule. Why then did the BJP make this ill-advised gamble? Who were the dramatis personae behind this unethical politics? And, should not, apart from the Governor, those at the Centre who took this decision, be named and accept culpability?

As I finish this column, the news has come in that the new Congress chief in Arunachal, Pema Khandu, has majority support, and has given evidence of this to the Governor. This, if proved right, is a further setback for the BJP, that was confident that in spite of the scathing judgement of the SC, its brand of politics would succeed.

The immediate priority is that Rajkhowa must resign; and, in future, all other Governors who transgress the SC's clear instructions should also be made to do so.

(This piece was originally published on 17 July 2016)

KASHMIR: THE WAY AHEAD

The beautiful valley of Kashmir is going through a phase of turbulence that should be a matter of concern to all political parties and all Indians. For weeks now, a curfew—partial or total—has been imposed. Several dozen lives have been lost, both of Kashmiris and of our police and armed forces. Anger and alienation have spread like a deadly pall across the state. There seems to be an impasse of a kind that obstructs any possibility of a light at the end of the tunnel. The Rajya Sabha has discussed this state of affairs at length, and it is a tribute to our democracy, that in spite of differences of approach of political parties, the House has unanimously passed a resolution emphasising the importance of restoring peace and trust in the Valley.

What should be the future course of action? There is a 'hardline' view that brute force deployed by the State is the only answer to deal with the anti-nationalism that is often on display in Kashmir. Hardcore terrorists, who have the backing of Pakistan, and who wave the Pakistani flag in rallies, and lethally attack our armed forces, need to be dealt with remorselessly and with greater force. Certainly, militancy and terrorism, and those openly espousing the cause of secession and unwilling to accept the supremacy of the Republic and its Constitution cannot be given any quarter. But, is the use of State force in perpetuity the only response we can think of to provide an enduring solution to the situation in Jammu and Kashmir?

I would think not. Statesmanship requires the ability to go beyond brittle simplicities that look at problems in only two categories of undifferentiated black and white. The crisis in Jammu and Kashmir has complex origins and no simple solutions. Quite apart from years of neglect and flip-flops in policies, there is the verifiable, planned and continuous support to terrorism by Pakistan. What can be done in these circumstances? I would suggest a four-point agenda for consideration.

First, we must work to restore normalcy. This means that those who resort to violence and terrorism must be dealt with firmly. Our armed forces and police are doing a very difficult job in highly adverse circumstances. Their morale and resolve must not be weakened. At the same time, a review must be made of the indiscriminate use of weapons like the pellet gun. Dozens of young Kashmiris have been blinded, and scores have been disfigured. Surely, our armed forces can acquire less lethal but equally effective instruments for crowd control.

Secondly, we must further beef up our abilities to prevent infiltration from across the border of terrorists trained and armed by Pakistan. I realise that given the difficult terrain and weather conditions, this is easier said than done. But, the effort has to be made, and whatever the requirements of our armed forces towards this end, must be met with expeditiously and on a sustained basis. At the same time, we must make the sponsorship of terrorism the principal focus of engagement with Pakistan. If Pakistan remains recalcitrant, as I suspect it will, then we should go all out to give this issue international resonance and seek the help of countries like the USA, which have considerable leverage in Pakistan, to apply the requisite pressure on that country. After all, we have the proof of Pakistan's complicity, and so has most of the developed world.

Thirdly, the government, both at the state level, and at the Centre, must work out a political roadmap that includes the vital elements of engagement and dialogue with the people of Jammu and Kashmir. Prime Minister Modi recently reiterated Atal Bihari Vajpayee's slogan of more than a decade ago of, *'Jamhooriyat, insaniyat and Kashmiriyat'* (Democracy, humanism, and the Valley's age-old legacy of amity). Although much delayed, the reiteration is welcome, but what is the follow-up? When the BJP–PDP alliance was formed, they released, in March 2015, an eleven-page agenda mapping out the future course of action. This agenda explicitly refers to a 'sustained and meaningful dialogue process with all internal stakeholders which include political groups irrespective of their ideological views and predilections,' thereby including the Hurriyat.

Has any attempt been made to pursue this explicitly stated goal? Even if we concede that there is little to be gained by talking to people like Syed Shah Geelani, has an effort been made to identify other interlocutors, less inflexible and more amenable to discussion, including segments outside the Hurriyat, such as opinion makers and representatives of the youth? I think that, however difficult this process may be, effort has to be made. The prime minister's meeting in New Delhi with leaders of all political parties last Friday was a good beginning, and it should be followed up, as a first step, by the visit of an all-party delegation to Jammu and Kashmir.

Fourthly, urgent steps need to be taken to expedite the developmental process in Jammu and Kashmir. The unprecedented floods of last year have taken a heavy toll, both on infrastructure and livelihoods. It is estimated that two-thirds of all Kashmiris are around the age of thirty, of which roughly half are unemployed. On

7 November 2015, the prime minister had announced a 'Diwali gift' of 80,000 crores for the state. Of this roughly half was for roads and highway projects, but significant amounts were also allocated for flood relief, power, health, agriculture, food processing and tourism. How much of this money has been spent? If this outlay is to be spent over five years, can we think of fast-tracking key sectors, especially those which rev up job creation and incomes?

The co-option processes of the Indian State have a great seduction. It is instructive to remember that since 1947, not a single secessionist movement has succeeded in India. Equally important is the fact that we have shown the maturity to negotiate with even those who have questioned the primacy of the Indian State—witness our interactions with rebel groups in Nagaland, in Assam, and even in Punjab. A tough stand against Maoists has not inhibited us in reaching out to those among them who wish to return to the mainstream. It is time now to turn our focus in a concentrated manner on Jammu and Kashmir, and try to apply the healing touch so as to win back the hearts and minds of the people of Jammu and Kashmir. The BJP–PDP government should try and overcome their internal contradictions and work to achieve this goal.

(This piece was originally published on 14 August 2016)

THE SURGICAL STRIKE

*F*ollowing the surgical strike carried out by our armed forces, many elements have come up in the national discourse and need urgent clarification. First, all political parties have stood by the government in support of this action. Nitish Kumar was among the first to congratulate the Central government and our brave armed forces for the decisive action against terrorism emanating out of Pakistan. Such action was, after the affront of Pathankot and Uri, and the daily cross-border infiltrations, sorely needed and needed to be made public.

Secondly, there is no imperative for the government to release evidence in support of this strike immediately, or at all. In a democracy, governments have to be trusted when they make public statements relating to national security, and our DGMO was authorised to make this statement. If the government feels the need, keeping all factors in mind, including that of national security, to release evidence, it is indeed its prerogative.

Thirdly, while the surgical strike has sent the right message to Pakistan, the action by itself is not enough. The goal of isolating Pakistan on its verifiable nexus with terrorism must be a multi-pronged strategy. A diplomatic offensive needs to be waged with vigour in the important capitals of the world, including Beijing and Washington. Evidence of Pakistan emerging as the epicentre of global terrorism needs to be provided, along with the argument that, while India may be facing the brunt of the terrorist attacks sponsored by Pakistan, terrorism is a global threat, and no country is insulated from its reach and impact. Hence there is a need for all countries to work to isolate Pakistan on this issue.

In addition, the government must do whatever necessary to ensure that the operational needs of our armed forces in Jammu and Kashmir, including in terms of material, equipment, funds and military hardware, is fulfilled. Simultaneously, there is an urgent need to upgrade our Intelligence apparatus. We cannot have a situation where fidayeens from across the border literally stroll into high-security military bases. In fact, regrettably, at Uri, where the terrorists struck, the perimeter of our base at that point was only ringed off by barbed wire. I understand that funds for a concrete wall have been asked for but not been sanctioned for years.

Fourthly, the politics unfolding on the surgical strikes must stop. This applies equally to the ruling party as to the Opposition. The strikes were authorised by the government of the day, and represented a national resolve to provide a befitting—and much needed—riposte to Pakistan. This was not an action taken by the BJP. Therefore, the attempt to use this by the BJP for partisan political gain, especially keeping the forthcoming UP and Punjab elections, is reprehensible. Why have posters come up all over UP depicting Narendra Modi as Rama vanquishing Nawaz Sharif as Ravana? The argument that this was done by some low-level *karyakartas* or workers is hogwash.

The BJP must understand that it cannot have it both ways. On the one hand, it deflects any queries regarding the surgical strike by saying that it is an act of national betrayal to question the achievement of the army. On the other, it sets aside the army and seeks to appropriate the credit itself.

Fifthly, however proud we are of the valour and sacrifice of our armed forces, we must resist the temptation to put them above all democratic interrogation. In a democracy, all institutions are subject to review and assessment. If a former Raksha Mantri says that similar strikes, albeit on a smaller scale, took place in the past, why is the BJP privileging the statement of a retired DGMO over that of a former Defence Minister? If tomorrow, a serving General of the army, on retirement, says something that indicts the current government or its Raksha Mantri, will the BJP say that he is right and their own Defense Minister wrong? This form of politicking is fraught with danger, and the BJP must think twice before encouraging such dangerous trends only to score immediate debating points. Moreover, even in a country like Israel, whose armed forces are held in very high esteem, there have been occasions when their conduct has been scrutinised in public interest. In the cacophony of the political slugfest now going on, any questions asked about the armed forces is now being equated with being anti-national. This must stop.

Lastly, in the competitive politics of praising our armed forces, sanction seems to be given to a wholesale denunciation of the political class and of the political leadership. There is every reason to be proud of our armed forces, but in a democracy, the armed forces work under the civilian government. There can be no compromise of this fundamental principle. Unfortunately, we are seeing today an entire array of retired Generals and others who almost seem to be saying that we know best what is needed for the well-being and security of our country, and anyone who interferes or is seen to be interfering in this role is working against national interest. Equally, unfortunately, the BJP appears to be encouraging this trend so long as the retired

Generals have praise for it. But has the BJP given a thought to what such a line of thinking means for the basic tenets of a democratic Republic, and what it could mean for the BJP itself when instead of praise, it is at the receiving end of this misguided hubris?

(This piece was originally published on 9 October 2016)

DEMONETISATION: GOOD INTENT, BAD IMPLEMENTATION

The overnight demonetisation of 500 and 1,000 notes announced on 8 November raises the fundamental issue of the link between intent and implementation. Is the laudable intent behind an action sufficient reason to excuse shoddy implementation? Or, does the inadequacy of the implementation devalue the intent itself?

This dialectic between concept and action is at the core of the current upheaval following the demonetisation decision. Many political parties supported the intent. Nitish Kumar was one of the first leaders who spoke up openly in support of the government's intent to escalate the fight against black money, the link between black money and terrorism, and the menace of counterfeit currency. Indeed, given the corrosive pervasiveness of black money in our economy, no right-thinking person can question the need for the government to take steps to eradicate it. But, he was also among the first to question the preparedness of the government to implement the scheme.

There is no contradiction in this stand. If the demonetisation in one stroke reduces roughly eighty-six per cent of all currency in circulation to mere paper, the legitimate expectation is that the government would have anticipated in full detail the consequences of such an action, and taken all measures to smoothen the process of transition. Rigorous and meticulous planning, including the ability to look at every micro detail, would not be asking for too much given the administrative resources of the government. But, it appears, that the government was so overwhelmed by the dramatic intent of its action that it largely ignored the detailed planning process that should have preceded such a move.

Not surprisingly, the transitional dislocation of the economy, including tremendous hardships for the ordinary citizen who may have cash but not black money, has been huge. The government's answer is that this is short-term pain for long-term gain. Most Indians would be prepared for this. But, in spite of their willingness to give the benefit of doubt to the government, if the impression grows that the short term pain may not be short, or could have been less through better planning and anticipation, then resentment is bound to grow.

Certain obvious facts must have been known to the government *before* the prime minister—no less—made the dramatic announcement at 8 p.m. on 8 November. Forty-seven per cent, or roughly half the total population, are not linked to the banking network; 300 million people lack identification papers; Rural India is a ninety-eight per cent cash economy. Cash transactions amount to almost eighty per cent of total transactions in the country. Some sixteen lakh crores would require to be infused into the economy in a matter of days, and so banks and ATM vending machines had to be, in great measure, ready for this consequence.

Given the magnitude of the task at hand, I don't think the government had done its homework properly. The size of the new 2000 rupee note could easily have been made compatible with ATM machines so as to avoid the need to recalibrate them. Although there is no 'right' time to take action against black money, some thought could have been given to the timing. The announcement was made at the height of the harvest season and the sowing of the new crop, where transactions happen almost entirely in cash. It was also the peak of the marriage season. According to some estimates, about 1.5 crore marriages are to take place in the next few days, and harried families are spending days standing in queues outside banks and ATMs.

It is also clear that the parallel economy will not go away only with demonetisation of notes. Figures vary, but by most accounts, only six per cent or less of black money is parked in cash. The rest is in benami properties, gold and bullion, or abroad. How is the government planning to tackle these forms of black money? The promise to bring back money from abroad has not amounted to much. Gold prices are soaring, so it is very clear that even as the demonetisation process is on, people are investing ill-gotten cash in the yellow metal. Nitish Kumar's call to attack benami properties must get a credible response from the government. There is a need also to go to the root causes for the generation of black money, of which the most important is electoral reform that severs the umbilical cord between unaccounted wealth and political funding.

Furthermore, the demonetisation exercise should not ultimately amount to innocent people, mostly middle-class householders, farmers, daily wage earners, and small shopkeepers and entrepreneurs being penalised while the big fish escape. Already, one is hearing about an entire infrastructure of touts and operators finding new ways to convert their unaccounted 500 and 1,000 rupee notes into white by misusing Jana Dhan accounts, and the legitimate savings of ordinary people. There are also reports—as yet unverified—of some select few having got to know about the demonetisation move in advance so as to give them enough time to dispose of their black money. If these reports turn out to be true, they will cast a very serious aspersion on the very intent of the government.

The real imperative now is for the government to do its best to alleviate the visible hardships of the ordinary citizen who may have cash but not black money. Some constructive suggestions have been made in this regard, both in the debate in parliament and by state governments. The government needs to look at these suggestions constructively, and stop this ridiculous business of labelling anyone who does not blindly endorse their actions as being in cahoots with black money hoarders. The jury is still out on how long the transitional hardships will continue, and what will be the degree and length of economic dislocation. But the one essential lesson to be learnt from this whole exercise is that even good intent needs proper planning and implementation. This is a lesson the government must accept with humility, not disdain.

(This piece was originally published on 20 November 2016)

THE UNIFORM CIVIL CODE

The thespian qualities of outrage that Ravi Shankar Prasad displayed when speaking of the BJP's views on the practice of triple talaq among Muslims in India were quite transparent. As a lawyer, he must have been aware that the matter is sub-judice before the Supreme Court. While the NDA government has filed an affidavit before the SC opposing the practice, the judgement is still awaited. Did the renewed burst of indignation then have less to do with a suddenly reignited desire for social reform and more to do with electoral politics?

The question of banning triple talaq is part of the BJP's stated goal of expediting the adoption of a Uniform Civil Code (UCC). The goal by itself has the sanction of the Constitution but in a specifically conditioned manner. Article 44, which states 'that the State shall endeavour to ensure for the citizens a uniform civil code throughout the territory of India,' was deliberately placed by the makers of our Constitution in the section on Directive Principles in order to stress the element of discussion and consensus that should inform such endeavours.

The problem is that the BJP has decided, somewhat selectively, to pick this one Article from among the Directive Principles, and then proceed to try and implement it in a manner that closely resembles a bull in a china shop. No one can deny the need for all religion-based personal laws in India to change in accordance with modern notions or reform, equity and gender justice. But, in order for this process to be sustainable and enduring, it is imperative to think about how these ends are best achieved.

On 7 October 2016, the Law Commission shot off a letter to chief ministers enclosing an objective-type questionnaire on the need for a UCC. Nitish Kumar was the first chief minister to reply to that letter. He said that he had examined the questionnaire carefully, but it was his considered view that the questions were framed in such a way as to force the respondents to respond in a specific manner. Complex issues, he said, cannot be tackled through such an amateurish approach. The UCC must be seen as a measure of reform for the welfare of the people, and not a political instrumentality to be hurriedly imposed against their wishes and without consultations with them.

Democracy is based on the foundational principle of a constructive dialogue. Where the UCC is concerned, such a dialogue, based on broad-based consultations with all religious denominations, is particularly necessary given the multicultural, multireligious nature of our society. In the absence of such in-depth consultations, any attempt at premature or hasty tampering with longstanding religious practices that deal with complex issues of marriage, divorce, adoption, inheritance and the right to property and succession, would, Nitish Kumar stressed, be inadvisable.

What the government does not want to understand is that the enforcement of a UCC would require all current laws applicable in such matters in respect of Muslims, Christians, Parsis and Hindus (including Buddhists, Sikhs and Jains) to be scrapped. Does the Central government have a draft of such a new law, with concrete details of which provisions of what religion are to be scrapped, and what will replace them? The truth is: no such draft has been circulated. The stakeholders are in the dark about what is being proposed and what is to be replaced. Nor has there been any discussion on this subject in parliament, the legislative Assemblies of states and other forums of civil society.

The essential point is that while the state must, indeed, endeavour to bring in the UCC, such an effort, in order to succeed in any meaningful way, must be based to the greatest extent possible, on a broad consensus within religious denominations in favour of such a move, rather than be imposed by fiat from above. If such an approach is not adopted, there could be avoidable social friction, and an erosion of faith, especially among minorities, in the Constitutional guarantee of freedom of religion.

Political maturity requires that on the issue of triple talaq, all parties await the judgement of the Supreme Court. Equally, on the question of the UCC, statesmanship requires the government to initiate a process of persuasion and consultation with different sections of the Muslim community on the desirability of reform.

It would be very unwise to reduce a serious matter like the UCC to an electoral ploy whose aim is the polarisation of votes for short-term electoral gain. It is also ironical that the government, when raising the issue of triple talaq, is claiming to speak for the interests of Muslim women when BJP leaders like Yogi Adityanath, Vinay Katiyar and Suresh Rana are at the same time busy demonising the Muslim community as a whole. No one from the top leadership of the BJP has condemned this fanaticism, and even if there is a token reproof, it hardly carries any conviction, given the fact that such attacks, especially at the time of elections, have become par for the course.

The Muslim community has many credible voices seeking reform of their personal laws in conformity with modern notions of gender equity. To hear more such voices would be very welcome, because the call for reform, when it comes from within the followers of a particular faith, lays the strongest foundation for the status quo to change.

(This piece was originally published on 12 February 2017)

THREATS TO THE FREEDOM OF SPEECH

I can understand that some people in our country don't agree with Umar Khalid. I can also accept that, according to some people, the views he holds are anti-national. But, what I cannot understand is that because such people disagree with him, they will not allow him to speak. Nor can I accept that the definition of being patriotic can be held hostage to some people's notion of what nationalism should be.

The Rashtriya Swayamsevak Sangh or RSS did not participate in the freedom movement. It was a conscious choice its leaders made on the basis of ideological differences with Gandhi and the Congress leadership in the freedom struggle. In fact, the British gave the RSS a certificate for 'good' behaviour. But, even though I disagree with the decision the RSS made then, and have deep reservations even today on some aspects of its ideology, I will not consider them anti-national. Their views must be fought politically, including through discussion and debate and argumentation, and in the arena of democratic discourse. For all my differences with the RSS, I will not say that it should be denied a public platform, or be dubbed seditious. It is for the same reason that I condemned the attempt by the JNU students association to prevent Baba Ramdev, or other speakers of the same ideological hue, including from the RSS, to speak in JNU.

Within the political spectrum, differences between the Left and the Right have existed ever since 1947. Liberals have questioned the fundamentalisms of the Right, and the Rightists have condemned the accommodative—and sometimes expedient—flexibilities of the liberals. But it is precisely the nature of a democratic State to allow both views to find expression. Article 19 (a) of our Constitution guarantees freedom of speech and expression, with such 'reasonable' restrictions 'in the interests of the sovereignty and integrity of India, the security of the State, friendly relations with foreign States, public order, decency or morality, or in relation to contempt of court, defamation or incitement to an offence.' The prerogative to decide what is an infringement of the fundamental right to freedom of speech and expression lies with the judiciary. Umar Khalid has not yet been convicted under the law. His matter is sub-judice, and he is out on bail. But, when he was invited to speak at Ramjas College last week, on a subject entirely different to the controversy in JNU, members of the BJP's student wing, the Akhil Bharatiya Vidyarthi Parishad (ABVP), decided that they were prosecutor, judge and jury, and declared that since Khalid, in their view, is anti-national he will not be allowed to speak and that if this *farman* (diktat) is not adhered to, they will violently enforce it.

The tragedy is that they succeeded. Ramjas College withdrew its invitation. The police did precious little to prevent the violence of ABVP members. In fact, it colluded with them and beat up not only those students who opposed the ABVP but also the media. It is reported that some policemen hid their identifications in order to reinforce the hooliganism of the ABVP. The impunity with which the ABVP broke the law is directly linked to the fact that as the youth wing of the ruling BJP government at the Centre, it believes that it has immunity from the law. And, although three policemen have been suspended, the truth is that, in general, the police is influenced by its own loyalties—not to the Constitution of India, but the political masters whom it serves. The net result was that Khalid could not speak, and nor could his colleague from JNU, Shehla Rashid. The undemocratic, illegal and condemnable tactics of threat and intimidation worked. Now, we hear reports that Khalsa College in Delhi University has also cancelled its street theatre festival because of repeated threats from the ABVP over the 'anti-national' content of some of these plays.

The danger is that every time such acts of vandalism, violence and intimidation in the name of nationalism succeed, they set a precedent that reinforces the possibility of their recurrence in the future. If the culprits are not punished—and those who are supposed to enforce the rule of law collude with them—they are likely to act in the same lawless manner with even greater impunity the next time around. In a concrete sense, we saw this demonstrated at Ramjas. The hooligans who beat up journalists and those opposed to their views when Kanhaiya Kumar was to be produced before the court at Patiala House in New Delhi—and remained both unpunished and unrepentant—are the role models for those who took the law into their own hands at Ramjas College a few months later.

In this increasingly brittle milieu, what is being forgotten is that our civilisation had never shown such aversion to dialogue and debate. On the contrary, we can with some pride claim that, in many respects, the foundation of our civilisational ethos was dialogic. Lord Buddha, who founded Buddhism, repudiated the Vedas, which most Hindus considered to be revealed text. Jainism did the same. Even within Hinduism, the Charvaka school of materialism went so far as to say that the Vedas are nothing but a compilation of untruths. But, the response of those who opposed them was not to beat them up or to say that their voice cannot be heard. Their response was to resort to vigorous debate and intellectual refutation, wherein the critique of their opponents was clinically analysed and refuted on the basis of reasoning and discussion.

Democracy is not only about the number of elections we hold. Democracy is about fostering the democratic temper, where people are free to disagree, and can debate the reasons. Unfortunately, a new kind of Indian is being provided all the encouragement to proliferate. This Indian believes that only what I say is right, and all those who disagree with me must be shut up or beaten up in the name of a new kind of insular 'anti-nationalism'. This is certainly not what the Constitution guaranteed to the Indian Republic.

(This piece was originally published on 26 February 2017)

THE RAM MANDIR DISPUTE: A NEGOTIATED SETTLEMENT

On 21 March this year, the Supreme Court while responding to an urgent hearing on the Ayodhya dispute by Dr Subramanian Swamy, said that the Ram Mandir matter is a 'sensitive' and 'sentimental' issue and should be settled amicably out-of-court by talks between all stakeholders. The court went further to say that it could arrange some principal mediator if so desired. Asked if he would like to mediate, Chief Justice Khehar said, 'If you want me I can, but will not sit on the bench,' adding that the court will 'come into the picture if you can't resolve the issue.'

The dispute has had a long and acrimonious history, and there is little to be gained by recounting it. Quite obviously, the matter is not only one about law; nor is it only about facts. This is a case where law, fact and faith intersect, and, therefore, the learned SC was right in urging all concerned to try and resolve the matter through discussions outside the formal arena of exclusive judicial intervention.

The reasonable mainstream of India, cutting across religious lines, has for long maintained that the dispute should be resolved either by the court or through a mediated settlement between the stakeholders.

Now that the SC has itself urged that a mediated solution should be given a try, should not all parties heed this call?'

Zafaryab Jilani, convener of the Babri Masjid Action Committee (BMAC) has welcomed the SC's concern but rejected its advice out of hand. 'Earlier also, out-of-court settlement efforts have been made at the highest level and failed,' he said. 'The Muslims are not willing for an out-of-court settlement. None of the demands made by the other parties are acceptable to us.' On the other hand, the Central government, and the newly appointed Chief Minister of UP, Yogi Adityanath have welcomed the SC's directive. 'I welcome what the Court has said. Both sides can sit down to find an amicable solution. The government is ready to extend any cooperation to facilitate dialogue.'

Between these two opposed reactions lies a gulf in perception that has identifiable reasons. Jilani probably has the not unfounded perception that impartial and sincere talks cannot take place given the acrimonies generated over decades by this dispute, the fact that similar attempts in the past have failed, and the present milieu where loud voices in the Hindu Right are proclaiming that the temple will be built come what may. The BJP leadership, in power both at the Centre and in UP, probably feels that in the backdrop of the party's massive victory in UP, this is the time to isolate those opposing the Ram temple, for which the out-of-court negotiations could provide a suitable platform.

The truth is that thanks to the SC's directive, a historic and game-changing opportunity has been presented to all concerned to make a genuine effort to find an amicable solution. For too long, inter-religious relations have been held hostage to this festering dispute. Law and faith, facts and beliefs, passions and emotions, politics and politicians, and a whole range of vested interests, have clashed with each other. Riots have taken place; the Babri Masjid was demolished; mobs have ruled the roost; the Archaeological Survey of

India (ASI) has intervened; the Allahabad High Court has pronounced judgement; and now, the SC has made its plea.

The challenge before India is whether all parties to the dispute can overcome the acrimonies and distrust of the past to find an amicably resolved solution to this matter. If they can, it would be a victory for the maturity and good sense of our civilisation and for democracy. If they can't, it will only further undermine the existing challenges to the composite and plural fabric of our polity.

To succeed in the task suggested by the SC, the BJP would need to rein in its ultra-Right-wing hotheads. It would need to desist from threat and intimidation or arbitrary deadlines. Brow-beating and public posturing would need to be eschewed. The talks would need to be approached in a spirit of give and take, in an open-ended manner, without absolutist positions, with a view to finding a solution, and not reducing the talks (if they take place) to a tokenistic exercise only to mobilise partisan political support.

The same advice would apply to Jilani too. Muslim representatives would do well to remember that the majority of those whom they claim to represent would rather get this dispute behind them. They need to recognise that for a great many of their Hindu brethren this is a matter of faith, and cannot be confined only to an adjudication of a point of fact. The position that Muslim interlocutors take would need to be guided by the larger good of the country as a whole, and not only a strictly narrow and defensive interpretation of the law. Provided of course, they are categorically assured that any 'concessions' or 'adjustments' they may make in this matter are not seen as a capitulation by their Hindu interlocutors, or used as a precedent for raking up Mandir–Masjid disputes elsewhere in the country.

The fact of the matter is that Indians in general, whether Hindu or Muslim, have had enough of this dispute. Most of them now want to swim away from the islands of religious exclusivism and the clutches of mullahs and mahants to the secular dividends of a modern, democratic and developed nation. The highest court of the land has provided an opportunity to move ahead. It must be seized in good faith and with sincerity. Legality is one aspect of this matter, but ultimately, what is crucial is goodwill and maturity. Will the BJP walk the talk on Narendra Modi's slogan of 'Sabka Saath, Sabka Vikas,' or will it allow hardliners to queer the pitch? Will Yogi Adityanath confound his critics by taking a statesmanlike approach in this matter, or will he tread the predictable line his track record indicates? And, above all, will the Muslims rise above their siege mentality and give a fresh chance to the possibility of opening a new chapter of inter-religious harmony?

(This piece was originally published on 26 March 2017)

COULD THE ATTACK ON AMARNATH
YATRIS BE PREVENTED?

On 10 July 2017, terrorists attacked a bus carrying pilgrims who were part of the annual Amarnath yatra. Such an attack on pilgrims, which claimed the lives of seven Hindu pilgrims of which six were women, took place after a decade and a half. It was a barbaric and inhuman attack, with the specific aim of creating communal tension and worsening the already tense situation in the Valley. All political parties emphatically condemned the attack, as did ordinary Kashmiris irrespective of whether they were Hindus or Muslims.

The terrorists who perpetrate such dastardly crimes know that the Amarnath shrine is a symbol of Kashmiriyat, where Muslims and Hindus have a common stake in the preservation of a religious tradition that has been nurtured by both communities. Although the shrine has very ancient origins, it is well known that a Muslim shepherd, Buta Malik, rediscovered the Amarnath cave some 150 years ago, and even today his family receives some part of the alms offered by pilgrims. The Hindu devotees who flock in lakhs for the annual pilgrimage provide income to Muslims in Jammu and Kashmir's tourist industry. The entire event binds the residents of the Valley in a shared project and is a symbol of the composite culture that underlines this troubled region.

It is true that there can be no fool-proof shield against a committed terrorist. This is particularly so in Kashmir where jihadis trained, funded and equipped by Pakistan are sent across the border and have misguided or brainwashed supporters among the local populace. It is precisely for this reason that elaborate security arrangements on a massive scale are made for the yatris every year. Terrorist attacks during the forty-eight-day July–August annual Hindu pilgrimage have occurred in the past. In August 2000, pro-Pakistan Islamic terrorists belonging to the Hizbul Mujahideen massacred twenty-one unarmed Hindu pilgrims, seven Muslim shopkeepers and three security force officers. In July 2001, terrorists threw two grenade bombs and fired indiscriminately on a pilgrim shelter killing thirteen and injuring many more. In August 2002, terrorist from al-Mansuriyan, a front group of the Lashkar-e-Taiba, massacred nine pilgrims and injured thirty (including several Muslims) near the Nunwan pilgrimage base camp.

It is no mean achievement that for the last fifteen years, our security forces managed to foil or prevent terrorist attacks during the yatra, in which the number of pilgrims measure in lakhs, and they trek unarmed through territory vulnerable to ambush and attack. And yet, if such an attack did recur, is it wrong to ask whether the attack was preventable? Was there any element of negligence or lack of planning and anticipation, or improper Intelligence appraisal that enabled the terrorists to strike again? For instance, there are reports that an Intelligence alert about the possibility of such an attack was issued by the SSP Anantnag in the last week of June. Was this Intelligence ignored, or was the Intelligence alert itself worded in much too generalised a way, so as to make concrete follow-up difficult?

To ask such questions is a perfectly legitimate exercise in democracy that is premised on the principle of accountability of those in authority. It is one thing to mindlessly politicise tragedy by blaming reflexively, and only for the purposes of short-term political gain, a political opponent. In the aftermath of a tragedy, there is something distasteful in trying to score political brownie points. But, is one 'anti-national' if he/she, in the interests of preventing such attacks in the future, asks for an inquiry into why this attack happened, so that the right lessons can be learned, and the guilty, if any, can be identified and responsibility be fixed. Can he or she be blamed for it?

I would think not. But, it was surprising that many in the BJP, both in the Central government and in the BJP–PDP alliance in the state, took precisely such an approach. Even more surprising was the endorsement provided by several media channels. A hysterical tirade, in the name of nationalism, was carried out against anyone who had the temerity to ask any questions on whether such an attack could have been prevented. Even those who constructively suggested that an enquiry should be held, so that any Intelligence failure, or administrative lapse, could be identified and corrective action taken for the future, were dismissed out of hand as anti-national.

Frankly, the attempt to invoke nationalism to cover every act of omission or commission committed by the ruling dispensation, has gone much too far. While many in the Opposition seek to play a constructive role, and unhesitatingly laud the government on many of its security initiatives, such as, for instance, the surgical strike against the Pakistan army along the border (even though the ceasefire violations by Pakistan and terrorist action has shown no sign of abating since then), the BJP, with full support from some sections of the media, has used nationalism as a shield to evade accountability whenever there is a security breach, by simplistically but aggressively labelling those who ask any questions as anti-national.

In this particular case, even the Shiv Sena, a BJP ally, minced no words in blaming the ineffective BJP-PDP alliance, and the BJP government, for the failure to stem the continuous terrorist attacks in Kashmir. Is the Shiv Sena then anti-national? And, would the BJP, if such an incident would have happened when a non-BJP government was in power at the Centre and in the state, been less than strident in its immediate criticism? Any attempt to counter such criticism would then have been labelled as anti-national! Double standards in politics can go only so far before they are revealed to be what they are.

This being as it may, the real hero in this ugly and tragic episode is Saleem Mirza, the driver of the bus that was attacked. It was his courage and presence of mind that saved the lives of many more of the pilgrims. When hailed for his act of bravery, he simply said: 'God gave me strength to save the lives of people.' In this simple statement lies the reason why India will survive all the attempts to break it.

(This piece was originally published on 16 July 2017)

THE IMPORTANCE OF
'COALITION DHARMA'

*I*t was an occasion of great personal happiness for me when Harivansh Narayan Singh was elected as the Deputy Chairperson of the Rajya Sabha. He is not only a close personal friend, but also a colleague in the JD (U), and in parliament. Frankly, a person of his temperament, innate humility, and many achievements in the field of journalism and creative writing, should have been elected by consensus. Those who only read English newspapers would not know of the decades of courageous effort he invested in making *Prabhat Khabar*, a Hindi newspaper with a circulation in hundreds, to a leading daily with a circulation of over a million copies daily, for which I am proud to write for.

His election prompts several interesting aspects. How did a person from the NDA, which lacks a majority in the upper House, manage to win? No doubt it was a consequence of far better coordination and planning. Apart from the efforts of the BJP, much of the credit must go to Nitish Kumar, for his political acumen and operational dexterity. He achieved first mover advantage by talking well in advance to Naveen Patnaik of the BJD in Odisha, and to KCR of the TRS in Telangana. He was also in touch with key players in the NDA, and with fence-sitters across party lines, so as to notch up a winning tally of numbers. I can vouch from my own election to the Rajya Sabha, which was fought under unexpectedly difficult circumstances, that at such moments, Nitish Kumar is veritably a general in command.

By contrast, the Opposition was transparently lacking in both strategy and planning. Nothing else can explain the defeat of the Congress candidate when the non-NDA parties had greater numbers. Even an agreement on who the candidate would be was taken at the last minute. There was no central coordinating agency, talking to those who could be persuaded, or cajoling those who were disinclined. The entire effort seemed to be mired in drift, with perfunctory consultations and absence of either proactive energy or preemptive initiative. By the day of voting, the result was a foregone conclusion.

The key question is: how do a collection of parties, who have the numbers, lose an election? I think the Opposition, as a whole, needs to introspect on this. Perhaps, it is time to convert periodical meetings over lunches and tea, or photo-ops on stage, to the rigour of demonstrably effective strategic coordination, not only at local levels but nationally. Ultimately, ideological agreement on certain issues needs to be buttressed by an organisational underpinning that focuses on micro detailing. The BJP has converted itself into an electoral machine. Maybe, the Opposition needs to try a little harder to emulate it.

There are some other interesting takeaways from this election. Firstly, there are many leaders of different parties that I have interacted with who said that the result may have been different had the BJP put up its own candidate, or conversely, if the Congress had not. In other words, more parties joined hands with the NDA—and could justify doing so on ideological grounds—precisely because the coalition's candidate was from the JD (U), and not the BJP. Equally, many parties that may have supported the Opposition, did not do so, because the candidate was from the Congress. This is not necessarily a reflection on the legitimacy of these parties or their indispensability in forging a winning coalition on either side of the political spectrum. What it is a pointer to is that, within a coalition, smaller parties cannot be ignored, and that there may arise several occasions, when it is, in fact, in the interests of the larger party, to accept this fact.

Any action as a consequence of such an acceptance should not be viewed as charity or largesse or concession. Coalition politics is about treating all constituents as equals, irrespective of their size. That is precisely why Atal Bihari Vajpayee coined the phrase 'coalition dharma'. As the 2019 national elections approach, this is the right time to ruminate on what coalition dharma actually means. This dharma recognises that smaller constituents within a coalition may be small in terms of their national footprint, but they represent, in their own regions, and beyond, a significant ideology, mass support, and, very often, towering leaders who have genuinely impacted the lives of vast numbers of people. True coalition dharma must accept this.

It follows then that coalition dharma must eschew politics of domination or imposition by the bigger partner. When that happens, coalitions begin to unravel. Coalition dharma must also accept that India is a land of diversities and that a 'one shoe fits all' policy may be, for very valid reasons, unacceptable to some of the other constituents. This dharma, therefore, requires all constituents to be able to have a civilised dialogue with each other. Such a dialogue cannot be dogmatic. It must not compel compromise which is contrary to the core beliefs of any one party, but it must foster, whenever necessary, strategic flexibility and accommodation in the larger interests of the coalition as a whole. One modality to achieve this is for coalitions to agree to a common programme, a charter of minimum goals to which all constituents must commit to. But this charter too must be negotiated, not revealed as fiat. And once agreed upon, it must promise cohesive functioning, and not only good—but democratic—governance.

Ultimately, coalition dharma is about human management. Political parties consist, after all, of people, and of leaders, who need to be deftly managed. This may require—especially by the larger party—humility, sacrifice, conversation, the willingness to listen and not to dictate, respect for opposing opinions, and the ability to build a consensus. To all of this, Atalji added something that was his special trademark: a sense of humour that could disarm the most hostile interlocutor.

My good friend, Harivanshji, may not realise that his election could prompt a great deal of introspection and rethink, both in the NDA and the UPA, and across the political spectrum.

(This piece was originally published on 12 August 2018)

VIEWPOINT

VIEWPOINT

DEENDAYAL UPADHYAYA

A week ago, the organisation Vichar Nyas brought out a special volume of their journal, *Think India*, dedicated entirely to Deendayal Upadhyaya. The journal is edited by NCP leader and parliamentarian, D.P. Tripathi. Among others, Dr Murli Manohar Joshi, Shashi Tharoor and I had also contributed articles. This special volume was presented in a formal ceremony to President Ram Nath Kovind, where we were present and had the occasion to say a few words.

The basic point that I had made in my article was that when a nation achieves freedom from colonial servitude, several voices emerge on what the new nation should aspire to be. One of these important voices was that of Deendayal Upadhyaya. Whether we agree with everything he has said or not is not important. What is relevant is that his defining idea of Integral Humanism, which he first articulated at the plenary session of the Bharatiya Jana Sangh in Mumbai in 1965, as a possible idiom for a new India, deserves to be judged for its sincerity, application of mind, ideological content and originality of thought.

As I have understood it, Upadhyaya sought to articulate an ideology that is first and foremost rooted in our own civilisational ethos. That endeavour cannot be faulted, because even if we achieved political independence from colonial rule only a few decades ago, the civilisational foundations of our nationhood go back to five thousand years. For a nation that is also one of the oldest civilisations of the world, it is only befitting that we chart a future, with a modern ideology that does not ignore the refinements and thought processes of the past.

There is a misplaced notion among many educated Indians that any reference to our past history, especially the wisdom of ancient India, is synonymous with communalism. In my view, such an approach is itself a consequence of a colonised mindset. One of the prime projects of colonial rule was to convince the conquered that their own history, culture, religion, beliefs and value systems were vastly inferior to the 'higher' knowledge and wisdom brought in by the colonisers for the benefaction of the 'natives'. The unfortunate fact is that this relentlessly biased critique was internalised by many of the ruled, especially the educated. The result was that, even after political independence in 1947, there were a great many influential voices that devalued our civilisational heritage, and considered the project of modernity only in Western terms. Deendayal believed that Bharat should not be reflexively imitative in its project of nationhood and should, while welcoming change and modernity, draw also upon its own belief systems.

How much of Deendayal Upadhyaya's philosophy animates the BJP today, as the successor of the Bharatiya Jana Sangh? There were many important strands to his thinking, and the BJP, which celebrated his centenary last year with a great degree of energy and sense of appropriation, must evaluate whether it is also working in accordance with his vision. It is my assessment that Deendayal was not exclusionist in his religious views. He did speak of the concept of 'chitti', which probably corresponds to the German concept of

Zeitgeist, but he clarified that chitti was meant to bring out the most positive or constructive content of each nation. Chitti, he said, is faith-neutral, and as per his Integral Humanism, all people have the full right to follow their respective faiths. As he wrote in 1962, 'So long as Hinduism is alive, there is no danger to Islam. A Hindu does not discriminate between Ram and Allah....The concept of Hindu nation is neither negative, nor reactionary, nor territorial, it is a cultural and civilisational concept connoting positive direction.' If this is the case, the BJP must ask itself why, while venerating Deendayal, it has not firmly dealt with those members of the larger sangh 'parivar' who practise violence, hatred and divisiveness in the name of Hinduism?

Deendayal Upadhyaya was also a great votary of social justice. This is clearly brought out by one of the lesser-known incidents of his life when in Rajasthan, in his capacity as the functionary in-charge of the Bharatiya Jana Sangh, he expelled seven of the nine MLAs of his own party for opposing the Zamindari Abolition Act. In this sense, his Integral Humanism had a strong 'socialist' content. This is evident too in his views regarding the labour class employed in production. The machine, he said, should not become a competition to human labour. To quote him: 'Machines cannot be blamed if the labours are displaced and subjected to privations. It is the fault of the economic and social system which cannot distinguish between the object and the instrument.' Why then has our current government, which otherwise pays rich tributes to Deendayal Upadhyaya, allowed for so much jobless growth, and paucity of jobs? And why, with an ideological mentor like Deendayal, with his strong commitment to a just and equal society, is the BJP perceived to be less than sensitive to the Dalits?

Deendayal was also particularly emphatic about the definition and role of the individual in society. A citizen, he argued, must be seen as an integral whole, and endeavours for his individual freedom must never be ignored. Given this straightforward position, the government must ask itself, to take a most recent example, why the ill-advised order was announced regarding punitive action against journalists who could be arbitrarily accused by the 'powers that be' of peddling 'fake news'? It is good that the prime minister promptly annulled his own Minister of Information and Broadcasting order, but questions remain as to how he could make such an announcement without his approval in the first place?

All political parties must ponder deeply about Deendayalji's central argument that if man is at the centre of the cosmos, no institution or system can function to optimal levels unless human beings themselves undergo a positive transformation. If good people helm even a sub optimal system, there are chances that it will resurrect itself; however, if less-than-good people run even good systems, it is a certainty that the system will deteriorate. True indeed!

(This piece was originally published on 8 April 2018)

TACKLING THE NAXAL MENACE

The manner in which India, in particular our media, has for some time become oblivious to everything except cricket, reminds me of the heedless revelries of the Mughal court even as Nadir Shah's invading armies were at the doorstep. This analogy becomes clearer when we see the continued preoccupation with cricket even when the Naxalites have made one of their most daring attacks in Chhattisgarh decimating almost the entire top leadership of the Congress party, and killing twenty-seven people in broad daylight.

Our cricket-obsessed nation seems incapable of grasping the magnitude of the Naxal threat. The Maoists, whose footprint now extends to over 200 districts in India, are not, as their propaganda machine projects to the ignorant or the gullible, disaffected youth or exploited tribals or misguided rebels. They are enemies of the State and seek to terminate a constitutional democracy by violence. Such an act is treasonable and needs to be dealt as such. But the response of our government is weakened by a sterile ideological ambivalence on whether the strategy should be development or punitive action.

Of course, poverty and lack of optimal development is a problem and provides fertile ground for the Maoist leadership to recruit cadres. But how can development be initiated when the State itself has ceased to exist within the country in an area as large as 40, 000 sq. km? The Naxalites run their jan adalats, zonal committees and military training camps with impunity in the areas they control (including twenty-four training camps in Chhattisgarh alone). They target the state economic infrastructure and eliminate so-called police informers at will. They extort and kidnap hostages, including senior officials, and use human beings as shields. They have no shortage of arms. And, in carefully prepared campaigns carried out with military precision, they kill ruthlessly. In Orissa, in June 2008, thirty-six policemen were murdered by the extremists. In Dantewada, Chhattisgarh, in April 2010, seventy-six CRPF men were slaughtered in an ambush; and, in Maharashtra, a landmine placed by them blew up scores of paramilitary personnel.

In such a situation, it becomes near farcical when the Home Ministry and the Planning Commission lock horns on which agency, the panchayats or the district administration, should deliver (under the Integrated Development Plan) development projects to Naxal-affected districts, when the truth is that neither of them can. The first priority must be to retake these areas, defeat the Naxalites and end their illegitimate rule. For this, given the violent nature of the enemy, there can be no other option except a national consensus on resolute, effective and punitive action by the State. Once the Naxalites are defeated, and their influence eliminated or significantly reduced, the State must with equal vigour move in to bring in development and progress for the deprived. If such a sequential two-pronged strategy is not followed, we will neither be able to promote development, nor will be able to tackle an enemy that, taking advantage of a weak State, continues to expand its area of control.

The Naxalites cynically exploit the ideological hesitation of the Indian State. They use every instrument of the very democracy they want to overthrow to create misguided sympathy for their cause. There are enough NGOs and human rights groups and, alas, opportunist politicians, brimming with the delusional milk of human kindness, to further their propaganda machine. While the government blunders along, the Naxalites choose their moment to strike and make national headlines when they do so.

A tragic consequence of a State's ideological confusion is the woefully poor quality of punitive response. In the last Chief Minister's conference, the then Home minister P. Chidambaram admitted that our capacity to deal with the Naxals is 'not commensurate with the nature of the challenge' and that results remain 'sub-optimal'. 'There are not enough police stations, not enough men, weapons and vehicles, not enough infrastructure....not enough roads, and not enough presence of the civil administration.' Chhattisgarh, which is India's tenth-largest state, covers a heavily forested area of around 2,00,000 sq. km; it witnessed as many as seventy-five Naxalite attacks in 2012. However, it has only 25,000 policemen and many of its senior police posts lie vacant. By contrast, Delhi where all the national decision-makers happily confabulate, has 70,000 policemen.

There is something pathetic about a country that is so flabby in dealing with a threat to its national sovereignty. The writing is clear on the wall: we urgently need a specially trained and dedicated crack-fighting force to fight the Naxal threat. Along with that, we need a comprehensive plan of action, including the machinery to follow up quickly with development plans, once an area is reclaimed from occupation by the enemy. An initial offer of amnesty to all those in the Naxalite movement who are willing to give up arms and work within the framework of the Constitution must be part of this multi-pronged strategy. The amnesty should, where effective, be accompanied by incentives. These could include cash grants, jobs in government, scholarship for children, housing and land allocation. The government should also be willing, as part of a conscious policy, to negotiate with the Naxal leadership (if it can be persuaded to come forward) on such demands that can be met within the Constitution. But, in the last resort, a State that hesitates to use legitimate force when its security and integrity is so gravely threatened or uses it so ineffectively or couldn't care less about such matters is capable of very little except the sordid politics of cricket.

(This piece was originally published on 9 June 2013)

THE GREAT INDIAN MIDDLE CLASS

*A*s we move towards the next general elections, questions that all political parties will have to answer are: what will be the role of the middle class in influencing votes and the outcome? Does this class really matter? What is its size? How interested is it in politics? Will it vote in significant numbers? Is it an organised entity? What are its divisions? Who are its leaders, if any? Does it have any discernible political biases? What issues appeal to it? In short, does the middle class have to be cultivated, and if so, will it yield the desired dividends?

For a long time after 1947, the middle class had a profile disproportionate to its size. With a presence in politics, the bureaucracy, media and other professions of the educated class, it made its voice heard much louder than other segments of the population, including the far more deprived. Paradoxically, however, the political class never gave it the importance it wanted. There was a simple reason for this: numerically, the middle class was far too small and much too fractured to show up on the radar screen of hard-nosed political arithmetic. Its voice had a higher decibel but its political punch did not. The general feeling was that the middle class talked more than it visited the voting booth; and, even if some of its members did, they did not account for a great deal. To a great extent, this assessment was valid. On voting day, most middle-class folk preferred to enjoy the holiday rather than get their finger smeared with indelible ink. Their approach to elections was apathetic. In fact, they had a disdain for both politicians and politics. Their agenda was also too narrow and simplistic: lower taxes, more consumer choices, lower prices for the things that mattered to them, better higher-educational opportunities, and more jobs for its own progeny. What happened to the rest of India and Indians did not concern them. There was little sense of larger causes, bigger communities, wider issues, societal well-being or bigger solidarities. Not surprisingly, the politicians had little time for this insular, disorganised, minuscule and disinterested class.

What has changed today, and why are politicians waking up now to the importance of the middle class? The change is that the middle class is no longer the inchoate and insignificant mass between the handful of the very rich and the hordes of the poor. It has, almost imperceptibly, grown to be a much stronger numerical reality. If we take a strictly economic criterion of defining a middle-class person as anyone who comes from a household that has a monthly income between Rs 20,000 to Rs 1,00,000, the middle class suddenly starts to look very substantial. Estimates reveal that in 1996, the size of such a middle class was around twenty-five million. Today, it is in excess of 160 million. And, by 2015, its numbers are expected to go up to 267 million. Such a large number constitutes a significant critical mass. Its importance is magnified by three key factors. First, it has emerged as a pan-Indian class. Its members are in all parts of India; they are beyond linguistic divides; they have had a similar education; they wear the same clothes; they nurture the same consumer aspirations; they watch the same TV and eat the same food in the same restaurant chains. Secondly, they are, thanks to the exponential growth of the electronic media, connected on a common informational platform.

Thirdly, because of the revolution in mobile telephony and social media, they are capable of being dynamically and instantly in touch with each other since mobile phones are literally an extension of their fingers.

This new middle class is angry, but not because it hasn't benefitted from economic progress. In fact, it would be fair to say that this class has been the largest beneficiary of the rising incomes and productivity of the reforms begun in 1991. The irony is that with greater money in its pocket, it wants more. What is equally significant is that shedding its past insularity, it is now, on occasion, and still in fledgeling and disorganised ways, willing to engage with a select few larger issues. The first signs of this change became visible on the Jessica Lal case, where, appalled by the initial dismissal case against the accused, the middle class came out to protest. Since then, corruption has been a galvanising issue as have the increasing rape incidents in the capital. The Anna Hazare movement was a catalytic moment for middle-class Indians. Consider these facts. There were 80,000 protesters, mostly from the middle class, out on the streets on 19 August 2011, the day Anna Hazare was released from Tihar Jail and drove to the Ramlila Maidan in New Delhi. The protests that he sparked engulfed over two hundred cities in the country. There were close to four lakh people supporting his campaign on Facebook. One and a half crore calls were made to the designated phone number in Mumbai in his support. And, in 'blasé South Delhi', as many as twenty Resident Welfare Associations held candlelight vigils to join their voice to his. Even if his subsequent agitation drew diminished crowds, and even if the movement has now split, it would be wrong to believe that the chord he touched in the collective psyche of the middle class has disappeared.

The middle class is thus on the verge of arriving as a potent political constituency. I say 'on the verge' because it is as yet disorganised, lacks ideological clarity, is still elitist in the issues it takes up, refuses to engage with ideas for long-term change, and, in the absence of a pan-Indian leadership, is sporadic in the display of its anger. But the day it overcomes these shortcomings and identifies with causes that are relevant to India as a whole, it can become a force that all political parties will have to reckon with.

(This piece was originally published on 21 July 2013)

WHY SHOULD A RAM TEMPLE IN AYODHYA NOT BE BUILT?

I cannot understand why anybody—Hindu, Muslim, or of any other faith—would oppose the building of a Ram temple in Ayodhya. Even an atheist would accept that purely in terms of numerical democracy, there are millions of Hindus who would like to honour Lord Rama by building a temple in his name in the city where he was born and to which he belongs. Those who are not atheists but believe that the money spent on constructing the temple can be better used for building a hospital or a school, are being naïve too. First, it is not an either–or scenario: we need hospitals and schools, but those of the faith need places of worship too. And, if the 'developmental' imperative is so strong, why not a campaign to convert the Rashtrapati Bhawan to a hospital, as Mahatma Gandhi wanted to do in 1947?

Lord Rama is a much loved and respected deity. He is Maryada Purushottam, the very epitome of rectitude. The Ramayana—whether of Valmiki or Kamban, or the vastly popular *Ramcharitmanas* of Tulsidas—are not only works of literary genius but deeply sacred texts. In the popular imagination, Rama is the touchstone of right conduct, and the divine guarantor of moksha or salvation. When a Hindu dies, the words chanted by those who take the body for cremation is: '*Rama naam satya hai*' (The name of Rama is the enduring truth). Gandhiji, who wanted independent India to be as righteous as Rama's kingdom—Ram Rajya—died to an assassin's bullets with these two words as his last exclamation: 'Hey Rama!'

So, there really can be no credible opposition to the construction of the Rama temple in Ayodhya. The question that can be asked is: how to build it, since the site where it is to be constructed—and where an earlier temple existed—was in Babur's time replaced by a mosque, the Babri Masjid. That masjid was condemnably demolished in 1992 by Right-wing hoodlums, but the question of title or ownership of the land itself is still contested between Hindu and Muslim groups. Currently, the matter of title is before the Supreme Court, and hearings are to start in January.

It is generally agreed that the matter should be decided either by the judgement of the Supreme Court or by mutual agreement between all relevant stakeholders to the dispute. This is the civilised way to proceed and would be in conformity with the 'maryada' always associated with Shri Rama. However, personally, I have my own reservations on whether a matter of faith can be definitively decided by legal intervention. The court can decide on title, and that won't be easy either, given the mass of conflicting evidence, much of it not of a judicial nature. But, even if a judgement is forthcoming and is interpreted to be against either of the opposed parties, will it put a final closure to the dispute?

The second option is a far better one. A dialogue would be the ideal way to put this acrimonious and divisive issue behind us. For this, both sides will need to curb their inflexible hard-line elements and find a modus vivendi. This is easier said than done. One way could be for Muslims to agree for a mosque to be built at an alternative site, and for Hindus to declare that if this is done, there will be a closure to all other disputes of this nature—whether at Kashi or Mathura or anywhere else. The mosque built by Babur does not have any special significance separate from the fact that it is one of the many mosques built by the Muslims after they invaded India. It has acquired significance because of the condemnable nature in which it was forcefully demolished in 1992. But that is a blot of the past from which lessons have to be learnt, the foremost of which is that such incidents should never happen again. Now, we must respond to the imperatives of the present, because so long as this dispute remains unresolved, extremist elements on both the Hindu and Muslim side will continue to draw sustenance.

For Hindus, the site where Rama was born—irrespective of whether this can be historically proven or not—has very special significance. It would be a grand gesture of great import if Muslims agree to allow a temple to be built here, in exchange for a mosque to be built in Ayodhya itself, but at another place. But such a gesture requires Muslim liberal opinion to assert itself and break the stranglehold that a handful of clerics and ulemas have currently acquired in the matter. The million-dollar question is whether moderate Muslim voices will be willing to take this initiative, given that the bulk of both Hindus and Muslims are keen to put this dispute behind them and get on with their lives in peace and harmony, by marginalising the *kattar-vadis* or fundamentalists among their communities.

It is sad, however, that while a great many Muslims I know privately agree to the possibilities of such a solution, very few are willing to come out in the open. It is true that a community that often feels under siege by the inflammatory statements and intimidating actions of Hindu extremists can retreat into a shell-like fear psychosis. But the question is still relevant: where are the Muslim liberals? Apart from a few, like Javed Akhtar, Shabana Azmi and Shahid Siddiqui, most appear to have opted for silence and ceded space to the stereotypical mullah, so visible—perhaps by design—on some TV channels.

It is time for Muslims, who have no vested interest in perpetuating this dispute, to become more visible, and if possible, in an organised manner. It is time also for Hindus to facilitate this process by robustly rebutting fanatical Hindu fringe groups. Only when sane elements among both Hindus and Muslims come together can we have a solution to the Ram Mandir issue. It would seem that the best way to do this is to take the negotiating process away from those who only have relevance if this dispute continues to remain unresolved.

(This piece was originally published on 17 November 2018)

A WAR IN THE CBI

There is a circus of the highest order going on in the Central Bureau of Investigation, the country's premier investigating agency. The top two officers of the agency were openly at war with each other. In a midnight drama, Alok Verma, CBI director, was issued orders to proceed on leave, as was his warring deputy, Rakesh Asthana; the Director was then reinstated in his job by the Supreme Court on 10 January this year; within twenty-four hours, the high-level committee that appointed him, comprising Prime Minister Narendra Modi, the then Chief Justice of India (CJI), Justice A.K. Sikri, and the leader of the Congress (the largest Opposition party) in parliament, Mallikarjun Kharge, met and removed him in a 2-1 decision, with Kharge dissenting. In the twenty-four hours that he was reinstated, Verma transferred some dozen officers. Now, he has been shunted out to the post of Director-General Fire Services. Nageshwar Rao has reassumed his post of interim Director. In all probability, those transferred by Verma will be transferred back again.

In this sordid spectacle, played out in full public view, one thing has emerged quite clearly: the CBI's public image has hit rock-bottom. I hold no brief for either Verma or Asthana. But, as a former bureaucrat, I believe that any public servant has the right to prove his innocence, and not be punished on the basis of unsubstantiated allegations. This is an important principle, irrespective of which government is in power, because if it is ignored, then any allegation would suffice to transfer or remove any bureaucrat at the will of the political powers that be.

It is true that, in this case, the Central Vigilance Agency (CVC) had gone into the allegations against Alok Verma, and submitted a report, on the basis of which the high-level committee that appointed him found sufficient reason to transfer Verma to the relatively inconsequential task of tending to fire services. But, what was the nature of the accusations brought against Verma in the CBI report? Again, purely from the point of view of a bureaucrat, the CVC report presents grave problems. It lists a menu of allegations, none of them fully substantiated or proven, and some found to be incorrect. How could this then be the basis for the high-powered committee to remove Verma from a post to which he had been reinstated by the SC only twenty-four hours ago?

Let us examine what exactly is the content of the CVC's findings. The first charge is that Verma took a bribe to influence an investigation. The CVC finding is that no direct proof for this is forthcoming, and the evidence, if any, is circumstantial, and needs further investigation. A second charge is that Verma attempted to call off the raids in Patna in the Lalu Yadav investigations. The CVC finding is that the charge is not substantiated. A third charge is that Verma delayed finalising investigation in a bank fraud in order to favour the prime accused. The CVC finding is that the charge is incorrect. A fourth charge is that he placed a CBI officer of his choice to monitor the bank fraud case in which his relative was allegedly involved. The CVC finding is that the charge is not substantiated. A fifth charge is that Verma did not share with other agencies Intelligence inputs on two industrialists. The CVC finding is that the charge is not substantiated. A sixth charge is that

Verma is linked to bribes in regard to enquiries on land-acquisition matters in Haryana. The CVC finding is that it could not look into these allegations for want of time and that further inquiry is needed. A seventh charge is that Verma failed to act in a gold smuggling case at Delhi airport. The CVC finding is that the charge is only partially substantiated and that the matter needs re-investigation. An eighth charge is that Verma helped cattle smugglers. The CVC finding is that the charge is not substantiated. A ninth charge is that Verma unduly interfered in a CBI case against an Enforcement Directorate officer. The CVC finding is that the charge is only partially substantiated and needs further investigation.

There are only two matters in which the charge is, as per the CVC, substantiated. The first is that Verma did not include the name of a suspect as an accused in the FIR in the Indian Railway Catering and Tourism Corporation or IRCTC case relating to Lalu Yadav. The second is that he tried to induct two officers about whom internal inquiries had raised integrity issues. But even these findings are based on circumstantial evidence. In summary then, of the eleven allegations levelled, as many as six are unsubstantiated or require more investigation and one is found to be incorrect, and four only show the possibility of wrongdoing on the basis of circumstantial evidence, or need further investigation.

Is such a CVC report sufficient ground for the removal of an officer, who, in any case, had but some twenty days left to retire? Surely investigation against him, where the CVC had so recommended, could have been initiated, without needing to remove him from a post on the basis of largely unsubstantiated allegations, especially since that post has a mandatory two-year tenure. And, while the correct procedure was followed, as per the SC's directive, for the high-level committee to decide on the removal or transfer of Verma, is it asking for too much if this very committee could have also given Verma a chance to present his point of view, before deciding that he needs to be shunted off to look after fire services?

Such questions have no partisan political provenance. They pertain to the fundamental need to protect the independence and impartiality of the bureaucracy and keep it insulated from unwarranted political interference, the very reason why certain posts were given a mandatory two-year tenure. Otherwise, all bureaucrats will work under the fear of unproven allegations, severely impairing both their functioning and effectiveness. The CBI has made a circus of itself, and no one knows when and how the curtain will finally come down on this unseemly spectacle, but it is incumbent on all of us to understand the full implications of what is unfolding before our eyes.

(This piece was originally published on 13 December 2019)

WHY SHOULD A STATUE FOR
SARDAR PATEL NOT BE BUILT?

*W*hy should a statue of Sardar Patel cause controversy? Is it because it is the tallest statue in the world? Or, is it because its inauguration was an extravaganza choreographed by the prime minister? Or, is it because it cost—as per reports—something in the vicinity of 3,000 crores? Other reasons have been cited too. Is erecting statues out of fashion and a waste of money? Or—as some people have said—would the Sardar have been less than happy at this kind of spectacle in his name? Perhaps, there are even those who feel that the Sardar does not deserve this kind of glorification. Or, maybe, the Congress is annoyed at the 'appropriation' of Patel by Narendra Modi and the BJP. And, finally, there could be some who feel that such tributes are best pursued only for the Nehru–Gandhi parivar.

To the critics of this statue, I say simply, choose from any of these options. As far as I am concerned, a befitting tribute to the Iron Man of India was long overdue. If his statue in his home state has been erected and is the tallest statue in the world, so be it. For too long, the Nehru–Gandhi family has tended to monopolise all such tributes, and by doing so, has pushed to the relative margins other iconic figures of the freedom movement, and of India's recent history. When Pandit Nehru died, his home was converted into a museum. That was the first overreaction. A home once designated for the first prime minister of the country should have been the residence for future prime ministers as well, much like, for example, 10, Downing Street is. I am of the firm opinion that there is no better address for the prime minister of our country than Teen Murti Bhavan. It has the right location, size and suitability for protocol requirements. Instead of that, we now have our prime ministers living in an improvised residence, which clumsily combines three bungalows.

We seem to be congenitally disposed to create museums to honour our prime ministers. Former Prime Minister Indira Gandhi's residence is also a museum now. The airport in the capital is named after her too. Connaught Place, another landmark in the capital, is now called Rajiv Gandhi Chowk. The capital's premier National Centre for the Arts bears Indira Gandhi's name. New Delhi's largest stadium is named after Jawaharlal Nehru. There is the Jawaharlal Nehru University too in the capital. The country's largest open university—also in the capital—is named after his daughter. Apart from this, there are huge swathes of priceless real estate marked for the final resting place of Nehru, Indira and Rajiv. The city's only planetarium is in the name of Nehru. The capital's largest cancer hospital is named after his grandson.

These are only some examples, and restricted to New Delhi, but they clearly indicate that there has been an excess. Since the Nehru–Gandhi's were in power for most of the last seven decades, it is not difficult to understand why this happened. The role of sycophants, forever ready to suggest what they believe will appeal to those in power, must have played a role too. Of course, none of this is intended, even for a moment, to belittle the contribution of Nehru, Indira Gandhi or Rajiv Gandhi. They served the nation with great distinction and need to be remembered. Indira Gandhi and Rajiv gave their lives for the nation. This can never be forgotten. Nehru, in particular, is someone I hugely admire. In fact, in my study, there is a black-and-white photograph of Mahatma Gandhi and Nehru, and this is the permanent backdrop to my participation in TV debates.

However, this does not make me blind to the fact that there were other leaders in the pantheon of our freedom movement, and in the making of more recent Indian history, who have not got their due. The allegedly shabby manner in which the Congress party—then in power at the Centre—dealt with the body of the late P.V. Narasimha Rao, is a case in point. Netaji Subhash Chandra Bose, and later, Lal Bahadur Shastri, did not get their due either. There were other iconic leaders, like Ram Manohar Lohia, who remained sidelined. Sardar Patel suffered the same neglect.

The BJP is obviously trying to do a course correction. Some leaders of eminence from the BJP stock, like Deendayal Upadhyaya, have suddenly shot into prominence, knocking off the name of well-established railway stations like Mughalsarai. But the BJP has a paucity of iconic figures linked to the freedom movement. Hence the need for appropriating figures like Sardar Patel. The appellation 'Iron Man' appeals, I think, to a person like Narendra Modi. There is, undoubtedly, an irony in this new-found deification. The BJP, which is joined at the hip to the RSS, has internalised a convenient amnesia about what the Sardar actually thought of the RSS. He was unrelentingly critical of the RSS ideology and made no secret of it. Perhaps, the BJP thinks that the size of the statue will make people forget this part of Patel's legacy.

But all this notwithstanding, a tribute to the Iron Man of India cannot—and should not—be made a matter of controversy. The money spent on the statue could have been less, but it is hardly a material factor, given the thousands of crores spent on remembering other great leaders, mostly from the Nehru–Gandhi family. The contribution of Sardar Patel to the freedom movement is immeasurable. The resolve of steel he displayed in uniting India—earning for him the sobriquet of the Bismarck of India—is something that can never be forgotten. He was a true Gandhian, a peasant leader of great sensitivity and acumen, and the founder of the modern all-Indian civil services system. As the integrator of the Republic of India, the Statue of Unity dedicated to him on 31 October 2018, deserves the support of every patriotic Indian.

(This piece was originally published on 4 November 2018)

ATAL BIHARI VAJPAYEE: A TRIBUTE

*I*f there was one thing about Atal Bihari Vajpayee that left no one unmoved, it was his eloquence. That oratorical dexterity was mesmerising not only because of his use of words. It was remarkably impactful because the words seemed to flow from his heart. Each sentence, crafted with just the right degree of complexity, was often followed by a pause, pregnant with meaning, allowing the audience to digest what he had said, and then, just at the right time, followed by another volley of sentences that gave the punchline.

But, paradoxically, Atalji could also be a man of few words. This became marked towards the later years of his life, when he would speak reticently, or sometimes—much to the discomfiture of his interlocutor—not at all! It was difficult then to imagine how the same person, when before a mike or on the podium, could so dramatically change and keep his audience spellbound, when in private he could lapse into long moments of silence.

Perhaps it was the contemplative poet in him that became dominant in later life. Indeed, this was the key to Atalji's personality. He was a politician for almost all his life, occupying the highest public office, including being prime minister thrice, and yet, in all of this there was one part of him that was transcendent, making him less a participant and more an observer. I personally believe that he was never seduced by the pomp and paraphernalia of power. The poet in him told him that all this was passing, a shadow play, a fleeting moment in the grand canvas of time. Behind it, ultimately, there was a loneliness that prompted a spontaneous sense of detachment, a *virakti*, a deliberate denial of ownership. It was this interplay between the participant, forever in battle for what he believed was right, and the observer, perpetually aware that for all the sound and fury, this was part of the overpowering transience of all human endeavour, that made Atalji the man he was.

The observer in him negated the ego. His infectious laugh, which could disarm the most trenchant critic, was a consequence of his poetic resolve not to take himself seriously, without diluting in the slightest way his commitment to pursue his goals seriously. Those who did not understand this were often stumped by his inexplicable silence, his habit of closing his eyes while the other person spoke, his undiluted concentration to the matter at hand simultaneously diluted by his essential *vairagya* or detachment to power and position.

Nevertheless, sometimes, encounters with him could be very challenging, precisely because of his elliptical style of interaction. I recall once I was with him at his residence when the legendary Nelson Mandela was to call on him. However, there was no sign of Mandela at the appointed hour. A frantic effort was on to trace where the grand old man was. Apparently, he had gone to meet some old friends of his in India, supporters of the anti-apartheid meeting, quite oblivious that he had an appointment with Atalji. There was no option but to wait for him to show up. While waiting for him, Atalji sat with his eyes closed in total silence. There was Brajesh Mishra, his Principal Secretary, a Joint Secretary in the PMO, and myself (in my capacity as Joint Secretary dealing with Africa) in the room. Suddenly, Atalji's eyes opened, and looking towards me, he said: '*Woh tasveer toh purani hai,*' (That's an old photograph).

Frankly, such a sentence, out of the blue, completely foxed me, and everybody else in the room. For a moment, I was not even sure he was talking to me! There was silence in the room. After what seemed an interminable pause, Atalji spoke again: '*Mere sirhane rakhi hai*' (It is kept on my bedside). This second sentence too made no sense. When, after a pause, he spoke a third time, I began to get the drift. He said: '*Shabana ne di hai mujhe padhne ke liye.*' It was then that the penny dropped. I had translated, on Shabana Azmi's request, the poems of her father, Kaifi Azmi. The cover of the book had Kaifi's photograph. That picture was of him in his younger days. Atalji was reading the book. That is why he said: '*Woh tasveer toh purani hai!*'

The poet in Atalji often made him reclusive, and prone to staccato sentences, which he left to the intelligence of the others to decipher. It is this silence that made him write poetry—which I had the great honour to translate into English—that was full of anguish and joy, pain and sorrow, triumph and reflection. I reproduce my translation of one of his most moving poems, dealing with his encounter with death, titled in Hindi, *Maut Se Thann Gayi*, for it provides, through his own pen, the most penetrating insight into the man he was:

A battle with death!
What a battle it will be!

I had no plans to take her on,
We had not agreed to meet at the curve,
Yet there she stood, blocking my path,
Looming larger than life.

How long does death last? A moment, perhaps two—
Life is a sequence, beyond today and tomorrow,

I have lived to the full, I will die as I choose,
I will return, I have no fear of letting go.

So do not come by stealth, and take me by surprise,
Come, test me: meet me head on.
Unheeding of death, life's journey unfolds,
Evenings sketched with kohl, nights
Smooth as the flute's notes,
I do not say there was no pain,
There were sorrows, of my own and of this world.
And much love I received from those not mine,
No grievance remains against those who were mine,
I grappled with every challenge thrown my way,
Lit brave little lamps in violent squalls,
A savage storm rages today,
The boat is a brief guest in the whirlpool's embrace,

Yet the resolve to sail across is firm,
The storm flashes its fury, this boat will take it on,
With death, what a battle it will be!

(This piece was originally published on 18 August 2018)

CHANGE THE STRUCTURE
OF THE HOME MINISTRY

Very often institutions of the past persist unchanged because of sheer inertia or the inability of those in charge to understand the need for change. No institution is created to exist in perpetuity as originally conceived. It must evolve, reflect new priorities and respond to new challenges. When governments fail to act on what needs to change and what is preserved, they blunt the efficacy of that institution and display critical lack of leadership. Chanakya's *Arthashastra* is a vivid testament to the vision that looks afresh at the institutions a polity has inherited and why and in what manner they need to change to serve changing needs.

In this spirit, I think a very serious fresh review needs to be undertaken about our Ministry of Home Affairs (MHA) as it currently exists, as also of some of the key institutions under it. The MHA was a creation of British times; that creation is still with us. At that time there were four key ministries—Home, Defence, External Affairs and Finance. Home was meant to broadly oversee all matters relating to internal administration and Intelligence. Over time, and after Independence, there have been ad-hoc additions to this original mandate, but no thought has been given to whether its omnibus structure is still relevant to the new and urgent priorities which now confront the Republic.

Today, there are two new and overwhelming priorities before the Republic: terrorism and insurgency. It is quite clear that the MHA as constituted is ill-equipped to deal with them. I would, therefore, propose that a separate Ministry of Internal Security (MIS) headed by a Cabinet minister should be hived off from the MHA. A minister with this portfolio has been a feature of some previous Cabinets, but without specific focus or clout and always subordinate to the minister of Home Affairs.

The new ministry must have two primary wings: one, an anti-terrorism unit that will unite under one umbrella to direct the nation's war against this threat; two, an anti-insurgency department, which will single-mindedly tackle the threat of Left-wing extremism and other insurgencies. With the creation of these two wings, the need for the Intelligence Bureau (IB), as it currently exists, must be seriously reviewed. The IB with generalised Intelligence responsibilities is something we inherited from the British. The nature of the Intelligence and the specific tasks for which it needs to be deployed have greatly changed since then. It is, therefore, only logical that the IB itself must be restructured and replaced by specific units that exclusively target specific threats.

The wing to tackle terrorism must in effect be a more effective and upgraded version of the National Counter Terrorism Centre (NCTC). It would be headed not by an additional director of the IB but the director of the IB himself, usually the senior most police officer. This would help to overarch bureaucratic turf wars and give the agency the heft it needs. The new wing would have three major subordinate agencies under it: one, the Natgrid, which must be made efficient enough to provide a nationwide database and track terrorist threats, and it must also have much more access to information than it currently does, including banking and financial transactions; two, the National Investigation Agency (NIA) with national jurisdiction and the authority to rigorously—and preemptively—investigate and prosecute terrorism-related offences including powers to arrest and interrogate suspected terrorists, working in tandem, of course, with state police agencies; and three, the National Security Guard, the elite special-response unit based in multiple hubs around the country so that it can be mobilised quickly against terrorist activity.

The second wing under the newly created ministry of internal security would be the Anti-Insurgency Department (AID). It could be headed by a secretary-level officer. Its first and foremost priority would be to stem and reverse Naxal activity in the country. For this, AID will be empowered to raise a crack operational unit of sufficient strength (an improved version of the Greyhounds in Andhra Pradesh) in each of the states where Naxalism is rampant; the possibility of exclusively assigning the Central Reserve Police Force to an anti-insurgency task could also be considered. Individual units of this force will be under the central command of AID, but the planning and execution of operations will be done in consultation with the state Director General of Police and the chief minister. AID will have an Intelligence wing to study the Naxalite movement, its planning, leadership, modus operandi, communications and ground support. It is clear that a nationwide campaign against a violent enemy whose avowed aim is to overthrow the duly constituted Republic cannot be run by state units, which lack equipment, expertise and training and are distracted by routine law and order duties. It is equally clear that the Intelligence required for dealing with an enemy that transcends individual state boundaries needs to have a federal agency.

The new AID department would also be the nodal agency to coordinate with identified insurgent groups in the Northeast. Such interactions would include punitive and preemptive action where necessary, and negotiations where desirable. The imperative is to have a focused agency at the national level to deal with all insurgency-related matters, because there are obvious areas of overlap, both in terms of collusion between different insurgent groups and the methodology to be adopted in containing them.

Nations that value their security and the well-being of their citizens, adapt, modify and retool the instrumentalities in dealing with changing situations. This strategic flexibility and ability of forward thinking is essential because threats do not remain constant. If the institutions that are supposed to deal with these threats remain fossilised in the structures of the past merely because no one has the courage or the vision to change them, the situation gets out of hand. Chanakya's dictum was to anticipate a problem and have the institutions ready to dynamically handle them as they arise. This is a lesson we should not forget.

(This piece was originally published on 14 April 2013)

WHY IS CHANAKYA SO
RELEVANT TODAY?

*S*ome days ago, I met a group of visitors from Europe. They had come on an official delegation to plan the Europalia Festival, scheduled for later this year. They were people supposedly informed about India. But I was stunned when one of them, talking about my latest book, asked me who Chanakya was. I was tempted to respond by a couplet of Ghalib: *Poochte hain yeh ki Ghalib kaun ha; Koi batlaye hamein, ki ham batlayein kya?* (They ask me who is Ghalib? Someone tell me, pray, how should I respond?) This little incident quite vividly illustrates the cultural asymmetry that still rules the world. If I had asked my interlocutor who Machiavelli was, the question would be considered laughable, and I would be presumed to be largely uneducated. But we, the once-colonised, must indulgently accept such egregious ignorance and be grateful that at least they asked!

Chanakya pre-dated Machiavelli by around 1,800 years. He wrote the world's first holistic and detailed political treatise. The *Arthashastra* consists of 6,000 Sanskrit shlokas, not all of which are relevant to our times. They deal with the specific situation of his times, and even the remedies prescribed for problems which overlap with ours, have to be seen in the context of his period. But there are certain elements that can be culled out from his magnum opus, and from his life, which we need to learn from, especially today when the Republic is at a critical crossroad, desperately needing change, but still caught in the grooves of the past.

In the course of one lifetime, Chanakya groomed a king, deposed another, helped to keep at bay the mighty Greeks, united a fractious territory, put his nominee on the throne of Magadha, and contributed in consolidating a great empire—the Maurya Empire—extending from the western passes adjoining Afghanistan to the Bay of Bengal and touching on the southern fringes; arguably the first true empire in India's history. To achieve this, what are the qualities he displayed? First and foremost, he had the clarity of vision to unsentimentally identify what was the root of the problem and what needed to be done to rectify it. This is easier said than done. Most people, especially today, are either mesmerised by the past or paralysed by the fear of change. Secondly, he had a clear understanding of human behaviour. This understanding was not a prisoner of unrealistic idealism, although he did not devalue idealism per se. Thirdly, he believed in the importance of leadership. The ship of State without the right person at the helm will sooner or later run aground. Fourthly, he had the ability to unerringly spot talent, and even more importantly, groom it for the responsibilities it must deliver. Conversely, he did not hide the fact that he found it very difficult to suffer fools; in fact, he stated that those without talent should stay away from leadership positions. For those who had it in them to lead, he laid down, such as for the king's council of ministers, detailed instructions on conduct, decision making, probity and behaviour.

Fifthly, he never lost sight of the fact that all politics must work for the welfare of the people. If that central tenet was ignored, no Constitution, however high-minded was worthwhile. Sixthly, he considered economic prosperity the backbone of a nation's strength. If the treasury is empty, all promises are mere slogans or populism, and all pretensions to service are so much hot air. Seventhly, he believed in analysing systems; this required an extraordinary prescience and precise knowledge of history, and a true understanding of how complex processes of society and of the government worked, something that most observers and leaders of the day were incapable of, preoccupied as they were with symptoms and not the source of the problem. Eighthly, he believed that systems must be just, and those who threatened the rule of law must be adequately punished. Ninthly, he had the courage, resolve and iron discipline to work to achieve what he believed was the right course of action. Many people know what the right course of action should be, but do not have the courage of conviction to pursue it. They are paralysed into following what the seemingly dominant are saying, and do not interrogate it with true courage of conviction. And finally, he never lost sight of the fact that there is one supreme goal that transcends all others when it comes to matters of the State—and that is national interest.

Today, India is at a historical crossroad: on the one side is the promise of governance that has elements which are divisive and polarising, and, on the other the assurance of governance that is inclusive and wishes to carry all of India under its awning. To make the right choice, it is essential first to recognise the consequences of making the wrong one. Do we want governance that rides roughshod over the weakest sections of society and resurrects communal strife to a point where the very project of governance is jeopardised? Or do we want verifiable good governance that imbues our polity with harmony and upholds the compulsion of co-existence that defines the very idea of India. To make the right choice, all Indians must become leaders, displaying the qualities that Chanakya invoked two thousand years ago. The people of India want to escape religious strife and get on with their lives in order to benefit from the secular dividends of progressive and effective governance. But, in order to be able to do so, they must first make the choice as leaders in their own right. Only then can they be the beneficiaries of the future they want to see.

(This piece was originally published on 23 June 2013)

DOES THE YOUNG POLITICAL BRIGADE LACK IDEALISM?

*W*hen Bhutan made its transition to a constitutional monarchy some five years ago, it wrote a new Constitution. That Constitution has one amazing article. It stipulates that even the King must compulsorily abdicate his throne at the age of sixty-five in favour of his successor. In other words, the new Constitution of Bhutan prescribes a retirement age even for the monarch! Naturally, this feature is applicable to politicians as well. No prime minister, minister or Member of Parliament can continue to hold office after the age of sixty-five.

I was reminded of this dramatic Bhutanese innovation when, in one of his recent speeches, Rahul Gandhi declared that he would lead the country by providing a younger leadership. Certainly, with two-thirds of all Indians being below the age of thirty-five, this would appear to be the right thing to do. India is, by the age of its population, one of the youngest countries in the world. Why is it then led by a leadership that is conspicuous by its near universal octogenarian profile? Do Indians like elder leaders, or are they left with no option but an ageing leadership that believes its hold on power is eternal and will not cede ground to those of the younger generation?

The emergence of a dramatically younger leadership appears to be a global trend. David Cameron and Obama were poster boys of this phenomenon. Even China, for all the opaque and largely unaccountable ways in which it selects its leaders, has seen the writing on the wall and opted for a younger collective at the helm. Is this generational shift likely to happen in India?

Before we answer this question we have to, in all fairness, ask a preceding one. Are younger leaders necessarily better in leadership qualities than their older counterparts? The conventional wisdom is that young is better, but does experience bear this out? Rahul Gandhi's young brigade, many of whom were ministers in the former UPA government, have so far hardly shown the leadership qualities that would entitle them to claim they are better. More often than not, they have huddled together in non-descript conformity, content to work routinely, and vociferous only in their assertion of absolute loyalty to the Gandhi family. Perhaps they have not been given due opportunity, but I see very little evidence of their seeking it out or bringing fresh ideas into the political or governance debate, with the courage of conviction to stick their necks out. Very few political parties have the inner democracy to allow constructive dissent and debate. The dismaying factor is that much of our younger leadership accepts this state of affairs, and is, by and large, content to hang on to their political perch within this accepted paradigm.

The truth is that young leaders in our political system are often the most bereft of idealism. They have grown up in the cynical political milieu of the last few decades and have taken to it like fish to water. If a generation twice removed from now emerged from the idealistic crucible of the freedom movement, and the one that succeeded it began to accept political compromise in the pursuit of power, the younger generation of politicians today seem to have embraced this rotten state of affairs enthusiastically, and shown little other inclination than the perpetuation of their own narrow ambitions. Strategic manipulation of the system, rather than robust new parameters of leadership, has been the hallmark of their contribution. Of course, there are exceptions to this trend, but such exceptions apply equally to the old or the young. The Delhi-based emergence of the Aam Aadmi Party is one example of such new thinking. But, generally, it is a pretty barren landscape where the potential of young leadership is concerned.

The octogenarians do bring in greater wisdom and experience, but not always of the kind the nation now wants. Their ideas and thinking are caught in a rut and their exposure to the possibilities of the new severely limited. Besides, although this is a subject we don't overplay out of deference or politeness, there is no denying the visible physical deterioration that occurs to their faculties after a point. This is the law of nature, and even politicians are susceptible to it. Reduced physical mobility, slower reflexes, impaired hearing, memory lapses, debilitating multiple ailments, flagging stamina, incapacity for sustained periods of work—all of these are routinely visible in the octogenarian leadership we now have.

Can we follow the Bhutan example and put a compulsory retirement age for our politicians? After all, if there is a retirement age for everybody else—judges, bureaucrats, corporate, professors, technocrats—then why not for politicians? India does not have to make a fetish about age or over-romanticise the potential of the young, but a cut-off of seventy for politicians holding public office is something the country could think about. At the same time, I think the nation is also waiting for a younger leadership worthy to step in the shoes of those who need to be eased out. So far, we have the rhetoric about the need for young leaders but very little to show that we have a credible alternative. The time has come for the young to enter the political mainstream, but not to perpetuate the old. They must have the courage to bring new ideas to the table and the courage of convictions to pursue them even if the immediate consequences are unfavourable. The youngest nation in the world is waiting for a genuine revolution to be led by the young. Only then will the old really begin to cede ground.

(This piece was originally published on 27 October 2013)

THE SHOCKING NEGLECT OF CULTURE

*I*f Chanakya had written about culture, what would his views have been? This may seem like an irrelevant question in the politically surcharged atmosphere of today, where only issues of what is going to happen in the forthcoming elections dominate all debate. But a nation is more than the sum of its political parties, more than merely the combined decibel strength of its vociferous politicians, and more than merely the competing claims of economists on what the rate of GDP should be. This is especially true of India, which is not only a nation but also a civilisation going back to the dawn of time, with a culture defined by antiquity, continuity, assimilation, diversity and peaks of unprecedented refinement.

Chanakya would have first understood that there is an inextricable link between growing political power and cultural efflorescence. A nation that has global aspirations must be the harbinger of a culture that has global credibility. Given his pride in the cultural ethos of which he himself was a product, he would have interpreted credibility to mean three things above all else: originality, authenticity and aesthetics. And, he would have wanted the ideal State to provide maximum support to the development of culture, since nations are a holistic entity, not merely the paraphernalia of authority and force.

These thoughts came to me due to two parallel exposures. The first was the sheer exhilaration of watching two women who made, on my commissioning, a large Madhubani wall painting at my residence. These artists, hailing from Bihar, lacked metropolitan sophistication perhaps, but they more than made up for it by the sheer deftness of their artistic skills so rooted in their authentic cultural inheritance. Without initial tracing or any pre-made design to guide them, they drew a bewitching tree of life and embellished it by brightly coloured birds and fruits, drawing free hand, and only from their inherent sense of space and format as resplendent on so many walls in the village of Madhubani.

The second exposure was to the ongoing retrospective at the National Gallery of Modern Art (NGMA) in New Delhi of the renowned artist Subodh Gupta. Subodh has won international acclaim for his large installations using symbols from our everyday life, including, most ubiquitously, the common *balti, chammach* and *kardhchi* or a bucket, spoon and a ladle. His work has a remarkable quality of spectacle, with larger-than-life creations, but his great redeeming feature is that his idiom is authentic, his symbolisms are rooted in the soil, and his creativity has the energy of innovation and new experimentation, thereby creating a pleasing aesthetic experience. To that extent, although Subodh's creative language is dramatically different, he has a resonance in terms of authenticity and continuity that could be seen in the works of the Madhubani painters.

This being said, my personal view is that much of what passes as installation art frankly borders very often on gimmickry and is an embarrassing attempt to copy Western trends of 'found art', popularised, among others, by the French artist Marcel Duchamp (1887–1968). Duchamp's installation of a common urinal, which he titled 'Fountain', was selected in 2004 by 500 renowned artists and historians in the West as 'the most influential artwork of the 20th century.' The elevation of common urinals may be comprehensible as part of a certain artistic evolution, but there is no need necessarily for Indians to be a part of it. Besides, installation art, embedded in our own cultural context, has a living tradition in the decorations for Indian festivals, marriages and a host of other celebrations that is part of the ebb and flow of everyday life. My suspicion, though—and several leading artists I have spoken to seem to agree—is that most artists experimenting with installations are merely copying Western idiom and themes and are encouraged by Western galleries and curators, and their hangers-on in India, to do just that.

One important reason why such developments go largely unquestioned is that there is hardly—and Chanakya would have been deeply concerned about this—any scholarly evaluation of our own artistic principles or discussion of what our aesthetic yardsticks should be. It is disturbing that even today, the curriculum of our art colleges is hopelessly outdated; they rely disproportionately on Western studio techniques and continue to make the invidious distinction between art and craft that is completely a Western construct. As per Indian aesthetics, a work of art is to be judged by its quality and not categorised by its origins. A painter making a Madhubani painting on the walls of a village in Bihar is as much an artist as a 'sophisticated' city-bred painter. When such distinctions are made mindlessly, there is the real danger of the vibrant and ancient folk art being de-contextualised, wrenched away from its natural environment and promoted only as a rustic curiosity. Should this happen, Subodh Gupta may survive, even flourish, but the two Madhubani artists, persevering so beautifully with a centuries-old art tradition, may vanish.

Finally, Chanakya would have emphasised that art in vibrant nations has vital people connectivity. It is not an elitist phenomenon, somehow nurtured by just about 500 serious art collectors in a country where the very rich at the very least number over twenty million, or celebrated only when some artist gets some hefty amount at an auction abroad. He would have been worried that the NGMA where Subodh's exhibition was held, although greatly upgraded, gets no more than 30,000 visitors per year when the Museum of Modern Art in New York gets 2.5 million visitors a year at thirty dollars a ticket; the Louvre in Paris as many at 12.5 euros per head; and the Tate in London four million at twenty pounds per person. High-decibel politics may be the flavour of the season, but there are issues of great import that go beyond who wins the elections.

(This piece was originally published on 19 January 2014)

BIHAR NEEDS SPECIAL
CATEGORY STATUS

*W*hat is the relation between the Centre and its parts? This was an important question that preoccupied Chanakya when he sat down to pen the basic features of an effective and functional polity. Is the Centre merely the mechanical sum of its parts? Or, is it greater than the parts and can act unilaterally and, if it so desires, arbitrarily? Chanakya compared the polity to a wheel: the Centre as the fulcrum, and its constituents as the spokes, each dependent on the other, none able to function independently of each other.

This paradigm assumes importance, since today, Nitish Kumar, the chief minister of Bihar, will hold a rally in New Delhi to highlight Bihar's case to be accorded the Special Category status. Our Constitution has been described as sanctioning a federal state with a pronounced unitary bias. His rally will test how federal is our thinking, and what are the limits to the Centre's unitary bias. In this sense, at a crucial juncture in the evolution of the Republic, it may help to create a new dynamic to the complex question of Centre-State relations.

In recent times, I have been asked by several well-meaning people what exactly is the substance and logic to the Bihar chief minister's request. As I have understood it, Nitish Kumar is making this demand not only in the interest of Bihar, but in the interest of India as a whole. His view is that the nation is an organic whole. The destiny of any one part influences the destiny of the whole. India cannot sustain an institutional structure of discrimination by which those already better off continue to avail of the bulk of Central assistance and investment opportunities, while those, for reasons not of their own making and in spite of best efforts to remedy matters, remain economically backward for lack of resources and investments.

Bihar constitutes almost nine per cent of India's population and is the Union's third-most populous state. For the last five years, as a result of good governance, it has had the highest growth rate of any state in the country, averaging twelve per cent. In spite of this, it will, even at this rate of growth, *take another twenty-five years to come up to the average national per capita income.* Why is Bihar locked into this vicious cycle of backwardness? First, there are verifiable historical reasons. During colonial rule, the British followed a conscious policy to de-industrialise Bihar. Further, the Permanent Settlement imposed by them in agriculture gave zamindars the right to nine-tenths of the farmers' produce in perpetuity, thereby institutionalising a terribly impoverished peasantry. Secondly, after Independence, the Centre imposed the Freight Neutralisation Policy, which allowed the developed states to get minerals and raw materials from Bihar at cheaper rates than they were available in Bihar! This terribly inequitable and arbitrary system continued for four long decades, from 1952 to 1993. In 2000, Bihar was bifurcated to create Jharkhand. All the minerals and raw material wealth, along with a huge chunk of the industrial belt, went to Jharkhand. Finally, there were long years of misgovernance, but that has been rectified dramatically in the last seven years.

The Centre has a policy to assist backward states by according them Special Category Status. The Centre's criteria being that the states must be in hilly and difficult terrain with low population density, have a strategic location along the border, and suffer from infrastructural weakness and non-viable nature of financial resources. Except for not being sparsely populated, Bihar qualifies on such counts. It has a 729-km border with Nepal; its northern terrain is endemically flood-prone due to rivers originating in Nepal; on the infrastructure side, its roads, power and teledensity is one of the lowest in the country; and, in the absence of investments and industrialisation, its financial situation, although greatly improved in recent years, is still precarious.

States that have been accorded Special Category status have greatly benefitted by receiving loans at concessional rates from the Centre, and through tax concessions, which have helped to catalyse private investment flows. Of the Special Category states, Himachal and Uttarakhand have a per capita income three and a half times that of Bihar, and even that of Assam is double of Bihar. The irony is that developed states like Punjab, Haryana and Tamil Nadu receive per capita central funds that are four times higher than Bihar. With over fifty per cent of its population below the poverty line, Bihar receives only 2.67 per cent of Central subsidies and 1.9 per cent of Central enterprise investment.

Nitish Kumar has argued at every level—the prime minister, the Planning Commission and the Finance minister—that Bihar needs the help of the Special Category regimen to fast track its development. In its absence, in spite of the remarkable track of good governance seen by the state in recent years, the 110 million people of Bihar will remain locked in a cycle of poverty. With nine per cent of the country's population, Bihar today contributes only 2.9 per cent to the national GDP. Imagine what would happen to the overall prosperity of India if Bihar was enabled to contribute as much as ten per cent, which is feasible. Bihar wishes to contribute to the growth story of India.

Chanakya believed that the Centre is only as strong as all the parts that constitute it. To ensure this principle is not a favour accorded by the Centre but a right of all those who are a part of the Union, Finance Minister Chidambaram, in his Budget speech, indicated that the Centre will reconsider Bihar's request. Nitish Kumar has welcomed the gesture. He is coming to New Delhi today to address a mass rally in order to strengthen that resolve.

(This piece was originally published on 17 March 2013)

DON'T INSULT THE INTELLIGENCE
OF THE VOTER

*D*o elections tend to devalue the intelligence of the voter? This is an important question considering the shenanigans of our leaders and political parties in the frenzy to win the political battle. False propaganda, wild promises, cynical compromises, and the invocation of principle for transparent manipulation become a daily occurrence. Leaders leave one party to join another for purely opportunist reasons and quote high principle for doing so. Parties which swear by the purity of their ideology admit defectors who have openly abused this ideology. Cleverly devised slogans seek to mask the absence of substance. Subjects are made black or white. Complex issues are reduced to simplified opposites. Expression becomes deliberately inflammatory. The stance becomes: what I say is right and what you believe is wrong. Lies are no longer considered immoral. In fact, the greater the ability to deceive, the more 'correct' their usage. It is a strange period of hyperbole and exaggeration, of larger-than-life misrepresentation.

In all of this, the voter is the most sought after 'commodity', but his good becomes secondary to his vote. He or she becomes a means to the coveted altar of power. To this end, seduction, in all its lurid colours, is the ultimate tool. Substance, truth and moderation become dispensable.

At some point in this larger-than-life battle, a strange alchemy occurs. Some leaders and political parties mistake their electoral message for the truth. They begin to believe their own propaganda. A sense of infallibility overwhelms them. They become victims of their own campaign. This is the dangerous point, when balance and good sense become permanently hostage to ambition and strategy.

The truth is that it is a big mistake to insult the intelligence of the voter. He is not a novice to the political game. In the past, he has been fooled by the invocation of caste and creed. He is still susceptible, but democracy is an educational process and by now, he knows what the game is all about. Leaders may refuse to answer his questions, but he still has questions to ask. He want to know why the Congress, which has vowed to make the fight against corruption its plank, has chosen to align with Lalu Yadav who has been convicted and sent to jail for corruption. It is a question they also want to ask the BJP, which condemns the corruption in the Congress, but aligns itself with Yeddyurappa in Karnataka and admits the tainted Bellary brothers. They listen patiently to declamations on the so-called 'Gujarat model' of governance but want to ask why Gujarat, a relatively developed state, has such a lacklustre record on providing better health and education to its citizens. They want to understand why as much as forty-two per cent of all investment in Gujarat has been made only in the petrochemical sector. They want to know who are the handful of businessmen who have benefited disproportionately from this one-sided investment. They are curious about why farmers are protesting in Gujarat and why such poor compensation was paid to them for land taken away to benefit a selective list of industries. They want to ask why some two lakh children below the age of fifteen are working in hazardous BT cotton fields when they should be in schools. They want to know why Gujarat has such a high level of public debt, and who is benefitting from the money borrowed. They want to ask from where certain political parties are getting the enormous amounts they are spending.

There are many more questions but nobody provides the answers. Does the BJP's slogan of 'India First' mean that all the subtle complexities and the many splendoured plurality of India must be subsumed soullessly under the awning of jingoistic nationalism? Is there a contradiction between the primacy of nationalism and the respect that is due to all the faiths of India? Must the goal of governance be posited as a polarity to the imperative of social and religious harmony? Why must the two be delinked, as if one can be pursued without ensuring the other? These are questions that have a direct relevance to the lives of all Indians. They know that governance would be impossible if there is endemic communal suspicion or strife. They know that a leader who cannot carry all Indians, irrespective of their faith, will ultimately carry no one, not even his own party. Our country cannot be reduced to the synthetic simplicity of one faith, one culture, one slogan, one model.

The voters hold the trump card, but the tragedy is the political leaders think they do. In many ways, the voter has begun to beat the politicians at their own game. He humour ambitious politicians. He attend political rallies. He applaud an eloquent speech. He listen to endless promises. He watch how alliances are made. He congratulate political opportunists for their unprincipled agility. He observe the blatant use of caste and creed in wooing voters. But in all of this, he know what the truth is. He knows what is good for him; who has worked to change the quality of his life; who will stand with him; and who really speaks for him and his good. And when it comes to casting his vote, he votes accordingly.

After sixty years and more of democratic elections, it would be foolish to think the voter remains a gullible puppet to be cynically manipulated by opportunist politicians. The big mistake now is to insult the intelligence of the voter. Alas, political leaders who hop from one political rally to another, without waiting to listen, forget this cardinal truth.

(This piece was first published on 30 March 2014)

WHY DOES THE UPSC GIVE WEIGHTAGE TO ENGLISH?

I had only recently written on the question of Indian languages. But I am constrained to write on a related subject again because of the reported reluctance of the Union Public Service Commission (UPSC) to amend its Civil Service Aptitude Test II to reduce the weightage of questions relating to the knowledge of English. I have the highest respect for the UPSC, but its alleged bias for English in this respect is something I have great difficulty in supporting.

When I took the Civil Services exam in 1975, aspirants could write their papers only in English. This gave an unfair advantage to those of a certain social background who had studied continuously in English medium schools as against those who had not. Not surprisingly, in my batch in the Indian Foreign Service, almost half the batch was from St. Stephen's College. Since then, a great deal of reform has taken place keeping in mind the imperative need to provide a level playing field to those whose proficiency and talent was perhaps even greater but whose knowledge of English was not.

Those grappling with this question in the hallowed chambers of the UPSC may do well to remember what Mahatma Gandhi, the father of the nation, had to say about this subject as far back as 1921: 'It is my considered opinion that English education in the manner it has been given has emasculated the English-educated Indians, it has put a severe strain upon the Indian students' nervous energy. The process of displacing the vernaculars has been one of the saddest chapters of the British connection .... No country can become a nation by producing a race of translators .... Of all the superstitions that affect India, none is so great as that a knowledge of the English language is necessary for imbibing ideas of liberty and developing accuracy of thought .... The system of education (in which the medium is English) was conceived and born in error, for the English rulers honestly believed the indigenous system to be worse than useless. It has been nurtured in sin, for the tendency has been to dwarf the Indian body, mind, and soul.'

Gandhiji's views did not change, for, in 1944, just a few years before Independence, he spoke in a similar vein, but this time with a great sense of foreboding about the consequences for the future: 'Our love of the English language in preference to our own mother tongue has caused a deep chasm between the educated and the politically minded classes and the masses. We flounder when we make the vain attempt to express abstruse thoughts in the mother tongue .... The result has been disastrous ... We are too near our own times correctly to measure the disservice caused to India by the neglect of its great languages.'

Significantly, Jawaharlal Nehru, whose first language was English and who, against his own will perhaps, became the patron of the English-speaking elite, had equally strong views on this matter: 'Some people imagine that English is likely to become the lingua franca of India. That seems to be a fantastic conception except in respect of a handful of upper-class intelligentsia. It has no relation to the problems of mass education and culture ... if we have to have a balanced view of the world we must not confine ourselves to English spectacles.'

The truth is that for too long now, English has become a language of social exclusion: the upper crust of the Indian middle class presides over this linguistic apartheid; the rest of India consists of victims and aspirants. The ability to speak with the right accent and fluency and pronunciation has become the touchstone for entry into the charmed circle of the ruling elite. For some people, still living in the prism of an Anglicised past, those who can speak English fluently are People Like Us. Those who cannot must be especially tested for their ability to claim educational and social competence. That is why Ram Manohar Lohia once said perceptively that in India, to be part of the ruling elite, you need three things: upper-caste status, wealth and a knowledge of English. That is also why a great leader in Bihar, Karpoori Thakur, gave permission to students, who were otherwise proficient, to be promoted to the next grade even if they had failed in English.

It is important to emphasise that this is not a diatribe against the English language. English, has for historical reasons, become an important medium to interface with a globalising world. Moreover, as a language, it has a beauty and dexterity of its own. Languages, by themselves, are not guilty of cultural domination; their usage is. For Indians, it is relevant to introspect on what the imposition of English has meant to them, as a people, a society and a nation. Even as more and more Indians queue up to learn English, we are witness to the most unacceptable linguistic shoddiness in a nation with an inestimably rich linguistic heritage. Anyone who sees the quality of English prose in government files will be left with no doubt about this assertion. V.S. Naipaul in *An Area of Darkness* said much the same thing. Calling English 'the greatest incongruity of British rule,' he added that a clerk in India using the English language is 'immediately stultified,' since he can never fully grasp the nuances of the foreign language, 'which limits his response and makes him inflexible.'

The UPSC's mandate is to test a candidate's abilities as an Indian administrator. It is not to judge his knowledge of English. There are many states in the Union where work of the administration is carried out almost exclusively in the language of that state. In Bihar, for instance, all work in the administration is done in Hindi. In any case, those who qualify for the IAS have to learn the language of the state allotted to them. The UPSC must provide a level playing field for all candidates.

(This piece was originally published on 20 July 2014)

U.R. ANANTHAMURTHY

*I*n the engulfing mediocrity that defines our intellectual discourse today, one voice that remained consistently refined and nuanced is no longer with us. In the passing away of U.R. Ananthamurthy on 22 August, our country has lost a powerful writer, thinker, philosopher and public activist. He was a man who consistently believed that a writer is not a neutral entity who expresses his views but is not required to fight for what he believes is right. For him, a writer was a spirited part of society and politics, and needed to use his pen to engage with the vital issues of the day. In the deadening expediency of 'public' debate now, he was the quintessentially cerebral non-conformist, who opposed when he thought he should and not merely to be noticed.

I first got to know Ananthamurthy well when he accepted my invitation to participate in the Afro-Asian Literary Festival. The festival was organised by the India Council of Cultural Relations (ICCR) in 2006 when I was its Director-General. The venue was the historic Neemrana Fort near Delhi, so beautifully restored by Aman Nath and Francis Wacziarg. At that time, Ananthamurthy's health was already fragile but he was still fairly mobile. The fort required a visitor to climb some considerable steps, and although I was afraid of his ability to do so, Ananthamurthy readily accepted the challenge.

That conference was memorable also for the presence of another great writer, Gulzar. In the case of Gulzar, our meeting at that memorable locale was, at least for me, path-breaking. It led to a friendship, which is one of my most treasured possessions, and to several books, which include several volumes of my translation of his poems, and his wonderfully evocative translation of my epic poem, *Yudhishtir And Draupadi*.

But to return to Ananthamurthy. He emerged at that conference as one of the most powerful voices on the importance of writing in our own mother tongue and the respect that must be given to our own languages. It was not a new argument, but in the context of this specific conference, where so many well-known writers from Asia and Africa were present, apart from literary figures from India, it made a great impact. Through his simple yet emphatic logic, the point came through that one of the greatest losses of colonised societies is the loss of their own languages. He reiterated this in a public lecture in Delhi a little later: 'We are going to lose our memory. We need English, but not of the "call centre" sort. It is not a gateway of knowledge. We need to create in our own language. The English elite in India are not as cultured as the masses. English must be taught but children in schools need to create in their own languages, because we don't think in English. It is a received language.'

This thought, so simply yet eloquently elucidated by Ananthamurthy, was shared by several of his noted contemporaries, both in India and abroad. Professor Namwar Singh has made the crucial point that no language can be *substituted* by another. Like mother's milk, our mother tongue is something we acquire in childhood; a foreign language can be an additional acquisition, but never an alternative to it. The brilliant Kenyan writer Ngũgĩ wa Thiong'o began his book *Decolonizing the*

Mind with the statement that this will be his last book in English, and henceforth, he will write only in Giyuku and Kiswahili, because a foreign language can only be a language of communication, not a carrier of culture and history. Sheldon Pollock, the great US Sanskrit scholar, has made the point that until 1947, and for centuries before that, India had scholars in philology who compared with the best of the world. These scholars produced pioneering works in all our languages, including Persian, Prakrit, Sanskrit and Urdu, which were invaluable reference works and constituted a window to the roots of our culture. Unfortunately, the last few decades have, seen almost no work on this literary treasure, so much so that foreign universities—and he cites the case of an important one in the USA, that failed to get a trained professor in Telugu who had a command over the entire classical Telugu tradition—are being forced to close down their specialities in our languages.

Ananthamurthy wrote almost entirely in Kannada and still had a huge following. He was fortunate that some of his noted works were widely translated into other languages, including English. His classic novel *Samskara,* written in 1965, was made into a much-acclaimed film and became a sensation for its fierce condemnation of the sterile and inequitable norms prevailing in a Brahmin village. It is significant that Ananthamurthy spoke of the humiliation and degradation of the caste system when he himself was a Brahmin. He was a beneficiary of institutionalised social inequity by birth but rebelled against it because he had the ability to think for himself and read widely and eclectically, including the works of Ram Manohar Lohia.

In recent times, even though unwell and on dialysis, Ananthamurthy spoke fearlessly on the dangers of communalism, the threat to India's pluralistic ethos, and the use of ethnicity and religion in the rise of Fascism. He was ruthlessly criticised for his views by the fanatical wings of the sangh parivar. There were even reports that on hearing of his death, some members of these organisations ignited crackers to celebrate. Had they even read his books? Were they even aware of the magnitude and depth of his intellectual corpus? The bigoted zeal of the illiterate fanatic has become one of the greatest threats to our society. The memory of the gentle but unbending legacy of Ananthamurthy will always be an inspiration for those who have a different vision of India.

(This piece was originally published on 31 August 2014)

LINK BETWEEN INTERNAL
HARMONY & EXTERNAL SECURITY

*C*hanakya believed that the unfolding present will cast its shadow on the configuration of the future. That is why he believed that analysing the situation as it exists today, provides the material for devising the strategy that must be shaped for the morrow. There is a causal continuity between the past, present and the future. Those who derive the right lessons from the past understand the present and are well-prepared for the future. Those who don't seek to thrive on short-term dividends without a thought for the long-term consequences of their wilful myopia.

This incisive intellectual heritage, which so many of us seem to have forgotten today, is exceptionally relevant for the India of today. For instance, there is a direct correlation between certain developments abroad, especially in our own neighbourhood, and consequences within our own country. To ignore this would be a monumental blunder for a country like India, which is situated arguably in one of the most dangerous regions of the world: we have a 4,057 km of disputed Line of Actual Control (LAC) with China; a 778 km-long disputed Line of Control (LoC) with Pakistan; a total of 15, 106 km of international borders with seven countries, and a 7,516 km long vulnerable coastline.

In addition, we have pivotally influential elements in the Pakistani establishment who are implacably hostile to us; we have the problem of externally sponsored terrorism, and now increasingly, homegrown terrorism; Afghanistan is endemically unstable with the Taliban regrouping in anticipation of American and NATO withdrawal; Nepal remains a vulnerable conduit for terrorism directed against India, as does Bangladesh; and large parts of Myanmar are under the sway of terrorism of various hues. In all of this, China is always willing to fish in troubled waters.

The purported video threat circulated by the Al-Qaeda recently, threatening to step up jihadi terrorism in India, acquires a dangerous salience in this context. There are some who argue that we should not take the video seriously and view it only as an attempt by Al-Qaeda to gain publicity to counter its own perceived decline in the face of the terrorist extremism of the rival nascent organisation, the Islamic State of Iraq and Syria (ISIS). This could be true, but it could also be false, and in any case, we have no reason to be complacent.

There are two important reasons for this. First, our security establishment is still flabby, ill-equipped, directionless and uncoordinated, with a multiplicity of agencies often acting in individual silos without a nodal strategic focus. Secondly—and this is far more important—the communal polarisation often witnessed on our soil will, if unchecked, provide the most fertile ground for the success of the Al-Qaeda threat.

Over two millennia ago, Chanakya stated the eternal verity that, ultimately, the ability of a nation to defeat its external enemies depends on how stable and healthy it is internally. The incendiary statements being made by the ultra-Right Hindu outfits and their members, which appear to be specifically designed to generate hatred and violence between religious communities, is a time bomb ticking away for the benefit of those who are waiting across our borders to exploit the consequential social instability. The BJP's choice of Yogi Adityanath as its mascot for the by-elections in UP is an inflammatory case in point. In speech after speech, he has spewed communal venom, disregarding a reprimand from the Election Commission and defying its instructions to restrain him through an FIR.

It is true that the majority of Indians are Hindus. But it is also true that we have large numbers of people of other faiths living across the length and breadth of our country. As Jawaharlal Nehru said as far back as 1948, religious co-existence is, therefore, not an option but a compulsion for us. For centuries, we have succeeded in living together, largely in peace and harmony. If this strength of our social fabric tears, or is ripped apart, no Indian anywhere will be safe. Governance and progress will come to a standstill. The USP of India has been, and must remain, its vibrant plurality, because that is the foundation of both our nationhood and our civilisation.

It is increasingly clear that some members of the BJP–RSS combine do not understand this. They seem to have adopted a conscious policy to talk of *vikas* or development at one level and to pursue *vinash* or destruction at the ground level. Obviously, they are unaware of the long-term consequences of such a policy. Two days ago, Home Minister Rajnath Singh said, 'We have enough strength to face any challenge from organisations like the Al-Qaeda.' The truth is that we are not particularly strong in the hardware of our defence preparedness and Intelligence apparatus; but even more alarmingly, we are weakening the software of our unity and social harmony, a software for which we have the unquestioned patent, and which has succeeded in keeping at bay those who have always sought to divide and destabilise us. The strength of such dangerous forces cannot be underestimated today.

(This piece was originally published on 14 September 2014)

INDIA'S SOFT POWER

*F*or perfectly understandable reasons, handling the economy is arguably the most important priority for any government. Defence and foreign policy come next and certainly grab the headlines. But India is not only a young Republic, it is also an ancient civilisation. That civilisation, over a five thousand year's journey, was noted for its antiquity, continuity, diversity, assimilation and peaks of unparalleled cultural refinement.

Culture represents a wide arena of achievement. It is not only about the performing arts or the visual arts. Culture, in its widest interpretation, is the cumulative level of excellence achieved by society in all the areas of creative and intellectual expression. That level of creative refinement constitutes the soft power of a country. It is now widely recognised that soft power is as powerful a tool of foreign policy as conventional diplomacy or military hardware.

In the not so distant past, this soft power gave India a much larger footprint than its geographically defined territorial limits. The impact of Indian culture, for over a thousand years in South and South-East Asia, amply proves this and must count as perhaps the world's only example in the ancient and medieval periods of significant cultural export without military conquest. From the sixth century BCE onwards, the tenets of Buddhism were taken abroad in Pali, a dialect of Prakrit that, much simpler than Sanskrit, was what the masses spoke at that time. Pali is still the language of Buddhists in Sri Lanka, Myanmar, and much of South-east Asia. From the Amaravati period in the second century, through the Gupta, Pallava, Pala and Chola dynasties in the succeeding centuries up to the twelfth, Hindu culture spread across all of South and South-East Asia.

The largest Hindu temple in the world, and one of only two dedicated to Brahma, is at Angkor Vat in Cambodia. The epic Ramayana has immensely popular local variations in Cambodia, Laos, Thailand and Myanmar. The Champa dynasty, which ruled for over a thousand years in present-day central Vietnam was Hindu and followed the cultural mores and practices of India, including the Sakya calendar. Tamil is an officially recognised language in Malaysia and Singapore; in Thailand, which is predominantly Buddhist today, the names of people and places are derivatives of Sanskrit. In fact, archaeological findings across the region, right up to the Philippines, show that Sanskrit, and its most important secular and religious texts, were part of local cultures. The Borobudur temple in Indonesia is a monumental example of the influence of Hindu philosophy and architectural principles, and the island of Bali is still a Hindu enclave in this overwhelmingly Islamic nation.

If culture can play such an important role, why do successive governments at the Centre treat it as almost an optional accessory? It must be understood, that the impact of soft power is not some coincidental occurrence. When culture achieves a level of irresistible excellence at home, it finds a natural spillover overseas. When culture stagnates or receives short shrift in terms of official patronage and opportunities of expression, even military might cannot guarantee its enduring export. Today, Indian culture does have a following abroad, but it is far below our potential, and far more the result of such non-government players like Bollywood and chicken tikka. It certainly does not reflect a concerted and defined cultural policy on behalf of the government.

There was an expectation, perhaps in some people, that a BJP government, which takes great pride in Indian culture, albeit in a selectively sectarian manner, would do much more for its promotion. But this hope has, at least on present evidence, been decisively belied. For inexplicable reasons, the UPA government did not have, for the longest period of time, a full-time Minister of Culture. Culture was clubbed with the department of Tourism. It is plain to anyone who has a sense of the potential of both tourism and culture, that one minister handling both would do scant justice to either. Now, the BJP government has again made one minister in charge of both these portfolios.

Almost all organisations associated with the government for the promotion of culture are languishing. The National Gallery of Modern Art or NGMA counts its visitors in thousands every year; the Louvre in Paris or the Tate gallery in London get visitors in millions at a hefty entrance fee. The Indian Council of Cultural Relations, created especially by Maulana Azad soon after Independence, as the autonomous arm of the Ministry of External Affairs for the export of our soft power, is headless and pathetically short of funds. Whatever little it can do is being arbitrarily usurped by the Department of Culture, with no clarity about the role of either. Apex bodies, like the Lalit Kala Akademi, the Sahitya Akademi and the Sangeet Natak Akademi have become hotbeds of sterile politics under the bureaucratic stranglehold of the Department of Culture. The Sangeet Natak Akademi is lying headless, as are the National Culture Fund, the National Archives, the Indira Gandhi Rashtra Manav Sangrahalaya in Bhopal, and the beauteous Salar Jung Museum in Hyderabad. The National Museum remained headless for months on end and finally got a DG only in

December last year. Art galleries are few, badly equipped and suffer from a huge shortage of professionally trained curators. Except for a few institutions of true excellence, and most of these are so precisely because they are outside the purview of government, the cultural landscape is a barren wasteland notable primarily for its red tape and lack of political will and imagination. Some state governments, notably Bihar, have worked to revive cultural institutions, but they too are short of funds.

Culture is not about the imposition of a narrow ideology. It is about the efflorescence of ideas, of rejuvenation and providing a supporting infrastructure for creative excellence. Will our new government wake up to this fact?

(This piece was originally published on 26 October 2014)

POLITICS BEHIND CHANGING
THE NAMES OF ROADS

There was a time when the magnificent Raj Path in New Delhi was called Kingsway. There was also a time when Janpath was called Queensway. When my father was posted to Delhi in the late 1950s, my first memories were of our bungalow on a road then called Queen Mary's Avenue. In 1961, it was renamed Pandit Pant Marg, in tribute to the memory of the towering Home Minister Govind Ballabh Pant. My Nana in Allahabad built his palatial home on Elgin Road. That was still the name of the road when he died many years after 1947. But today Elgin Road has become Lal Bahadur Shastri Marg.

Roads rarely change their axis or alignment or direction. Rajpath still majestically connects Rashtrapati Bhavan to India Gate and Janpath is still the most important gateway to Rajiv Gandhi Chowk, earlier called Connaught Place. But identities, associations and memories change. Such a change reflects changed priorities or reformulated notions of patriotism or a deliberate choice to change the narrative of history, not all of which are misplaced. When recently, Aurangzeb Road, one of the most prominent boulevards of Lutyen's Delhi, was changed to Abdul Kalam Road, all the above were invoked, with some people in support of the change and others against.

222

The British came to rule us, and when defeated, left. When they ruled us they named roads and buildings and institutions after their own. When we won Independence, we reclaimed our own patriotic narrative. Most of the roads that were renamed bore British names. Even cities reverted to their pre-British nomenclatures: Bombay became Mumbai, Calcutta became Kolkata and Madras became Chennai.

The Aurangzeb–Kalam transference falls in an entirely different category. It connotes a preference of one kind of iconic individual over another but from within the non-colonial historical narrative. In other words, both Aurangzeb and Kalam were people who were our own, not firangis or outsiders. But, if this is the case, the obvious question that pops up is why did a *choice* have to be made, between one and the other? A choice is not a neutral decision, nor can it be random. It indicates selectivity through the conscious application of the mind, and is, therefore, inherently judgemental: Aurangzeb, the last great Mughal emperor, is not worth remembering. Is this a rewriting of history or a rectification of past mistakes or a course correction or, even worse, a somewhat hasty and arbitrary genuflection before religious stereotypes?

If this is not the case, I cannot, for the life of me understand why a road other than Aurangzeb Road was not anointed in the name of our late and revered president? Not far away from the erstwhile Aurangzeb Road, we have Dalhousie Road, recalling a British Governor-General who began the infamous policy of annexation that, among others, ended the kingdom of Awadh and introduced the theory of lapsed states by which the East India Company grew into an empire. Since we have so effortlessly renamed so much that recalls our colonial servitude, why could this improbably surviving remnant not be jettisoned to the dustbin of history and resurrected as Abdul Kalam road? My problem is that when such options are ignored, and deliberately provocative decisions are taken projecting the preference of one individual as against another, controversy and grievance are a totally unnecessary consequence. Aurangzeb, for all his faults, was the last great Mughal emperor. Does he deserve to be punished after so many years of remembrance? And, if he is to bear this fate, why not also rename an existing road named after Mohammad bin Tughlaq, who, in hindsight, inflicted only a great deal of pain on his subjects, both Hindus and Muslims? Why not, indeed, rename the Qutub Minar too, since it recalls the 'conquest' of India and was probably built on the debris of temples broken by the 'conquerors?'

The truth is that those who name roads, either now or in the past, have had a rather narrow vision in terms of choices. Political rulers and politicians abound. But there is no place for writers, poets, artists, thinkers and philosophers. Delhi, as the capital of not only a young Republic but also one of the most ancient and refined civilisations of the world, must have the least number of roads recalling this heritage. For instance, why is there not a road in our capital named after Shankaracharya, perhaps one of the greatest philosophers the world has seen? Why don't we have a road named after Thiruvalluvar, undoubtedly one of the wisest of our ancient thinkers? Why does Delhi not boast of a Kabir avenue or a Mirza Ghalib chowk or an Amir Khusro street or a Ramdhari Singh Dinkar road? Why is there no road named after Jamini Roy or Bharata who wrote the immortal *Natya Shastra* 600 years before the birth of Christ or Nagarjuna the great Buddhist philosopher?

In London, a blue plaque reminds every visitor of a home where a great writer or artist or thinker resided. This can be seen in many other countries as well. By contrast, till very recently the house of Mirza Ghalib in Gali Qasim Jaan in old Delhi was a *kabari wallah's* (scrap dealer's) workplace. Nations that have a very narrow sense of their own civilisational refinements are usually considered uncultured.

India has a great culture, but the resolve to recall it is certainly not visible in the capital of the nation. On the contrary, what we are witnessing is an ad hoc and arbitrary rewriting of history, guided by a selectivity that is hasty, subjective, whimsical and downright divisive. Dr Abdul Kalam needs to be venerated, but not at the cost of pursuing such policies.

(This piece was originally published on 13 September 2015)

THE REALITY OF AN ILLUSION

*I*n the febrile world of politics, what appears as real is often illusory, and what is devalued as illusory is actually real. Shankaracharya's much-quoted analogy of the serpent and the snake is not only illustrative of the philosophical difference between the real and the unreal; it is also the template of much of the so-called strategic planning of the political class. The magical powers of 'maya' or illusion are truly beguiling and hard to fathom. But, the hypocrisy and double standards of politics are far easier to identify.

What, for instance, is to be made of the ruling party's agenda to devote the first two days of the winter session of parliament to a re-affirmation of our commitment to the Constitution, and to pay tribute, on his 125th birth anniversary, to Babasaheb Ambedkar, who was the Chairman of the Drafting Committee of the Constitution? The government has decided to commemorate 26 November every year as Constitution Day. This was the day in 1949 when our Constitution was finalised. It was adopted on 26 January 1950, a day celebrated since then as Republic Day.

On 26 November 1949, the parliament in India was still functioning under a Resolution of the British parliament. The Constituent Assembly that met for nearly three years to discuss and debate the contours of India's future Constitution, was, as Sitaram Yechury, the leader of the CPI (M) in the Rajya Sabha, cogently pointed out, itself constituted, technically, under an enabling sanction of our erstwhile colonial masters. That legal regimen bearing the stamp of the British parliament remained in force until 26 January 1950 when independent India adopted the Constitution and resolved to become a Republic.

Republic Day, which falls on 26 January every year, and has been so commemorated and celebrated for the last sixty-five years, is the day when we reiterate our allegiance to the Constitution. What then, could be the motivation of the government to bring in another day, 26 November, as a day to express our commitment to the Constitution? On the surface, it appears to be a case of patriotic exuberance, but in reality, like the reality of the rope underlying the serpent, it is quite simply a Machiavellian attempt to appropriate a role in the making of history in which, regrettably, the BJP (and its earlier avatars) had no significant role.

The tribute to Babasaheb Ambedkar, on the occasion of his 125th anniversary, is a gesture all political parties emphatically support. Dr Ambedkar is a living example of the victory of human tenacity and courage against the greatest odds. Imbued with penetrative intellectual insight, great scholarship, remarkable courage of conviction, and an exceptional awareness of the real challenges to the values of democracy, equity and social justice, his role as the chairman of the Drafting Committee of the Constitution, was invaluable.

But, there is something, indeed, suspect in the manner in which the BJP has suddenly discovered Ambedkar. Underlying the expedient euphoria is a desire to appropriate another icon of the freedom movement in order to compensate for the fact that Right-wing Hindu organisations, especially the RSS under M.S. Golwalkar, had very little to do with either the struggle against the British or the making of independent India's Republican Constitution. Politics may justify such cynical tactics, but the clumsiness with which it has been attempted fools no one. Ambedkar would have been the first to admit—and that was the sign of his greatness—that the Constitution of which he was a principal architect was the collective effort of many stalwarts of the freedom movement, not least of whom was Nehru whom the BJP has sought to downplay, and, was, indeed, the combined contribution of the remarkably intense and substantive sessions of the Constituent Assembly.

This is not the first time since it came to power in 2014 that the BJP has sought to distort or rewrite history. An earlier attempt was made involving Sardar Patel. The BJP's transparent effort was to privilege him over all other giants in the freedom movement and to project his muscular, no-nonsense sense of patriotism as a reflection of the party's own image. A series of events were planned to implement this policy, including the construction of a gigantic statue of the Sardar. In doing so, however, the BJP conveniently forgot that it was the very Sardar Patel, who they were now claiming as their own, who had banned the RSS, and who believed that the RSS had created a social milieu that led to the assassination of Mahatma Gandhi. Vallabhbhai Patel had no illusions in this regard, and would have been very amused at the selective historical amnesia of the BJP in its attempt to rewrite history.

This dual policy, of ostensible projection to camouflage real intent, was in full display during the BJP's interventions in the two-day debate on the Constitution in both the Houses. In the Rajya Sabha, Prime Minister Narendra Modi gave a conciliatory, even statesmanlike speech, while in the Lok Sabha, his seniormost colleague, Home Minister Rajnath Singh came straight to the point and began his 'reaffirmation' to the Constitution by questioning the need for the word 'secular' in the Preamble. The prime minister said that the

Constitution is our only holy book, while maintaining a cynical silence on the words and deeds of ministers in his own cabinet like Giriraj Singh, V.K. Singh, Mahesh Sharma and Sadhvi Niranjan, and MPs like Sakshi Maharaj and Yogi Adityanath, who have rubbished the cherished values of the Constitution. The fact of the matter is that you can fool the people once, even twice. But, ultimately, however clever you may think you are, the people are cleverer and see through your tactics.

(This piece was originally published on 6 December 2015)

QUALIFIED VOTING RIGHTS: SUBVERTING THE CONSTITUTION BY STEALTH

The Constitution of India, to my mind, is being violated through a process of deliberate stealth. Our founding fathers, debating at great length in the Constituent Assembly, decided to give India universal adult suffrage. This means that all citizens over the age of eighteen can exercise their right to vote. At the same time, they ordained that anyone who is of eligible age can stand for elections to parliament and the state Assemblies. There were some, even at the time of the Constituent Assembly, who were of the view that such rights should be qualified in some form or another. However, in a far-sighted and bold decision, the makers of our Constitution decided otherwise.

But the governments in the states of Rajasthan and Haryana seem to believe that the principles animating our Constitution are flawed. Last year, the Rajasthan government decided that not every citizen of that state can contest the Panchayat Samiti and District Council elections. Through an Ordinance issued by the Governor, the government made an amendment to the Rajasthan Panchayat Raj

Act, 1994, and made it mandatory for candidates wishing to stand for Zila Parishads and Panchayat Samitis to be Class X pass, while those contesting Sarpanch elections must be Class VIII pass. In Scheduled areas, the eligibility has been kept at Class V pass.

Following the lead taken by Rajasthan, another BJP ruled state, Haryana, has now amended the Haryana Panchayat Act. For the elections coming up in January 2016, it has decreed that a matriculation degree would be essential for general candidates contesting the elections. The qualification for women (general) and Scheduled Castes has been fixed at Class VIII. The proposed amendments were challenged before the Supreme Court that has upheld their validity.

We must, of course, abide by the ruling of the highest court of the land. But, with due respect, a question does arise: can state governments dilute the categorical letter and spirit of the Constitution through separate legislations pertaining to elections to local bodies? It is true that they have the powers to do so. However, should not Panchayat elections follow the same principles of eligibility that have been prescribed for elections to our state Assemblies and to parliament?

There are valid reasons to ask this question. In Rajasthan, the literacy rate of women in rural areas is only 45.8 per cent. In tribal areas, the situation is much worse with only 25.22 per cent of women being literate. The new law means that in both these categories, the majority of women will be automatically excluded from their fundamental right of being active participants in the democratic process at the grassroots level. The arbitrarily applied exclusion hits men as well. The literacy rate for men in rural Rajasthan is 76.6 per cent. This means that roughly one-fourth of men will also be ab initio denied their right to stand for elections.

The literacy rates in Haryana are better, but only marginally. According to the 2011 census data, Haryana has a literacy rate of 76.6 per cent.

Within this overall figure, women's literacy rates are much lower at 66.8 per cent. Even in urban areas, where literacy rates can be expected to be higher, only 60.97 per cent women are literate. In other words, even in Haryana, the new amendments make one-fourth of all men and more than one-third of all women ineligible to stand for election to local bodies.

Is such an arbitrarily imposed exclusion democratic? People are not illiterate by choice. They are so for the lack of opportunity, for which the State itself must take the bulk of the blame. Moreover, the majority of those who are still the victims of illiteracy are from the most marginalised sections of society. Is it the intention of the imperious lawmakers in these states that those at the bottom rung of the ladder must be specifically excluded from their democratic rights of representing the people?

The argument given by both the Rajasthan and Haryana governments is that Panchayats deal with money transactions, and that, therefore, those who are illiterate are not qualified to handle them. This is hardly a credible defence. A Class VIII or Class X pass does not overnight possess the qualifications to handle complex financial matters. Panchayats have officials to maintain accounts, and those who are not illiterate are certainly not imbeciles. Moreover, our democratic experiment has shown that the capacity to serve effectively as elected representatives is not exclusively undermined only by the fact of illiteracy. Of course, ideally, all Indians should not only be literate but at least graduates too. But, the makers of our Constitution realised that given the poverty, lack of equal opportunity, and social deprivations in India, exclusionary criteria will work against democratic equity and, in particular, against the poorest and most marginalised sections of society. It was their thinking that it's precisely when such sections are given the opportunity to be fully involved in the democratic process that they will create the pressure to change the system to provide them the opportunities for education and health and other social benefits that are presumed as rights by the more privileged sections.

There is, of course, a final irony to this whole matter. To become a Member of Parliament, a candidate does not necessarily have to be able to read. To stand for State Assemblies, a candidate does not necessarily be able to write. But, to stand for local elections, candidates must have an educational eligibility! There is another reason too for indignation. These amendments to the law have been made just before the Panchayat elections. Why could they not have been made prospectively, or in a phased manner, to act as a feasible incentive for the people? Democracy cannot become an instrument in the hands of the privileged to exclude large sections of India, who have been given this precious right by no less than the makers of our Constitution. The Supreme Court, in my view, must review its decision, for it is unlikely that the state governments in question will.

(This piece was originally published on 20 December 2015)

RESERVATIONS IN THE CORPORATE SECTOR?

There was predictable outrage when the National Commission for Backward Classes (NCBC) recommended that there should be twenty-seven per cent reservation for backward classes in the private sector. I say 'predictable' because any proposal that seeks to further the cause of social justice is met with expected howls of protest by those who believe that they alone have the sacrosanct right to be the primary beneficiaries of economic development.

The fact of the matter is that even after sixty-nine years as an independent nation, India has the largest number in the world of the abjectly poor, the illiterate and the malnutritioned. Moreover, in spite of a great deal of empowerment—both political and socio-economic—in the last few decades, the numerical majority in our nation, consisting of the Dalits, the Scheduled Tribes and the backward classes, does not as yet have a level playing field in terms of opportunities.

Can one segment of a nation grow and another languish in perpetuity? A nation is an organic whole. All its parts are inter-related and must benefit with equity from the fruits of economic growth. However much they wish to, the successful cannot secede to form their own Republic. We must either swim or sink together.

That is why, when the visionary founders of our nation wrote the Constitution, they included the element of affirmative action in the form of reservations in government jobs for the Scheduled Castes and Scheduled Tribes. Later, this reservation was extended to include the Other Backward Classes (OBCs), with the caveat, as laid down by the Supreme Court that reservation should not exceed fifty per cent of the total jobs available.

These reservations were restricted to government jobs. But after 1991, when we opened up our economy, government jobs have reduced in number. In the period between 2006 and 2012, they fell from 18.2 million to 17.6 million, a 3.3 per cent decline. In the same period, jobs in the private sector grew by 35.7 per cent, from 8.7 million to 11.9 million. In other words, if we accept that social justice was an article of faith enshrined in our Constitution, the opportunities to implement it have constricted where government jobs are concerned and grown exponentially in the corporate sector.

Is it unfair to ask the corporate sector, for which I have the highest respect, to partner with government in furthering the cause of social justice? I believe not, because I am convinced that this will be, in the long run, in the corporate sector's own interest. Some corporate houses—alas, by far a minority—have volitionally implemented a policy where, along with profits, they have invested in welfare programmes for the underprivileged and the marginalised. They understood that by doing so, they were increasing the market size and the catchment area from which talent could be recruited.

In fact, in 2004, the corporate sector gave a categorical assurance that it will volitionally implement a programme of affirmative action. In a letter written to then Prime Minister Manmohan Singh, 218 of our top corporate houses and their associations promised to expand their 'current activities for disadvantaged persons with regard to scholarships, company run private schools, vocational training ... and we will implement in letter and spirit a programme of affirmative action to empower persons who are socially and educationally backward.' More than a decade has passed since then, but can the corporate sector say with honesty that it has fully, or even in substantial measure, implemented this pledge? Any objective survey will show that SCs, STs and OBCs even today constitute a minuscule minority in the senior managements of the top 500 BSE companies.

For all its entrepreneurial energy, the corporate sector cannot become an island unto itself. Many, if not all private firms are beneficiaries in some form or the other, of government support policies. The other day, the prime minister himself remarked sarcastically that when financial interventions are made by the government in favour of the underprivileged, they are called 'subsidies', but when the same support is given to corporates, it is called 'incentives'. If the private sector has grown with the help of the government—and that support is valid—why should it not lend its support to goals of social inclusiveness that is the unambiguous intent of our Constitution?

The argument that merit will be compromised by affirmative action is an elitist fallacy. In fact, the opposite is true. If more people are given the opportunity and exposure to become full participants in the national mainstream, we will increase the talent pool, as also the scope of the competition to select the best. To argue that only those who have been the beneficiaries of societal benevolence for centuries are entitled to have a monopoly on opportunity is the worst form of unsustainable elitism. The Constitution specifically speaks of affirmative action for the 'socially and educationally backward' because under our repressively hierarchic caste system, certain castes were for millennia kept socially and educationally backward. The privileged do not have an extra cranium that makes them inherently superior. And, no democracy can be truly effective unless all its citizens are provided with the opportunity of a level playing field.

At this stage, what the NCBC has recommended is precisely that: a recommendation. Parliament will have to consider it to take matters forward. I would suggest that in the interim, the leaders of our dynamic corporate sector do some introspection on their own. It would be best if they voluntarily accept a substantive and verifiable programme of affirmative action as they had promised to do in their letter to Dr Manmohan Singh twelve years ago. The government and our private sector must become partners in the great project of making our nation a more equitable and egalitarian entity. Economic growth with social justice should be the goal, not only of the government but also of the captains of business and industry.

(This piece was originally published on 14 February 2016)

DESECRATING THE BANKS OF YAMUNA: SRI SRI RAVI SHANKAR

*I*have nothing against Sri Sri Ravi Shankar. In fact, on a isit to Bengaluru, I had the privilege to meet him and receive his blessings. I have nothing against the Art of Living (AoL) movement either. If it gives peace and fulfilment to the millions who practise it, it must be effective. However, I have everything against spiritual gurus who leverage their spiritual legitimacy for acts of omission and commission that appear to be directly against the larger public good. In organising a mega cultural festival on the banks of the Yamuna in Delhi over 11-13 March, in spite of the vocal concerns of qualified environmentalists and the trenchant observations of the National Green Tribunal (NGT), Sri Sri Ravi Shankarji has, in my view, got embroiled in an avoidable controversy that will dent his spiritual credibility.

It is important to remember that the NGT did not mince its words on what the grand cultural event would do to the flood plains of the Yamuna. In its order of 10 March 2016, the Tribunal said: 'It is the consistent views of the Experts and is sufficiently evident from the documents placed on record that the flood plains have been drastically tampered with while destroying the natural flow of the river, reeds, grasses and natural vegetation on the river bed. It has further disturbed the aquatic life of the river and destroyed water bodies and wet lands on the flood plains.' For this damage caused to 'the environment, ecology, biodiversity and aquatic life of the river,' the NGT held the AoL Foundation to be liable, and asked it to pay an 'environmental compensation,' initially of five crores, *'prior to the commencement of the event.'*

Sri Sri Ravi Shankar's response to this notice opens up serious questions of propriety, as one would expect from a spiritual guru, and of legality. He said that he would rather go to jail than pay the fine. Displaying a remarkable indifference to a duly constituted apex Tribunal set up under the law of the land, he decided, suo motu, that he had not violated any rule and hence was not liable to pay any penalty. Given the imminence of the event, the NGT had no option but to accept his offer to pay only twenty-five lakhs prior to the event.

The pointed question that begs an answer is whether spiritual gurus can become a law unto themselves? In its order, the NGT also highlighted another disturbing aspect of this case. It said that the Foundation had not yet (that is, until one day before the event) obtained permission from the Police department, Fire department, the Ministry of Water Resource and the River Development and Ganga Rejuvenation authority and that 'all these authorities have failed to exercise due diligence in fulfillment of their public duties.' It added, more damningly, that the information provided by the Foundation was 'incomplete, vague and uncertain since it did not provide any specific data, supporting documents, comprehensive plan with regard to carrying on of such a huge construction, levelling activity and also construction of other approach roads, pontoon bridges, ramps, parking and a huge stage measuring 40 feet high, 1000 feet long and 200 feet wide to any of the Authorities.'

Why did the AoL Foundation behave in such a manner? It did so because of the hubris that affinity to power brings. The prime minister was invited to the event, as was the President of India. The president did not go, but the prime minister did. Was it appropriate for him to do so in the light of the observations of the NGT, Sri Sri Ravi Shankar's open declaration that he will flout its orders, and the knowledge that necessary permissions under the law had not been obtained by the Foundation?

There are two other aspects of importance. How was the Army deployed to assist in the making of bridges etc., for a private function? What kind of precedent is set by this kind of decision? Will the Army assist other private events, including those by Sikh, Christian, Muslim or other Hindu organisations? On the one hand, the government constantly speaks of the valour and sacrifice of our armed forces, and on the other hand, it has no compunction in using scarce defence facilities for a private event, thereby actually comprising the resources available for the defence of the nation.

Secondly, the prime minister spoke of this event as the 'Kumbh Mela of Culture,' and emphasised the need to 'take pride in our cultural legacy.' Are mega one-off events of this nature the way to revive our cultural legacy? Almost every major institution related to culture in our country is languishing and struggling for funds. The capital city has no auditorium remotely close to world standards; our art galleries are moribund; there is an acute shortage of trained curators; the apex akademies are mired in unproductive politics; our museums are in shambles; and State patronage at the grasroots for genuine work to nurture and revive our cultural legacy is far below what is needed.

The truth appears to be that Sri Sri Ravi Shankar is prey to the malaise of 'giganticism', where the spectacle is more important than the substance. And, Sri Sri Ravi Shankar believes that by creating a mega 'cultural' event that may enter the Guinness Book of Records, even if it means fatal damage to an environmental ecosystem, he is putting India on the world stage of recognition.

This is an illusion and can only be pursued at the cost of the real good of the country.

(This piece was originally published on 13 March 2016)

MONEY POWER & POLITICS: BEEJ OF ALL CORRUPTION

A few days ago, the Delhi High Court made an important judgement relating to political parties and funding. The court was dealing with a case of the Congress party regarding tax exemptions for the year 1995–96. Without prejudice to the merits of this case, the pronouncements of the court are significant because they deal with the critical issues of electoral reform and the deadly nexus between unaccounted money and politics.

'Money power,' the court observed, 'should not be allowed to distort the conduct of free and fair elections. This will in turn infuse transparency and accountability into the functioning of the political parties thereby strengthening and deepening democracy.' According to the learned judges, political parties must maintain 'properly audited accounts' of income received through voluntary contributions, and unless this is done, parties cannot claim an exemption on income tax. The sum and gist of the judgement was that the time has come to implement an 'effective check over the influence of money in electoral politics.'

It is apparent to everybody that India needs a substantive and comprehensive Electoral Reform Bill for changes in our democratic system. But the task is easier said than done. The record bears this out. The Goswami Committee on Electoral Reforms was set up twenty-two years ago in 1990. Subsequently, there have been a host of other committees and reports, including the Vohra Committee in 1993, Indrajit Gupta Committee on State Funding of Elections 1998, Law Commission Report on the Reform of Electoral Laws 1999, National Commission to Review the Working of the Constitution 2000, Election Commission of India Report on Proposed Electoral Reforms 2004, and the Second Administrative Reforms Commission (ARC) 2008. None of these have been able to bring about comprehensive change and have remained confined to proposals, ideas and intentions. Some matters of electoral reforms have also been pending before the Supreme Court for years.

The blame, however, does not rest at the threshold of the Supreme Court. The blame rests primarily with political parties and politicians who have no overriding motivation to change the current system because they are the biggest beneficiaries of it. According to the Association of Democratic Reforms (ADR), a widely respected NGO, eighty-five per cent of donors to political parties are faceless. Informal estimates indicate that actual collections are as much as ten times more than what is disclosed. The nexus between black money and political parties is the principal cause of all corruption in India. If those who are supposed to make laws against corruption are themselves the products of a corrupt system, how can the rest of society be clean? When parties take money in cash from 'unidentified' donors, they work for tax evaders. When candidates illegally spend many times the prescribed limit on elections, their first priority is to milk the State to recoup their 'investment.' India is among the lowest scoring countries on political finance regulation according to the Global Integrity Report, scoring a zero out of a hundred on implementation and disclosure of political party and candidate financing. India also scored a zero on the effectiveness of party financing regulations.

What practical and theoretically doable preliminary steps can be taken to remedy this unfortunate situation? First, the current law that allows parties not to identify donors contributing less than Rs 20,000 must be scrapped. This is the principal (but not only) channel for parties to collect vast amounts of undeclared funds. Every paisa given as a donation to political parties must be accounted for, and, wherever possible, transacted through auditable and transparent bank transactions. Reducing the ceiling from 20,000 to 2,000 rupees hardly serves any purpose. Secondly, all payments made by political parties, exceeding Rs 20,000 must be made by crossed account payee cheques or bank transfers. The Core Committee on Electoral Reforms sponsored by the Election Commission and the Ministry of Law and Justice have strongly recommended this. (The scheme introduced now for anonymous donations through electoral bonds does not, I am afraid, contribute to rectitude or transparency.) Concurrently, the EC must harness our vaunted prowess in IT to devise an online accounting framework leaving as little place as possible for political parties to hide income and expenditure.

Thirdly, all political parties must compulsorily make public their audited accounts every year. Currently, candidates are required to disclose their assets and liabilities but not political parties. As far back as 2004, the EC recommended that 'political parties should be required to publish their accounts annually for information and scrutiny of the general public and all concerned, for which purpose the maintenance of such accounts and their auditing to ensure their accuracy is a prerequisite. The auditing may be done by any firm of auditors approved by the Comptroller and Auditor General (CAG). The audited accounts must be made public.' My personal view is that they should also be brought under the ambit of the Right To Information or RTI.

Fourthly, careful thought needs to be given to strengthen the enforcement and regulatory role of the EC in such matters. Currently, political parties merely obtain a certificate from the EC that they have submitted their annual audited statement of accounts. Perhaps the time has come for the EC, strengthened by experts from other financial enforcement agencies, to be authorised to issue show cause notices at any time to any party where there is verifiable evidence of expenditures exceeding known sources of income. Of course, an impartial and independent EC is a sine qua non for such powers.

With these measures in place, the State funding of elections, as recommended by the Indrajit Gupta Committee in 1998, may not be necessary. State funding would only add an unnecessary burden to the exchequer and not succeed in inhibiting parties and candidates from illegally deploying funds over and above what is provided by the State. Given past experience, a far more practical way would be to stringently implement the monitoring, surveillance and deterrence measures mentioned earlier.

It is not enough for India to be merely labelled the world's largest democracy. We must also be a credible democracy in every sense of the term. Currently, the magnitude of illicit money power in the hands of political parties diminishes our democratic credibility. It is time for all political parties to voluntarily—and urgently—rectify this situation.

(This piece was originally published on 27 March 2016)

ANIMAL RIGHTS OVER FARMERS:
A DIFFICULT DILEMMA

Recently, I was on a panel discussion on a TV channel on the question of the culling of animals. Maneka Gandhi, who must be India's most vocal, consistent and eloquent animal right's activist, had publicly attacked her Cabinet colleague, in charge of environment, Prakash Javadekar, for his 'lust for killing animals.' Javadekar had given permission to certain state governments to kill, for a specific time period, certain animals whose proliferating numbers were causing large-scale damage to farmers. These animals included the nilgai or blue bill, wild boar and monkey.

For me, this debate presented a painful dilemma. At a personal level, I am a committed animal lover. I have five dogs at home, that include strays my family has adopted from the streets. One part of me is revolted by the thought of trained marksmen being brought in to mercilessly shoot animals brought up in the wild. I am deeply moved by stories of how their young ones are orphaned, and how some unfortunate ones linger on for days in pain before they die of their bullet wounds. I also understand that the root cause of this conflict lies in the drastic reduction of natural habitats for animals, and the haphazard and insensitive encroachment of humans into

246

forests and areas that were traditionally animal reserves.

At the same time, I understand that there are some very genuine concerns of farmers. When a herd of nilgai decimates an entire crop within hours, a farmer loses the labour of months of hard work. Already on the verge of bare survival, most small holding farmers have no other source of livelihood. If their crop is destroyed, they can neither earn nor feed their families. The Annual Economic Survey of the Central government acknowledges that one of every two farmers is already under a personal debt of Rs 47,000. The vast majority of small farmers are in the vice-like grip of moneylenders who charge usurious rates of interest. For entire farming communities, the only hope is that the seeds they planted with such loving care fructify into crops. When, just as this is about to happen, a herd of monkeys or wild boar destroys the crop within a matter of minutes, who can overlook the agony farmers go through?

Wilting under Maneka's very public and acerbic attack, the hapless Prakash Javadekar quoted the rulebook. Under the Wildlife Protection Act of 1972, there is an article that allows the Central government, on receiving an application from states, to downgrade specific animals from the Schedule 1 list of endangered species, to other categories, where, if necessary, they can be culled for a certain period of time. On receiving a missive from Javadekar's ministry requesting states to make their proposals, the government of Bihar sought permission for culling the nilgai, Himachal Pradesh sought it to for rhesus monkeys and Uttarakhand for the wild boar. Such provisions are not unique to India. In Africa, official permission is given for the culling of elephants when their numbers increase beyond a certain number leading to damage to crops and human settlements. In Australia, too, kangaroos are culled for the same reason.

In the case of Bihar, nilgais have become the nemesis for farmers, across the Gandak and Ganga basins that cover a vast swathe of territory from Bhojpur in the west to Bhagalpur in the east. Bihar is predominantly an agricultural state where farmers, especially those with small holdings who are the majority, are helpless against the nilgai onslaught. The numbers of the nilgai have gone up exponentially, primarily also because, unlike cattle, nilgais mate twice a year. Other methods such as sterilisation or relocation have been tried, but these are very difficult to implement given the scale of the problem. I understand that the problem with regard to monkeys and wild boars in other states is equally acute.

What then is the solution? Who is right, Javadekar or Maneka Gandhi, animal rights activists or farmers? My own view is that it would be wrong to take a black or white position in this matter. Good environment policy requires the preservation of habitats for animals, while good agricultural policy requires that when a problem threatens the very livelihood of farmers, it must be dealt with. Javadekar and the BJP government need to deal with environmental issues in a more holistic manner, devising a medium- to long-term policy that gives due place to our flora and fauna and agriculture. At the same time, animal rights activists should seriously try not to make their outrage so completely one-sided.

Some thirty years ago, I bought a two-acre farm on the border between Delhi and Gurugram. My wife, who is fond of gardening, planted vegetables in one part of the farm. Every year, hordes of nilgai, which used to then raid the farm from the nearby Aravali foothills, destroyed our vegetables. We had the choice to both mourn our lost vegetables and love the nilgais. For us, the veggies were a boutique indulgence. Our income and survival did not depend on them. But for millions of farmers, the choices are much more stark.

Nilgais don't come any more to our farm. Gurugram has largely eaten up their natural habitats. Should India have prevented

Gurugram from coming up? Could we have consciously put a ceiling on urbanisation even when the demand from the urban elite for office space and new living areas was immense? Are some of us guilty of asserting the rights of animals over humans when it is someone else's problem and does not affect our own lives? Ultimately, the escalating animal-human conflict is everybody's problem, and must be tackled more pro-actively, with both Maneka Gandhi and Prakash Javadekar putting their heads together. But, in the interim, I cannot resist mentioning that a great many of the animal activists I know live in Gurugram.

(This piece was originally published on 19 June 2016)

PERUMAL MURUGAN: FREEDOM
OF EXPRESSION

*A*new name has been added to the illustrious list of those who have fought to strengthen democratic India post-1947: Perumal Murugan. Until a few years ago, few outside Tamil Nadu would have heard of him, much less read him. This fifty-year-old remarkably talented scholar and writer, the author of several novels, short stories and anthologies, was happy to be away from the glamour lights of Chennai, and taught Tamil at the Government Art College in Namakkal. But destiny was waiting to catapult him from a Tamil writer of eminence to a national icon standing for the preeminence of freedom of expression and speech in India.

In 2010, Murugan wrote a Tamil novel titled *Madhurobhagan*, later translated into English as *One Part Woman*. It is a story about a childless couple desperate to have a child in order to escape social stigma. In the narrative, Murugan wrote about a traditional custom in which a woman could have consensual sex with a stranger on the fourteenth day of the temple car festival. This tradition, at one time, had the sanction of the community and was one way to resolve the predicament of childlessness. The decision was that of the woman, often with the support of her husband. It was not considered immoral and was part of customary law.

Murugan uses this custom as a powerful metaphor to highlight the anguish and humiliation of a childless couple. The curious thing is that for four years the novel did not provoke any protests from any section of society. But, suddenly, in December 2014, some elements expressed great outrage. Perhaps it is happenstance that in May of that very year the BJP had come to power at the Centre. Did this embolden 'fringe groups' of the Hindu Right to a new form of aggression? Readers are free to draw their own conclusions, but the fact is that for four years prior to 2014, there were no voices of protest or intimidation.

It is curious also that when these protests escalated, the government of Tamil Nadu stepped in to bring about 'peace' by 'unofficially' proscribing the circulation of the novel. What was the locus standi of the state to intervene in the matter? And was it becoming of it to so meekly succumb to the aggression brought to bear upon Murugan by such threatening fringe groups? Is it the dharma of the state merely to somehow enforce 'peace' without objectively assessing the merits of the case, or evaluating what the impact of this decision would have on the expressly guaranteed right to freedom of speech and expression under Article 19 of the Constitution?

Abandoned by the state, and devastated by the illiterate ferocity of the venom directed at him, Murugan took a landmark decision. He wrote on his Facebook page: 'Perumal Murugan the writer is dead. As he is no God he is not going to resurrect himself. He has also no faith in rebirth. An ordinary teacher, he will live as P. Murugan. Leave him alone.'

Rarely in the annals of creativity will we find such a public announcement of literary suicide. Why did Murugan resort to this extreme step? Essentially, he was left with no other option. Those opposing him were not open to reason. Their modus operandi was to threaten, intimidate, use violence and drum up hysteria against anyone who had the temerity to slight their notion of what is socially right or permissible in terms of creative expression. Almost none of them would have read the works of Kalidasa or Bhartrihari or Vatsyayana to understand the degree of freedom sanctioned in Hindu literary tradition. Nor would they have been familiar with the fact that the great Shankaracharya defeated his intellectual opponents not by threatening to kill them, but by shasthrath or discussion. With the government refusing to protect him, and with the examples of what happened to Dabholkar, Pansare and Kalburgi before him, Murugan decided to just die as a writer.

But judicial intervention has made Murugan rise from his literary grave. In a landmark judgement delivered on 5 July 2016, a division bench of the Chennai High Court comprising Chief Justice Sanjay Kishan Kaul and Justice Pushpa Sathyanarayana, decisively pronounced: 'Let the author be resurrected to do what he is best at: Write.' Recognising that the novel refers to a social practice, if at all it ever existed, to somehow solve the problem of a childless couple, the learned judges said 'the novel shakes you, but not in the manner its opponents seek to profess. It jolts you, because it succinctly depicts the pain and sufferance depicted through the words of this childless couple. That is the takeaway from the novel.'

'No one reading the novel,' the judges said, 'would be persuaded to draw a definite conclusion as sought to be canvassed by the opponents of the novel that the endeavour of the author was to portray all women coming to the car festival as prostitutes. This is a complete misreading of the novel and its theme.' Pronouncing that the so-called settlement arrived at with the intervention of the State authorities had no 'binding force or obligation,' the court, annulling all cases against Murugan, directed the State to provide him adequate security so that he could continue to write fearlessly. Finally, in an admonishment of historical proportions against those seeking to stifle creative freedom, the judges thundered: 'If you do not like a book simply close it. The answer is not its ban.'

Hindutva fringe groups may think that they are omnipotent today, but they should never underestimate the power of Indian democracy, especially the judiciary. Perumal Murugan, the writer is alive again, and may all creative people continue to have the freedom to 'jolt and shake' society, notwithstanding what the Hindutva brigade feels.

(This piece was originally published on 28 August 2016)

THE GURU

*C*onviction to be enduring requires ideological mooring. And, ideology, in order to go beyond tokenism, requires organisational rigour. In the absence of the resolve to work for what you believe in, ideology devalues itself to rhetoric. Rhetoric, however mesmerising, will ultimately be exposed. It cannot endure, for people increasingly judge words against output, promises against delivery, and posturing against concrete efforts that can be measured for their sincerity in verifiable terms.

These ruminations come to the fore in the backdrop of the recently concluded Prakash Utsav in Patna to celebrate the 350th birth anniversary of Guru Gobind Singh, the tenth Guru of the Sikh faith. Poet, philosopher, warrior and spiritual beacon, Guru Gobind Singh was born in Patna Sahib on 22 December 1666, and became the leader of the Sikhs at the tender age of nine when his father Guru Tegh Bahadur, was beheaded by Aurangzeb for refusing to convert to Islam. During his lifetime, he lost all four of his sons, two in battle and two interred alive in a wall, but notwithstanding such supreme sacrifices, he succeeded in institutionalising the Khalsa and enshrining the *Guru Granth Sahib* as Sikhism's eternal Guru.

To celebrate the 350th birth anniversary of the last Guru, the

Bihar government under Nitish Kumar spent months in meticulous planning and preparation, so much so that Patna took on the profile of a 'mini Punjab' from 22 December 2016 to 7 January 2017.

The task was nothing short of a mammoth. Lakhs of devotees were expected to visit from all parts of India, including thousands from abroad. Systematic and thorough planning was the key to making the event a success. Three massive tented cities were set up at the Gandhi Maidan, Kangan Ghat and the Malaichak Bypass. Detailed arrangements were made for food and transport. Parking sites were identified in advance. Water and electricity were ensured and hundreds of mobile toilets installed. Around Patna Sahib roads were widened, houses repainted and, for smoother connectivity, a new flyover constructed. The Patna Ghat railway station was reopened. New electricity poles were erected, along with new wiring. In addition, hundreds of solar-powered streetlights were put up. The entire city was cleaned and spruced up and new drains constructed. Special attention was given to security. Some 200 new CCTV cameras were put into operation.

A daily programme for devotees was drawn up. Dozens of tourist information centres were opened. Special vehicles of the tourist department were mobilised for publicity. A special Exhibition on 'Emperor Prophet-Guru Gobind Singhji' was organised at the Bihar Museum to display historical paintings, miniatures, hukumnamahs, coins, pictures of forts, and other rare artefacts associated with the life of the tenth Guru. The exhibition will be open till 31 January and then taken to different museums in Bihar. In the heart of the city, at the historic Gandhi Maidan, a massive replica of the Patna Sahib Gurudwara was erected.

These massive arrangements were supervised by the chief minister on a daily basis. In the lead up to the festival, there was hardly a day when he did not personally inspect ongoing work, or devote time to planning and preparation. His eye for detail was relentless, including, for instance, the provisioning of heaters for devotees to ward off the winter cold. This is what illustrates best the dialectics between conviction, ideology and planning vigour. Nitish Kumar is not a Sikh, but for him, the central issue was to give respect to the many faiths that make up the glorious plurality of India. Within a hundred-kilometre radius from Patna are situated some of the most important sites of almost every major religion in India. Patna Sahib is in Patna itself. Not far is Bihar Sharif, a Sufi destination next only in importance to Ajmer Sharif. A short drive from there is Pawapuri, the place where Mahavira attained his parinirvana, one of the most sacred sites for those of the Jaina community. Bodh Gaya, the most revered pilgrimage destination for Buddhists, is close to Pawapuri. And, next to Bodh Gaya is Gaya, a must visit for any Hindu wishing to pay homage to his ancestors. In this sense, Bihar is a microcosm of the multi-religious, Ganga-Jamuni tehzeeb of India, the preservation of which is an article of faith for Nitish Kumar.

Accolades have poured in from across the world for the organisation of the Prakash Parv. Prime Minister Narendra Modi, who visited Patna for the Parv on 5 January, was fulsome in his praise for the chief minister's successful organisation of the event. Captain Amarinder Singh on seeing the arrangements said that the Bihar chief minister was the 'original Sardar'. Parkash Singh Badal was as effusive in his compliments, as was Arvind Kejriwal. The important thing is that this appreciation transcended party lines. Equally gratifying was the overwhelming response of the lakhs of Sikh devotees who had come from outside Bihar or from abroad. One of them tellingly summed up the sense of the rest when he said: '*Bihar wale, tussi great ho! Sadey dil vich bas gaye,*' (People of Bihar, you are great! You have made a home in our hearts).

Ultimately, the Prakash Parv was an illustration of the organic link between ideology, conviction and governance. In this case, the respect for the Sikh faith could not be shown until it was accompanied by the effort required to make such an important event for the Sikhs a successful, fulfilling and well-organised event. The effort required a vision to go beyond the macro picture into the micro detailing of all aspects of planning. And, the respect in Bihar for Guru Gobind Singh made the hours upon relentless hour of planning and preparation an act of homage.

(This piece was originally published on 15 January 2017)

A SENSIBLE DIALOGUE

Kolkata is less warm than Delhi but more humid. At this time of the year, the haze of heat is punctuated by the scintillating red of the Gulmohar trees that, unlike their slightly reticent cousins in Delhi, are in full bloom. I am in the eternal city on the invitation of the Kolkata Ladies Study Group, a fifty-year-old institution run by the most influential women of the city, to speak, along with P. Chidambaram, on the subject of 'Positive Conflict: On the Democratic Chess Board of India'. Senior journalist, Jyoti Malhotra, is to conduct the discussion.

I can sense some apprehension in the audience on whether the debate would be fiery enough, considering that both Chidambaram and I are, broadly, on the same side of the political divide. After all, what is the use of a discussion where decibel levels don't clang, panellists don't speak to each other but at each other and sparks don't fly around to illuminate the slanging match? But thanks to Jyoti's provocative style, and the questions that popped up from the floor, I think the audience was not very disappointed.

One issue that cropped up more than once was the BJP's emphatic victory in the recent elections in Uttar Pradesh, and what it means for Indian politics in the future. Chidambaram's view was that the Congress' poor performance was due to organisational weaknesses, which the party must work to rectify. I said that UP's results connoted not so much the victory of the BJP as the failure of the Opposition. The gathbandhan (alliance) between the Congress and the Samajwadi Party was last minute, ad hoc and perfunctory, created a few days before the last date of filing nominations for the first phase of the elections. By then, both alliance partners had already announced their respective candidates, not to speak of rebels from factions within their parties. There was no groundwork to take the alliance up to the poll booth or to systematically structure outreach to the electorate. From the point of view of preparedness, such a show was in complete contrast to the systematic electoral planning done by the BJP for the last eighteen months. There was near total neglect of the large segment of non-Yadav OBC votes, which, as a consequence swung largely to the BJP. Besides, no attempt was made to co-opt Mayawati. Hence, this was not a mahagathbandhan, or grand alliance, as was forged in Bihar.

The prospect of Opposition unity was also discussed. Is it possible for a disparate group of regional satraps to eschew their personal egos and local priorities to come together as a convincing force to oppose the BJP? P. Chidambaram appeared confident. He said that in any vibrant democracy, a strong Opposition is needed. What would be the role of the Congress, given that it is the one party in the Opposition with the largest national footprint? Chidambaram was frank that the party should play such a role, but for this, it would be essential for it to also focus inwards for vital structural changes that can revive its traditional support base right up to the block level. It was his view that this process has already begun, but many in the audience were less than convinced.

I ventured to add that Opposition unity as an arithmetical equation means little. To be effective, it must be able to present a credible alternative vision of India and also show why this vision would be in the greater interest of India. A rag-tag coalition, without ideological clarity and organisational rigour, cannot be sold to the people of India. The question of who should lead this coalition can only be taken up after questions of ideology and organisation are sorted out.

A lady in the audience asked how long identity issues, focused on caste and religion, would dominate Indian politics. It was my view that this is a complex issue with no simple answers. At one level, societal inequalities continue to nurture identity issues. In a highly entrenched hierarchical system, how can a Dalit forget, or be allowed to forget, where he stands in the traditional social order? Perhaps, this is less visible in the more cosmopolitan environment of our metropolises, but as Chidambaram rightly pointed out, such identities are still a big factor in most of India. Equally, as a consequence of the ultra-Right-wing Hindu groups proliferating under BJP patronage, a Hindu is being asked to see himself as a Hindu first and a citizen later, while a Muslim is being forced to withdraw further into the confines of his own community. Moreover, the truth is that all political parties take into account identity issues in planning their electoral strategies.

Chidambaram made the point that the BJP is trying to impose a Hindu–Hindi hegemony. He was also worried about authoritarian trends in the polity, including through the practise of neutralising the Constitutionally mandated role of the Rajya Sabha by categorising non-money bills as money bills, a point I strongly concurred with. The way in which self-anointed groups, like the so-called gaurakshaks, or the Yuva Vahini, were taking the law in their own hands, with the powers that be benignly looking on, was also a matter of deep concern. The disastrous situation in Kashmir was also discussed. We both made the point that while security issues were paramount, some form of engagement with our citizens in Kashmir was essential. The policy paralysis of the BJP in this endeavour, both in Srinagar and Delhi, was both obvious and incomprehensible.

At the end of a rather spirited debate, one question, like Banquo's ghost, remained invisible but palpably present in the room: if some of the policies of the BJP need to be opposed, how can the Opposition come together effectively to do so? That question remained inadequately answered, although I suspect both Chidambaram and I were not unaware about what needs to be done.

(This piece was originally published on 7 May 2017)

THE ROMANCE OF RAIN

Would Chanakya have paused for a moment from his relentless pursuit of politics and political theory, when the first raindrops of the monsoon drenched the parched earth, and the irresistible smell of wet earth filled his nostrils? I would think yes, for human beings as talented as he was cannot—and indeed should not—be monochromatic. The change of seasons—from winter to the short-lived spring of north India, to the monsoons, to the clear autumnal nights of October and November, and then the winter again—tug at your heartstrings, a curious mix of elation and nostalgia, for one such year that passes by means one year less to witness this great pageantry of nature.

I recall one year when the monsoons were delayed but later came with a vengeance. I was then a bureaucrat, entombed in one of the rooms of the ministry of External Affairs in South Block. Suddenly, the light outside my window darkened, and the first big drop hit the pane. I was dictating a note to my private secretary, but I left my work to run to the corridor from where I could see the sky open up in all its splendour. When I returned, my secretary, otherwise a quiet, even reticent man who hardly made conversation, sought my permission to narrate two lines of the poet Bihari:

Lagey saawan maas bidesh piya
Morey ang pe boond pare sarsi
Shath kaam ne jor kiyo sajani
Bandh toot gaye chaitya darsi

(The monsoons are here but my beloved is away
A raindrop touches my body suddenly
Cruel Kama wrought his effect, O friend
The strings of my garment snapped abruptly)

Frankly, I was left quite stunned. I took my colleague to be someone who was entirely a prisoner of the humdrum routine of office, weighed down with the pedestrian burdens of life, far removed from poetry and the magical seductions of the monsoons. But, here he was, shyly reciting to me the sublime poetry of Bihari, as much—if not more—a participant in joyously welcoming the rains.

After the intense heat of summer, the monsoons in India have always stood for release, relief and romance. So much of our folklore and classical poetry are linked to the rains. Such poetry is not only about the fulfilment of love but also of *birha,* the pangs of separation if the beloved is away when the skies become grey and the moist winds of saawan (the fifth month in Hindu calendar heralding rains) blow. If, in the West, a beautiful day has to be sunny, for us a romantic day is when the clouds have hidden the sun, and there is the promise of rain. In the fifth century CE, Kalidasa, in his play *Meghdoot,* immortalised such a cloud by making him the bearer of the exiled Yaksha's message to his wife, Alaka, in the Himalayas.

In more recent times, who can ever erase from memory the song *Zindagi bhar nahi bhoolegi woh barsaat ki raat,* from the eponymous film *Barsaat Ki Raat,* where the ethereal Madhubala meets Bharat Bhushan in a rain-filled night? Or, Raj Kapoor and Nargis, singing

Pyaar hua ikrar hua, in the 1955 film *Shri 420,* the rain cascading around them as they come closer to share an umbrella? Perhaps, for the younger generation, these films are much too old, and there are as many rain-drenched songs from more contemporary films. But, these black and white tributes to the romance of the monsoons are, in my view, quite unmatched.

The monsoons are also a time for hot cups of tea and garam-garam pakodas (piping hot pakodas) and the whiff of *bhutta* (corn on the cob) being roasted on a makeshift fire along the roadside. If it is possible, this is the time to take a short break, and while sipping a cup of tea, listen to the raga Malhar. Every time I listen to Malhar during the monsoons, I wonder at the genius of our musical legacy. How can a raga so wonderfully correspond to the mood of the monsoons? As the sky begins to darken, listen first to the slow elaboration of the raga, and reach the fast-paced *drut* as it begins to pour. It is quite an unforgettable experience. Or, if you are inclined to poetry, recall the lines of the poet:

Yun barasti hain tasawwur pe purani yaadein
Jaise barsaat mein rimjhim ka sama hota hai

(Like a drizzle in the monsoons
Old memories rain down on me)

There is, alas, the ugly underbelly of the monsoons too. Floods are a recurring experience. The coming of the rains brings relief, but also the foreboding of a great deal of misery. People are rendered homeless; crops are destroyed; landslides occur; rivers in spate create havoc; lives are lost. In cities, roads become rivers; traffic jams last for hours; electrical lines snap. In Bihar, for instance, floods are an annual occurrence, given the silt depositions in the Ganga (which have made it shallower), and the rivers coming in from Nepal. If north Bihar suffers floods, there is always the fear that south Bihar, in the shadow of the monsoonal curve, may be afflicted with drought.

The problems created by the monsoons need institutional and enduring responses as urgently as possible. But whatever the downsides, the monsoons are awaited with great anticipation by all Indians, most of all by the farmer. So, as the skies darken, and a sheet of water surrounds you quenching the thirst of the land, pause for a moment, and salute the miracle of nature. Chanakya would readily agree that while politics may be a 24x7 preoccupation, there must also be a little time kept aside for poetry and music and a hot cup of tea with pakodas on the side as a humble offering to the Rain Gods.

(This piece was originally published on 2 July 2017)

THE MAHATMA

Every year, as we approach 2 October, the birth anniversary of Mahatma Gandhi, I have often wondered what the British must have made of him. Here was a man who spoke their language—English—impeccably, but wrote his first book, *Hind Swaraj*—in Gujarati. He could have worn a suit and a tie, as he did, indeed, when he was a barrister in London, but took to wearing only a dhoti in India. He could have, while opposing the British, lived in a home that was a replica of a colonial bungalow, but built his ashram, in terms of design, space and furnishing, in an entirely Indian way that was authentic, yet beautiful. He knew the Bible, perhaps in greater detail and with more understanding than most, and was particularly fond of the Sermon on the Mount, but was thoroughly rooted in the scriptures and philosophy of his own faith—Hinduism—and the other religions of his country.

When Gandhiji emerged as a leader of reckoning in the freedom movement, the British must have wondered why he was not, like most others they had encountered, a *photocopy* of his colonial masters. How were they to deal with a man who, against every consciously planned consequence of colonial rule, had the courage, quite simply, to be himself, without affectation or hate.

This one lesson has often escaped the Westernised elite of our country. Somewhere, in the pursuit of 'modernity', they have failed to realise that, ultimately, outsiders respect only those who are culturally rooted, and not nondescript imitators immersed in a 'cosmopolitanism' that has made them adrift from a knowledge of their own culture, even as they will always remain, in more ways than they realise, perpetually alien to the 'foreign' culture they wish to emulate.

Essentially, Gandhiji understood that the fight against colonialism is incomplete without the assertion, without xenophobia or chauvinism, of one's own culture and identity. In this sense, he was echoing Chanakya's view that a nation is not only about territory and an administrative structure, but a cultural construct, based on identifiable markers of a civilisational legacy. When the nation, and the culture that underlies it, are not in sync, you produce a Republic that has the paraphernalia of nationhood, but without a soul.

The year 1947 brought us political freedom, but the battle to free ourselves from the colonisation of our mind is still incomplete. One sees this in almost every sphere of creative endeavour, in lifestyles, aspirations, status symbols, sartorial choices, and above all in the denigration of our own languages in preference to badly spoken English. It is my firm belief that the entire politics in our country about languages will cease once we begin, first of all, to *respect* our own languages.

India is a young nation. The majority of our people are below the age of thirty-five, and from these, the bulk is at least ten years younger. This is, undoubtedly, a demographic dividend, but it is equally true that our youth are the most adrift from their cultural roots. Cultural rootedness does not mean chauvinistic exclusion, but informed inclusion. Our young may be nationalistic, as they should be, and, on occasion ultra-nationalistic, as they should not be, but they are largely abysmally ignorant about the fundamentals of the very culture that underpins the nationalism they are proud of. The result is that they know the rituals but not the philosophies underlying them; they will fight for their regions' language but have not read any of the classics written in that language; they will speak of the greatness of Hinduism but have not read the Upanishads; they will celebrate Valentine's Day—which is quite cute—but know almost nothing about the sringara love poetry about Radha and Krishna; they are happy with 'Hinglish', unsure about Shakespeare and unaware about Kalidasa; enthusiastic about 'designer' Navratri thalis, but ignorant about the profound philosophy of the Shakti doctrine in Hindu philosophy; indignant about the 'intrusion' of Western culture but without a clue about *Bharata's Natya Shastra*; proud to be Indian, but, often, unable to provide a line by line meaning of the National Anthem.

That is why the one lesson we need to learn from Gandhiji is that you can only be really Indian if you make the effort to be one. Once, at the Viceroy's Palace, where he was invited for talks, Gandhiji demonstrated this in his own inimitable way. To the surprise of his hosts, during the lunch break, he benignly smiled at them, and spread out a *chattai* (mat) on the ground and began to eat. A horrified British official recorded a note about this incident: 'I remember Gandhi squatting on the floor and after a while a girl coming in with some filthy yellow stuff which he started eating without as much as a by your leave.' On another occasion, Gandhiji responded to the urgent summons of Viceroy Mountbatten by walking into his study with a finger on his lips to indicate that it was his day of silence. That left Mountbatten to do all the talking, while Gandhiji, as the Viceroy later recalled, 'scribbled a few notes on the backs of used envelopes.'

As I have written in my book *Becoming Indian,* such idiosyncrasies, if this is how some would wish to see them, were not only about the virtues of silence, or the merits of sitting on the floor while eating. They were symbolic of a revolution of spirit, a proclamation of intent, that even under British subjugation he would meet with the rulers as *himself*. His persona was, therefore, at once rid of both deference and mimicry.

The question is whether he can inspire us even today—for the issue is as important now as it was then—to be Indian through a conscious decision not to be imitative or unthinkingly derivative. If he can, then we would be equipped to authentically preserve our self-respect and dignity while simultaneously enhancing our stock as global citizens.

(This piece was originally published on 24 September 2017)

KHUSHWANT SINGH

I had the opportunity last week to attend the Khushwant Singh Literary Festival at Kasauli. For the last four years, I had confirmed that I will, but something or the other had intervened at the last minute to make me change my plans. This year, I was able, at last, to fulfil my commitment. Kasauli, a quiet cantonment hill station on the way to Simla, is quite lovely in early October. The Kasauli Club, the venue where it is held, dates back to the nineteenth century, and the lovely deodar trees around it look that old. But, for me personally, the real dividend was that I was able to participate in an event dedicated to the memory of a man whom I had the great privilege to know very well, and for whom I had the highest respect.

Khushwant Singh (KS), loved to deliberately project an image that would provoke some kinds of people to hate him. This was an image he had conjured up about himself: a Scotch-loving, womanising, atheistic, irreverent old man with 'dirty' ideas in his head. But the reality was quite starkly different. Yes, he did love his evening drink, which he had at sharp 7 p.m., but he was by no means a drunkard. In fact, his 'happy hour' would end exactly at 8 p.m. He would eat early, wake up around 4 in the morning, was very particular about his exercise—tennis, swimming, walking—and worked with a discipline that was as unwavering as it was admirable. That is why he was such a prolific and thoughtful writer.

His home was a salon where, for that period between 7-8 p.m., only the very lucky were invited. The guests could include the talented but unknown, as also the most powerful and the most famous. It was always the right mix of people, and during these small soirees, the conversation was far more important than the spirits. It is true that he had a weakness for beautiful or unusual women, but he was very far from being a letch and treated them with great respect. His wife, who died only a few years before he did, was always present, and his occasionally flirtatious or outrageous remarks were never in bad taste, but only a way to jolt people out of their complacency or hypocrisy.

KS' greatest strength was his ability to speak and write about what he believed was right, irrespective of who this would annoy, and it was on this aspect of his personality that I dwelt upon in my intervention in Kasauli. He believed that religious fundamentalism of all kinds was wrong—Hindu, Muslim, Sikh or of any other faith. Thus, he was as devastatingly critical of the demolition of the Babri Masjid as he was of the Khalistani movement. In fact, the Khalistanis had planned to assassinate him, but fortunately this was foiled by the Delhi police in the nick of time. Many religious charlatans, who claimed to be god, were the focus of his acerbic critique. Although he claimed to be an atheist, the truth is that he was deeply knowledgeable about all religions at the level of spirituality and philosophy, but was dismissive about rituals and had little time for blind religious orthodoxy.

He also believed that, as a citizen of India, he had the right to voice his opinion on any subject of public importance, without anyone having the right to question his credentials to do so. In a democracy, the right to dissent was fundamental, and he never failed to exercise that right, much to the annoyance of both his 'powerful' friends and others who were congenital conformists. For instance, upon his request, the Kasauli Lit Fest is dedicated to the brave Indian soldier. But, this notwithstanding, if he felt that there have been lapses with regard to the security of the country, he would not have hesitated to say that for one moment lest someone accused him of lack of patriotism.

He was also an iconoclast where personal morality was concerned. He hated hypocrisy and loved to provoke the self-righteously pious, who looked upon anything sensual as an affront to 'Indian' values. Such people, he felt, were woefully ignorant about either the philosophy behind the *Kamasutra* and Khajuraho, or human psychology as part of a balanced life. In this sense, he was but a link in a powerful Indian tradition of lampooning the *vayiz* or ritualistic sermoniser. In one of his couplets, Ghalib writes:

Kahan maikhane ka darwaza Ghalib or kahan vayiz
Bas itna jaante hain kal woh jaata tha jab hum nikle

(The tavern's door and the sermoniser—the two are far apart
But this I know that yesterday, he was going in when I came out)

Even the right to dissent is a well-established tradition. Adi Shankaracharya, who revived Hinduism in the eighth century, and was one of its greatest thinkers, said that nothing mattered, not dharma, nor artha, nor kama, not even salvation, the teerthas (pilgrimages), the Vedas or yagnas. The only thing that mattered was bliss and awareness—chidananda rupa—and he who understood this could say: 'I am Shiva! I am Shiva!'

Unfortunately, today, KS, if he was alive, would probably have had to face, for his refusal to conform, and for asserting the right to state fearlessly what he believed in, the threat of assassination, or the crime of sedition, or the label of being anti-national. At the entrance to his apartment in New Delhi was a wooden plaque that said: 'Please do not ring the doorbell if you are not expected.' Kalburgi did not have such a notice on his door. When the bell rang, he opened it and was shot dead. His killers have still not been traced, and Dabholkar, Pansare and Gauri Lankesh have also been killed in a similar manner.

Perhaps it was best that KS, having lived for almost a hundred years, died when he did. He would have found it very difficult to accept the brittle atmosphere that is threatening the very idea of India today.

(This piece was originally published on 8 October 2017)

THE SACRED RIGHT TO PRIVACY: SUPREME COURT'S ROBUST JUDGEMENT

At the height of the Communist oppression in East Europe in the 1970s, when individual liberties had been entirely crushed in the name of the State, a Polish poet, made an impassioned plea for his right to privacy. Instead of the Marxist slogan—'Workers of this world, you have nothing to lose but your chains!'—which was then chanted with tedious and predictable unison, he simply wrote: 'Workers of this world, leave me alone!'

That basic human proclivity to privacy, in areas where neither the State nor non-State actors, or for that matter anybody, has the right to intrude, has been accorded by the Supreme Court's latest judgement the status of a fundamental right, under Articles 14, 19 and 21 of the Constitution. In doing so, the nine-judge Supreme Court bench overturned a sixty-three-year-old judgement that had refused to recognise privacy as a fundamental right. Echoing the plaintive but powerful plea of the Polish poet, Justice Chandrachud pronounced: 'Privacy postulates the reservation of a private space for the individual, *described in the right to be let alone* (italics mine).

The concept is founded on the autonomy of an individual. The ability of an individual to make choices lies at the core of the human personality.'

Beyond legalese, the court has addressed itself to many larger and fundamental philosophical questions. In recent times, we see the development of two mutually opposed trends. First, there has been a phenomenal advancement of technologies that have the capacity to intrude in the personal lives of individuals. Second, and precisely for this reason, there is a felt desire in individuals to ensure that, notwithstanding such technologies, their right to privacy is not whittled. Can these opposing trends be reconciled, and if so, what is that modus vivendi?

I don't think any citizen, however evangelical about the protection of personal privacy, is unwilling to part with some aspects of that privacy for his or her own benefit. For instance, if I want a smooth transfer of a tax refund directly to my bank account, I have to give details of that account to the bank. Similarly, if I am the legitimate beneficiary of certain monetary welfare measures of the government, I will not be averse to cooperating in a system, such as the biometric-based Aadhaar, to ensure that such benefits reach me, and are not diverted to someone else, as used to happen rampantly in the past. The Supreme Court has, therefore, said that digital platforms that work towards this end are valid. To quote Justice D.Y. Chandrachud: 'In a social welfare state, the government embarks upon programmes which provide benefits to impoverished and marginalised sections of society. There is a vital state interest in ensuring that scarce public resources are not dissipated by the diversion of resources to persons who do not qualify as recipients.'

On the other hand, if the information that I voluntarily and in my own interest part with, is misused for mala fide purposes by State authorities, such as for illegal surveillance, I would have strong objections. This would be doubly so if the only reason why this is done is because I do not agree with everything the government does. The issue of privacy then becomes linked to the larger ideological question of the right to dissent in a democracy. Appropriately, therefore, the Supreme Court said: 'Criticism and critique lie at the core of democratic governance. Tolerance of dissent is equally a cherished value. The conditions necessary for realizing or fulfilling socio-economic rights do not postulate the subversion of political freedom.'

Similarly, while discussing the issue of privacy, the Supreme Court has pronounced on several other fundamental issues that are of vital interest to a democratic society, such as the beef ban, abortion rights, sexual orientations, euthanasia, and even—like the wish of our Polish poet—the right to be left alone. On matters like the beef ban, Justice Chelameswar said, 'I don't think anybody would like to be told by the State what they should eat or how they should dress...' On abortion, the court was of the view that 'a woman's freedom of choice whether to bear a child or abort her pregnancy fall in the realm of privacy.' On the question of sexual orientation, the court was particularly blunt: 'That a minuscule fraction of the country's population constitutes lesbians, gays, bisexuals or transgenders is not a sustainable basis to deny the right to privacy.'

In fact, broadening this argument, the court made the foundationally important ruling: 'The purpose of elevating certain rights to the stature of guaranteed fundamental rights is to insulate their exercise from the disdain of majorities .... The test of popular acceptance does not furnish a valid basis to disregard rights which are conferred with the sanctity of constitutional protection.' On the right to be left alone, Justice Sanjay K. Kaul made a far-reaching comment: 'An individual who is no longer desirous of his personal data to be processed or stored should be able to remove it from the system, where it is no longer necessary, relevant, or is incorrect.'

Quite clearly, under the awning of pronouncing on the right to privacy, the jurisprudential majesty of the Supreme Court has specifically included a great many other issues that will greatly strengthen the fabric of our democracy. At the same time, the unanimous judgement has retained the right balance by stating that the State can, for bona fide and transparent reasons in the interests of definable public good, exercise reasonable restrictions on such a right, especially for welfare measures for the poor and deprived, national security and criminal investigations.

However, at rock bottom, citizens now have been given the right to contest unwarranted encroachments on their right to privacy. This is a giant leap forward. Private firms that collate data in an era of internet and data mining must be on their guard. The government must also expedite its efforts to bring in a robust data-protection regime. We live in times when technology has made us both a beneficiary and a victim. Thanks to this landmark Supreme Court judgement, we are now in a position to distinguish between the two and fight for our rights to do so.

(This piece was originally published on 27 August 2017)

INDIRA GANDHI

$\mathcal{T}$here is a story, perhaps apocryphal, that Narendra Modi, when preparing for the bid to be prime minister, had a choice to model himself on one of India's two leading politicians, one from his own party, the BJP, and the other from the party he wanted to defeat. The choice was between Atal Bihari Vajpayee and Indira Gandhi. Unhesitatingly, he chose Indira Gandhi. Like her, he wanted to be seen as decisive, authoritative, resolute, determined, focused, strong, and unemotional in dealing with opponents.

Today, on her centennial birthday, it is interesting to ruminate on why India's only female prime minister still occupies so much of the mind space of the Indian people. It is equally plausible to argue that a leader who imposed the dreaded Emergency in 1975–77 should be remembered only for this direct assault on Indian democracy. But, Indira Gandhi returned triumphantly to power in 1980 and, even today, is remembered more for her remarkable political acumen than for the—brief but undeniable—authoritarian streak in her.

Legendary leaders become part-mythology part-history. With the passage of time, their aberrations diminish and their achievements amplify, or vice-versa. In the case of Indira, people remember her more for her persona, an elegant woman who never accepted defeat, had her hand on the pulse of the people, displayed an uncanny sense of political timing, was shrewder than the shrewdest of politicians, dealt with opponents ruthlessly, had an unmistakable aesthetic sensibility, took decisions firmly when required, and died a martyr.

What people also find fascinating is the manner in which she transformed as a person. An insecure child with an unsettled childhood, overshadowed by the towering image of her father Jawaharlal Nehru, trapped in a less than happy marriage with Feroze, diffident, reclusive and withdrawn, transformed in the space of a few years, from the *gungi gudiya*—dumb doll—her opponents derisively called her, to a leader who was like a fish in the treacherous waters of Indian politics. Her great moment of glory came when she successfully dismembered Pakistan during the 1971 war. Then, even the Leader of Opposition, the ever-magnanimous Atal Bihari Vajpayee hailed her as Durga in action.

As a politician, her real test came after she lifted the Emergency, and in the ensuing elections in 1977, was decisively defeated. This was the time when, in a period of great adversity, her adroit political skills stood out in stark contrast to the bungling shenanigans of the motley Janata Party coalition that came to power. For every ill-planned move they made to pillory her, she had a rapier response. When Charan Singh, the Home Minister, sent the police to arrest her, she took her time to get ready—and in that period alerted the entire media and her party workers—and then, when the time came to leave for jail, refused to go without being handcuffed. The police were not carrying handcuffs, and what is worse, did not even have clear instructions where to incarcerate her! She spent one night in jail and was unconditionally released the very next day.

In December 1978, she was arrested again. There is an incident of this time which illustrates her remarkable political acumen. Charan Singh's birthday on 23 December was being celebrated with great fanfare at the Ramlila Maidan in Delhi. From the jail, Indira gave meticulous instructions to a senior leader of the Congress party. He was asked to take a taxi to a specific florist on Janpath and purchase a large bouquet. Then, he was told to go to Ramlila grounds, and seek to reach the podium. She warned him that he would be stopped by security, but since he was a known face as a former minister, he must find a police officer who recognises him and manages to reach him to the podium. Once on the podium, he was to ensure that the bouquet is presented to Charan Singh on her behalf, not anonymously, but publicly. There must be, she instructed, a public announcement that the flowers had been sent by Indira Gandhi. The Congress leader managed to implement these precise instructions. Charan Singh, in fact, himself announced with glee that Indira Gandhi herself has felicitated him. Three days later, Indira was out of jail. Next year, Charan Singh ditched his own alliance partners to become prime minister with Congress support, only to have the Congress withdraw support within days. Fresh elections were called, and Indira stormed back to power with a huge majority in 1980.

The enduring image of her on an elephant reaching Belchhi is also a tribute to her political instincts. In May 1977, nine Dalits were burnt alive by an upper caste mob in Belchhi, Bihar. No prominent leader of the Janata Party went to express solidarity with the victims. Indira decided to do so. She landed in Patna by plane; from there, she drove in a car; after a point the road became so bad that she moved to a jeep; a little later even the jeep failed, so she sat on a tractor; when the tractor could not make headway, she climbed onto an elephant and reached Belchhi. That photograph was on the front page of every paper the next day.

No great leader is without her faults or infallible. Indira trusted few; over centralised power; had little compunction in diluting the autonomy of democratic institutions; was excessively tolerant to the wilfulness of her younger son, Sanjay; remained unacceptably vulnerable to mediocre sycophants; and made fatal mistakes by tolerating people like Jarnail Singh Bhindranwale for too long.

But she had great redeeming features too, including a private, lesser-known aspect, where, as a woman and an aesthete with a fine sense of taste and an enduring commitment to the great legacy of India's arts and crafts, she was the natural inheritor of the cerebral refinements of her father. If anyone is in doubt in this regard, I would urge them to read the book, *Two Alone, Two Together*, which is a fairly bulky compilation of the letters between her and Jawaharlal Nehru. What will surprise readers is not the erudition of Nehru—for that is known—but the remarkably intellectual, insightful, informed and thoughtful responses of Indira.

(This piece was originally published on 19 November 2017)

NEED FOR AN UPRIGHT BUREAUCRACY

*T*here is a story, perhaps apocryphal, of a very distinguished member of the Indian Foreign Service, who was, many years ago, our Ambassador in Washington. As his date of retirement approached, he was expecting to get an extension, something still not so common in those days. In lobbying for this cause, he cited several reasons why his continuation was indispensable for the well-being of Indo–US relations. When, after several missives, and undoubtedly many long-distance calls with people who mattered, he heard nothing from the ministry of External Affairs, he sent a final letter requesting for a decision. In reply, he received a telex (the normal fast track mode of communication then) from a junior Under Secretary, informing him, with biting brevity, that when an officer joins service he is aware of his date of retirement, and it would behove him to proceed accordingly. Needless to say, our Ambassador packed his bags and came back, without any great damage ensuing to our relations with America.

This little anecdote is important to illustrate how much things have changed since then. Today, almost every senior bureaucrat expects to get some assignment, either on extension, or on contract, or on re-employment after his retirement. The practice has become so pervasive that it now threatens to undermine the independence of the bureaucracy, once called the 'steel frame' of the government.

The bureaucracy is meant to be apolitical, to give free and frank advice, and to uphold the rules and ethics that should govern the decision-making process, without bowing to any extraneous pressure. As against this, co-option is the natural proclivity of the political class, so that all key agencies of the government become more amenable to sub-serving its interests. In the case of the bureaucracy, one of the most effective ways of achieving this undesirable end is to dangle before a retiring officer the possibility of continued office, and all the perks that it ensures. How can a bureaucrat, in a key position in government, continue to give fearless advice if he is promised, on the unstated condition of 'good' behaviour, the possibility of a post-retirement sinecure, along with the bungalow, staff and salary that goes with it? There are, of course, exceptions to this understandable human vulnerability, but they are, as can only be expected, very rare exceptions.

The very real fear is the emergence, over a period of time, of an unacceptably compromised bureaucracy that is willing to toe the line of political bosses, and, indeed, on occasion collude with them for ends which are manifestly questionable. More importantly, even if there is no unethical issue involved, there is the real danger that officers will, under the temptations offered to them, forfeit their real dharma of stating their views frankly irrespective of the consequences. Officers close to retirement are usually in influential jobs; their ability to give objective advice is all the more crucial, a distinct possibility if the officer has nothing more to lose or to gain. But this is often subverted by the seduction of another coveted assignment, in handing out which politicians have near unfettered powers of selectivity and decision-making.

The time has, therefore, come to seriously take stock of the existing situation. The posts against which a retiring bureaucrat can be 'adjusted' have grown exponentially over the years. Some of these are relevant, and some are not. Unfortunately, the dilution of the independence of the steel frame has grown in corresponding measure. Some sanity, in the form of rules and procedure and norms, are essential. First, there is no reason why a compulsory two-year cooling-off period should not be applicable to all retiring officers; until this two-year period lapses, they would be barred from employment, in any form, either in government or in the private sector. There are some existing rules regarding the taking of jobs in the corporate sector, especially if the private company is in a field directly related to the work done by an officer before he retired. However, this rule is discretionary, and very often breached, including in sensitive sectors, where any decision a bureaucrat took before his retirement, could disproportionately benefit a private player. Even if there is no concrete proof of any correlation, why is the inference wrong that the officer while still in government was not influenced by the 'reward' of being offered a lucrative assignment by the very firm whose cases he was probably involved in deciding?

Secondly, certain jobs, like that of the Central Vigilance Commissioner (CVC), or Director, CBI, or the Comptroller and Auditor General (CAG) or the Chief Election Commissioner (CEC), should not be eligible for *any* government employment after the tenure ends, including governorships, or nomination to political office. Thirdly, certain sensitive and key assignments in government, such as that of the Home Secretary, the Defence Secretary, the Finance Secretary (among others) get a mandatory two-year term on appointment, which normally implies a de facto extension of service. The Foreign Secretary is among the latest to join this select list. If, however, the job is so central to crucial decision-making to merit an extended term, why should the incumbent not be insulated from the lollipop of another job, so that his advice remains free from any extraneous consideration? Fourthly, there is a need for transparent guidelines and a stringent screening process, to curb the arbitrary selectivity and cronyism in doling out these jobs. Fifthly, if a particular officer is transparently indispensable and needs to be kept on (although, no bureaucrat, except in his own eyes, is indispensable), he could, as a rare exception be re-employed, but on contract on a fixed lump sum salary, without the perks of housing, car, etc., which is the real 'carrot' in these assignments.

Officers must know when it is time for them to pack up their bags and retire with dignity. That is good for them, and for their junior colleagues. Otherwise, they become cannon fodder for the political class and accessories to the subversion of a key institution of the polity.

(This piece was originally published on 26 May 2013)

DIPLOMACY

THE CONUNDRUM OF OUR
PAKISTAN POLICY

I have great personal respect for Sushma Swaraj. She is, by far, one of the most competent ministers in the current Cabinet. It is for this reason that I am at a loss to understand what is happening with regard to our policy towards Pakistan.

It is abundantly clear to anyone remotely in the know that Pakistan is absolutely clear about how to deal with India. Pakistan's policy is, as I have said on countless occasions, one of explosive aggression followed by tactical appeasement. This policy has undergone no change with Imran Khan becoming the prime minister of Pakistan. In fact, any civilian prime minister of Pakistan is a puppet of the Deep State consisting of the ISI and the army. Prime ministers may come and go, but the policy of the Deep State remains unchanged, and the incumbent civilian, who is ostensibly 'democratically' elected, has no option but to follow this policy.

This situation explains why Imran Khan, on assuming power, held out an olive branch to India, while Pakistan relentlessly continued its support and sponsorship of terrorism against India. Ceasefire violations have escalated; the Pakistani army has upped its shelling from across the border, killing and displacing civilians; terrorists sponsored by Pakistan have claimed with impunity the lives of our brave armed forces and paramilitary personnel. Aggression, followed by appeasement, has been the consistent policy.

What has been our response? I am afraid we have neither been consistent nor prepared or armed with a strategic response of our own. On the one hand, we have publicly maintained, for some time now, that there can be no talks with Pakistan, in the shadow of terrorism. The formal comprehensive talks were suspended by the previous UPA government precisely for this reason. Even though Prime Minister Modi invited former Pakistani Prime Minister Nawaz Sharif for his swearing-in ceremony, and later air-dashed to Lahore to give a hug to Sharif on his birthday, these talks were not resumed, because Pakistan's transparent nexus with terrorism directed against India not only continued, but escalated, with such brazen attacks as that of Uri and Pathankot.

While not agreeing to the resumption of the composite dialogue process, we have, in addition, made countless statements that *no talks* with Pakistan will be our policy so long as it does not end its verifiable nexus with terrorism. Sushma Swaraj herself said that until the perpetrators of the Mumbai carnage are brought to book, any talks with Pakistan are out of the question. But, just a few weeks after her statement, Modi met with his counterpart, Nawaz Sharif, on the sidelines of the Ufa Summit, and issued a rather ambivalent and questionable joint statement after that.

Imran Khan's offer of talks with India was something we should have expected and been prepared for. In fact, even better, we should have proactively preempted Pakistan's move by becoming the prime mover ourselves. Immediately after his election, we should have issued a formal statement expressing the hope that the new prime minister of Pakistan will eschew the path of terrorism, so that the comprehensive dialogue process can be renewed, with terrorism as the first item on the agenda. Then the ball would have been in Pakistan's court. It would have to respond, and we could manoeuvre the response trajectory.

However, since we were not proactive, the opposite has happened. Pakistan has made the offer of talks, and we are scurrying around to respond. And, our response has been—to say the least—rather egregious. First, we said that the two Foreign ministers will meet on the sidelines of the UNGA in New York. Then we clarified that this will be a meeting, not a dialogue. What is the difference between the two? When two people meet at the level of Foreign ministers, what they say to each other—unless they are on 'maun vrat', a vow of silence—constitutes a dialogue. Such a dialogue may not be at the level of the structured comprehensive dialogue, but it is a dialogue. Hair-splitting on what is a 'talk' and what is a 'dialogue' is, frankly, quite silly.

But more egg on our face was to follow. The very next day the MEA said that the meeting had been cancelled. The reason given for this reversal was the killing of our security personnel by Pakistan-based entities, and the release of postage stamps by 'Pakistan glorifying' militant Burhan Wani, who was killed in an encounter by our security forces. The MEA spokesperson said, 'The evil agenda of Pakistan stands exposed, and the true face of the new Pakistan PM, Imran Khan, has been revealed to the world.'

This is truly mystifying. Were 'Pakistan-based entities' not killing our security personnel when we agreed, just twenty-four hours earlier, for Sushma to meet with her Pakistani counterpart, Shad Mehmood Qureshi? Were we in any doubt that Burhan Wani was a terrorist trained and supported by Pakistan, for us to suddenly realise, in the space of twenty-four hours, that a stamp issued in his name by Pakistan showed the 'true face of the Pakistan PM?'

The truth is that our response was a plain and simple

flip-flop, whose underlying cause is the transparent absence of a well-thought-out strategic policy to deal with our hostile neighbour. In the absence of such a policy, our responses become ad hoc. We appear as diplomatic dilettantes on the international stage, and the advantage, quite unnecessarily, accrues to Pakistan. In this instance, while we were busy explaining the reasons for the abrupt reversal of our decisions, Pakistan has conveyed to the world that India has spurned its offer for talks. Qureshi said as much: 'It is unfortunate that India has not given a positive response. India has once again wasted an opportunity for peace.'

Diplomacy to be effective must be embedded in a strategic matrix. The question is not whether we should talk to Pakistan or not. The real issue is that whatever we do must be in accordance with a well-calibrated strategic policy. There is no point in diverting attention from this basic issue by planning the celebration of anniversaries of the surgical strike. That was a move we welcomed and which paid tribute to our brave soldiers. However, one strike alone is not enough to overlook the continued violence against us from across the border. Nor is a muscular posture a substitute for strategic clarity.

(This piece was originally published on 23 September 2018)

SHOULD INDIA WASH ITS DIRTY POLITICAL LINEN ABROAD?

*P*erhaps I am just old-fashioned. Or, perhaps, the DNA of being a former diplomat still compels professional restraint in me. Or, perhaps, I have not made the transition to being a full-blooded politician. Whatever the reason, I do believe that when the Prime Minister, or the President, or the Vice-President are on a State visit abroad or are attending a multilateral event outside the country, the perennial slugfest of internal politics should momentarily be put on pause, or at the very least, not used to embarrass the dignitary who is, in that constitutional role, representing the country as a whole.

I say this, because on several occasions in the past—and most recently during Prime Minister Narendra Modi's visit to London for the Commonwealth Summit—the Opposition did nothing to reduce, postpone or put on hold, the adrenaline rush of political acrimony directed against him. The result was that even as he was interacting with the leaders of other countries, or speaking at the Summit, anyone who was watching the Indian electronic media or monitoring social media or reading about what was being said about him and his government in India by his political opponents, would have wondered whether he was worth talking to in the first place.

It is a matter of pride that India is a vibrant democracy. With the next parliamentary elections around the corner, and with the Karnataka elections imminent, it is but natural that the political atmosphere will be charged and accusations and counter-accusations will fly fast and thick at the slightest provocation. It may also be true that many of the accusations of the Opposition are not off the mark, and that certain incidents in the country at this time, such as the horrific Unnao and Kathua rape incidents, where the role of some BJP leaders was shockingly deplorable, had outraged the entire country. It is but natural that some of the anger and hostility of this backdrop would cast a shadow when the prime minister was abroad and could not be camouflaged merely by the pageantry of ceremonial pomp and sartorial elegance that is so visible when dignitaries go abroad.

But even so, it is hardly edifying when India publicly washes the dirty linen of its internal political acrimonies before a foreign audience. I believe Opposition leaders would be far more dignified—and, in the process, win far more public respect—if they said that so long as the prime minister is on a State visit abroad and is speaking for India as a whole, there will be a temporary moratorium on the vicious slanging matches directed at him. Visits of this nature are but for a few days. Let the political attacks continue unabated until he leaves the shores of India, and let them resume the moment he returns. But, in the interim, some form of volitional restraint is perhaps desirable.

This advice also applies to the prime minister himself. There have been instances in the past when he has brought up internal politics on foreign soil, especially when he is interacting with NRIs or the Indian community. This is equally undesirable, and—just like with the Opposition—he would win far more respect if he were to say that he would not like to speak of political differences at home. This feeling was voiced by a long-term ally of the BJP, the Shiv Sena. In the latest editorial of its mouthpiece, *Saamana*, it asks the question: 'Is it right for the PM to speak on rape cases in a foreign country? Why should a picture be painted of India as witnessing a rise in corruption and rape cases and as an unsafe country?' The editorial also mentions that Prime Minister Modi had made the same mistake by speaking about black money and corruption, and attacking the Opposition, when he was in Japan. Of course, this criticism, while valid, also begs the question that if the Opposition is so sensitive about the right projection of India's image when the prime minister is abroad, is it prepared to also put in abeyance the virulence of its attacks on him during this period?

When Modi was in London, there were some protests against him there. Peaceful protests are not uncommon by some sections among those living abroad when a Head of State or government comes visiting. But surely, no one can condone the fact that in London, some protestors tore down the Indian flag from an official flagpole for the Commonwealth Summit. According to reports, an Indian journalist was also attacked at London's Parliament Square. It was entirely appropriate for our High Commission to strongly protest against such behaviour. In a statement, the MEA said, 'The UK side has regretted the incident, including at the highest level. The flag was immediately replaced. We expect action, including legal, against the persons involved in the incident and their instigators.'

A spokesperson of the UK Foreign Office said: 'While people have the right to hold peaceful protests, we are disappointed by the action taken by a small minority of in Parliament Square.' More importantly, the spokesperson reiterated, 'The visit to the UK by Prime Minister Modi has strengthened our relationship with India and we look forward to working even more closely together on a number of important areas.' This is precisely the point. When a prime minister goes abroad, he is there to discuss, at the highest level, issues that are vital to India's interests, including economic interaction, investments, security, defence collaborations, technology, multilateral collaboration, and the fight against terror, apart from bilateral specific matters. His brief, and that of his political detractors in India, must be to ensure substantive gains in these matters, and not a continuation of the incessant linguistic vitriol that goes on at home.

Mature democracies run as much by the letter of the law, as they do by the spirit of national interest. When there is an enlightened combination of both letter and spirit, conventions emerge, of behaviour and custom, practice and restraints. It is time for all political parties to think of such conventions when India's interests are being pursued abroad.

(This piece was originally published on 22 April 2018)

THE CHALLENGE OF THE
SPOKEN WORD

The Official Spokesman of the Ministry of External Affairs does not have an easy job, and I should know because I have done that job myself when I was in the foreign service. He or she has to often try and convincingly explain foreign policy decisions that are ab initio inexplicable. On 26 December 2017, the National Security Adviser of India, Ajit Doval, and his Pakistani counterpart, Lt General Nasser Khan Janjua (Retd) met at an undisclosed destination in Bangkok, as part of, what was described as 'operational level talks'.

Not surprisingly, Raveesh Kumar, the Spokesman, was asked about this meeting and how it had taken place when we have publicly said that 'terror and talks cannot go together.' It was not an easy question to answer, and certainly, Kumar was not the maker of the policy that had put him in this predicament. His response, however, took the diplomatic cake as far as words without meanings go: 'We have said terror and talks cannot go together,' he pronounced, 'but talks on terror can definitely go ahead.'

This statement must rank as a classic of self-contradictory assertion. It accepted that talks will not be resumed so long as terrorism from across the border ceases. But, simultaneously it asserted that talks can happen on the issue of terrorism. Since terrorism is the reason why we put talks with Pakistan on hold, what does a statement mean when it says that terrorism will be the reason why talks 'can definitely go ahead?'

Since I am reluctant to attribute a complete lack of strategic clarity to the MEA, I am inclined to believe that the statement it put out represents one of the best examples of the philosophical ambivalence of Hindu metaphysics, wherein empirical reality exists as maya at one level and does not at another level, wherein all is subsumed in the attribute-less omnipresence of Brahman. What appears as real, is unreal; what appears to be unreal, is actually the real. The universe is a conjurer's play, where contradictions that seem to exist are an invention of the mind. All binaries are false, and all binaries are true. Everything depends on the vision of the observer; negation is assertion, and assertion is negation. Opposites are subsumed in a larger unity, known only to the one who knows, but opaque to the mundane world. In such a philosophical vision, talks with Pakistan do not happen even when they happen, and happen even when the official policy remains that they cannot happen!

Or, perhaps, our foreign office has borrowed the sublime notion of *syadavada* of Jaina philosophy. In support of such a carefully thought out doctrine of relativity, Jainism cites the parable of seven blind men examining an elephant, and depending on what part they are in touch with, arriving at a different conclusion of what it is. At a philosophical level, this revolt against absolutism is enshrined in the *saptabhangi* or seven-step theory whose purpose is to establish that only a singular assertion of reality can be deceptive. The seven possibilities are: maybe it is; maybe it is not; maybe, it is, and it is not; maybe it is inexpressible; maybe, it is and is inexpressible; maybe, it is not and is inexpressible; maybe, it is and is not and is inexpressible.

Jainism formulated this remarkable doctrine to counter dogmatism. Our foreign office seems to have adopted it to hide the complete absence of strategic clarity. The saptabhangi for our foreign policy with Pakistan is: talks with Pakistan cannot happen; talks with Pakistan can happen; talks with Pakistan cannot happen unless Pakistan agrees to stop its sponsorship of terrorism; talks with Pakistan can happen because Pakistan will not stop its sponsorship of terrorism; if NSAs of the two countries—arguably the most influential interlocutors from either side—meet, they met, but talks did not happen; if talks did not happen, then presumably they visited Bangkok coincidentally at the same time to take a respite from the cold of Delhi and Islamabad; talks, until terrorism stops have no meaning, but NSAs can meet to see if talks can have meaning.

The fact of the matter is that our foreign policy with Pakistan is replete with unpardonable contradictions and zig-zags in policy formulations that would leave even our most insightful metaphysicians stumped. The reason for this is the absence of strategic policy, and a resort to a never-ending series of ad hoc steps. If we need to review our earlier policy of suspending the formal dialogue process with Pakistan, we should do so in a carefully calibrated manner. Engagement has its own dividends, provided it is carried out in a way that is anticipated and planned for. On the other hand, if our policy remains one of no talks unless Pakistan-sponsored terrorism ceases—or at least reduces—then talks without talks in the manner in which our NSAs met in Bangkok makes a mockery of that decision. While the USA can play a key role in putting pressure on Pakistan on its nexus with terrorism, a country of the prowess and size of India cannot expect others to do for it what it refuses to do itself.

It appears that the only policy we have for our western neighbour is the absence of policy, both in the short and mid-term, and to lurch along from one event to another, alternating between mindless bravado at one level and surreptitious talks at another. Can we expect our foreign office to devise a strategic framework to deal with Pakistan, taking into account its internal situation, the level of ceasefire violations, the need for engagement, the importance of people-to-people contacts, the value of humanitarian gestures, the geopolitical imperatives, including the role of China, and developments in Afghanistan, while retaining a firm riposte to Pakistan-sponsored terrorism?

Given our track record thus far, it seems to be a tall order. Until then, our hapless foreign-office Spokesman will have no option but to forget foreign policy and adopt the wondrous ambivalences of philosophy.

(This piece was originally published on 14 January 2018)

WHY DO WE KOWTOW TO CHINA
ON THE DALAI LAMA?

*I*n diplomacy, foolhardiness is as damaging as pusillanimity. To show bravado, without the ability to implement it, displays a lack of maturity. To show timidity, when the situation does not warrant it, shows a lack of strategic resolve. These thoughts come to mind in light of the recent directive sent by Cabinet Secretary P.K. Sinha to the Centre, and states that senior leaders and government officials should refrain from attending functions marking sixty years in exile of the Dalai Lama. The directive was reportedly prompted by a note by Foreign Secretary Vijay Gokhale that such a step was advisable in view of the fact that India–China relations were going through a sensitive phase. As a result, the Tibetan government-in-exile has cancelled two events in Delhi: one, an interfaith prayer meeting at Rajghat, and two, a 'Thank You India' function, which has been shifted to Dharamshala.

Is this genuflection before Chinese sensitivities justified? Perhaps there are facts, or new developments, to which the MEA is privy to, but, prima facie, this deference to China is difficult to understand. The Dalai Lama has been in India for the last sixty years. India has reiterated to the Chinese that we recognise Tibet as a part of China and that His Holiness will refrain from any political activity. That this has largely been the case is verifiable and becomes manifestly clear through the nature of activities planned to commemorate the sixtieth anniversary: special prayers, mass tree plantations, yoga events, cleanliness drives, the feeding of the hungry and homeless, and the distribution of blankets to the poor. There is nothing 'political' in this, or different from what the Dalai Lama, a deeply revered religious figure internationally, has been promoting all these years. Why is China then taking umbrage, and even more importantly, why are we so suddenly deferential to their sensitivities?

Has China done anything in recent times to deserve a more compliant India? I don't think so. In fact, it has been particularly hostile. It has blocked India's efforts to designate dreaded Jaish-e-Mohammad chief, Masood Azhar, as a terrorist by the UN. It has done its best to block India's entry to the Nuclear Supplies Group. It has brazenly gone ahead with the proposal to build the Belt Road Initiative (BRI) in Pakistan through Gilgit–Baltistan, a territory that India claims as its own. Last year in June, it also escalated the Doklam crisis by attempting to build a road in the disputed area at the tri-junction between India, China and Bhutan. Geopolitical strategist Brahma Chellaney has now reported that, in spite of the Indian government's claim of disengagement, the Chinese are continuing to build sentry posts, trenches and helipads in Doklam.

Over the years, China has consistently implemented its policy towards India of 'engagement with containment,' which has meant showing India its place whenever necessary and with impunity. At the time of the visit of President Xi Jin Ping to India in September 2014, Chinese troops invaded India in significant numbers at Chumar in Ladakh. We predictably downplayed this outrageous behaviour. On bilateral trade—which is hugely in China's favour—China milks the Indian market while limiting market access to our exports. Geo-politically, China has penetrated deep into our sphere of influence by acquiring strategic assets in Sri Lanka, such as the Hambantota port, and by meddling against our interests in Nepal, Bangladesh, and more recently, in the Maldives. It regularly gives sanctuaries to anti-India insurgents in the North East. While we seem to have looked the other way, it has invested billions of dollars in Pakistan Occupied Kashmir or POK, an area recognised internationally as disputed, but resisted our attempts to foray for oil in the open waters of the South China Sea.

On Arunachal Pradesh, which is undeniably a part of India but which China continues to designate as disputed and calls 'South Tibet', the Chinese have been unrelentingly intimidating. Earlier, the Chinese government announced that Indian citizens from Arunachal Pradesh will be given stapled visas to travel to China. We protested but rather mutely. An effective retaliatory response to this affront should have been to say that we shall give stapled visas to Chinese of Tibetan origin. When Narendra Modi visited Arunachal Pradesh last month, the Chinese lodged a formal diplomatic protest! In April 2017 when the Dalai Lama went to Arunachal Pradesh, the Chinese lost all diplomatic restraint and unilaterally named six places in that state on their own map.

The problem is that we have too low a threshold of happiness about Chinese behaviour. In April this year, China appeared to be a little 'nice' to us at the Financial Action Task Force (FATF) meeting in Paris, by withdrawing its opposition to a US proposal to place Pakistan on the FATF's watch list of countries that have financial links to terrorism. We took it as a huge victory. But China plays this game of aggression and conciliation as per a strategic plan, and support to Pakistan, notwithstanding this 'concession', will remain an integral part of its policy to contain India.

So, with such a track record, why are we so readily willing to kowtow to China? Are we a natural punching bag? In diplomacy, perceptions greatly matter. Nations respect nations that respect themselves. This is particularly so in the case of China. A timid and submissive India reinforces the Dragon's self-belief in its ordained destiny of global dominance as the 'middle kingdom' and strengthens its conviction that India can be easily bullied. We need to understand that while China may be militarily stronger than us, we are not a walk-over either. Such meekness, particularly from a government whose leaders took pride in their muscular approach to diplomatic relations, hardly does credit to them, or to our national interests. We need to have good relations with China and should do what is required for this, but only in conformity with our self-esteem and as part of a strategic game plan. A little bit of attitude will do our diplomacy good. Perhaps, this couplet of Ghalib can inspire us: *Mat pooch ki kya haal hai mera tere peeche; Tu dekh ki kya rang hai tera mere aage:* Don't ask how I will fare under your sway; You see how you will fare under my watch!

(This piece was originally published on 11 March 2018)

FOREIGN POLICY: STRATEGY NOT AD-HOCISM

*F*oreign policy has been much in the news recently, but for all the wrong reasons. The moves by Pakistan and China mostly have us on the back foot. Our handling of Maldives leaves much to be desired. And, our relations with Sri Lanka have plummeted as we struggle to deal with our own internal contradictions.

The real problem is that we deal with foreign policy on an ad-hoc basis. We react to events rather than anticipating them. We are absorbed with the surface symptoms but are unable to pinpoint the central malaise. The central malaise is that our approach to security, of which foreign policy is an integral part, is sloppy, unplanned, reactive and completely lacking in focus and will. In short, the real problem is that modern India has not developed a clear-cut, unequivocal and well-thought-out *security doctrine*.

Strategic vision requires the ability to adopt that policy which is best suited for a particular situation. That is why Chanakya articulated the four tools of *sama, dama, danda, bheda*— reconciliation, inducement, deterrent action and subversion—and the lesser-known asana, the strategic art of deliberately sitting on the fence. Each tactic has a specific use. The need for us today to have an effective security doctrine incorporating each of the elements above is self-evident, given the fact that we are located in one of the most troubled neighbourhoods of the world. We have two implacably hostile states as our neighbours: Pakistan and China; Afghanistan is endemically unstable; Nepal is flirting with China; large parts of Myanmar are under the sway of terrorists of varying hues; the entire region is in the grip of fundamentalist and violent radicalism; China's policy of encircling India by finding strategic bridgeheads in our neighbours is known; we have the problem of externally sponsored terrorism, and now increasingly home-grown terrorism; and as many as 200 districts in eight states are infested with Naxal violence.

Given the gravity of this scenario, it is unfortunate that our foreign-policy establishment has been devalued to an unprecedented extent in recent times. The routine day-to-day requirements of diplomacy have overwhelmed any cerebral policy-making, both short-term and long-term, which must be the prime purpose of a foreign office. Institutions are devalued when they forget their principal focus and allow minutiae to crowd out the fundamentals. For instance, a critical component of the MEA should be the Policy Planning Division (PPD), which is currently near defunct. It needs to be managed by the best and the brightest who, free from the routine work of diplomacy, present policy options on a continuous and dynamic basis. In particular, security diplomacy must be embedded in a first-rate PPD. In an ideal situation, the External Affairs minister should see a memo prepared by the PPD the first thing in office, and only then go about his official routine.

It is equally important that the MEA independently provide policy inputs to aid decision making on the part of the government. This means that as an institution, it must carefully weigh the pros and cons of any situation, and make its voice heard in the Prime Minister's

Office or PMO. There was a time when, at least partially, the MEA had a point of view that—even if it was at variance with the PMO—it was prepared to defend. This enriched policymaking and gave to the institution a sense of defined purpose. Today, the MEA has become a mechanical adjunct of the biases of the PMO.

Not surprisingly, our foreign policy is mostly reactive. This is particularly evident in our reaction to Pakistan and China. China follows a policy of 'containment with engagement' with single-minded focus. Pakistan has perfected a policy of explosive aggression and tactical appeasement. India remains undecided on which to respond to, without a cohesive policy framework that anticipates both. China openly arms Pakistan when it knows that the latter's arsenal is directed against us. It makes major economic investments brazenly in POK, but when India contemplates a 'quadrilateral' dialogue with the US, Japan and Australia, or a trilateral dialogue with Japan and the US, China protests and India is deferential.

There is no harm in talks or negotiations or other forms of engagement so long as we see them as a means to an end of our own making. But that is rarely the case. The initiative is always taken by the other party, secure in the well-justified belief that our reactions will follow predictable lines. In fact it sometimes appears that China and Pakistan have mastered Chanakya's strategic thinking to the same degree that we have forgotten them.

The earlier improvised handling of the Maldives, and the way we responded to the UNHC resolution on Sri Lanka, which neither served our purpose nor that of Sri Lanka or the Tamils, are symptoms of a major country in an explosive neighbourhood still struggling to craft a well-thought-out security doctrine, and as importantly, demonstrating the will to carry it through. The cause of the Tamils is undoubtedly important, but it must be dovetailed with the understanding that a security-oriented foreign policy needs to be insulated from the pulls and pressures of coalition or regional politics. Any country willing to sacrifice its overall and long-term security concerns for short-term political gains does not deserve to be in power.

(This piece was originally published on 31 March 2013)

THE GREAT INDIAN RAILWAY BAZAAR

*A*irports can sometimes be the venue for unexpected rendezvous. On a recent visit to Germany, while sitting at the lounge at the Frankfurt airport, I ran into fellow writer-diplomat Navtej Sarna, who was one of my successors, many times removed, as the official spokesperson of the MEA. Since we both had time to kill, we talked of many things. One of them, for some random reason, was the remarkable transformation of rail services in China. I recalled this especially after the recent scandal at Rail Bhavan broke.

Navtej told me of his high-speed train journey from Shanghai to Beijing. The magnetic levitation track allowed the train to travel without the slightest jerk, as though it was floating in the air, at a speed of over 300 km an hour, covering the 1,318 km journey to Beijing in a little over five hours. It was, Navtej said, one of the most exciting rail journeys he had experienced. On my return to Delhi, I did some more reading on the state of the railways in China. Today, China has the world's largest high-speed rail network covering a route of 9,300 km. It also has the world's longest high-speed line, stretching for 2,295 km from Beijing to Guangzhou. High-speed trains were introduced in 2007; the aim is that they will cover 18,000 km by 2015. To begin with, the country had collaborations with global giants like Siemens and Kawasaki, but now all trains that can reach an operational speed of 380 km an hour are produced indigenously.

Of course, there is corruption in the Chinese railways too. In 2011, the Rail Minister Liu Zhijun had to resign on charges of corruption following a fatal high-speed train accident at Wenzhou in July of that year. But while corruption is always to be condemned, and China has its own share of the corrupt, particularly in the ruling elite, the fact of the matter is that China is making giant strides in a great number of important spheres, of which the railways is an outstanding example.

Contrast this with our record. Our railways, which started out in 1947 as superior to the Chinese, is today on the brink of disaster. In 2011, a major train accident occurred almost every month; some months recorded more than one accident, the worst being July 2011, when there were as many as seven accidents claiming over a hundred lives. From April to July 2012, there were ten accidents claiming over a hundred lives. Forget high-speed trains, the Railway ministry is woefully lagging even in safety measures, the procurement of new rolling stock, track renewals, training, electrification and electronic signalling. Our fastest trains average a speed of eighty km, and more often than not, not even that. In spite of this, ministers in charge have in the past spent more time in their state capitals than in Rail Bhavan. In fact, it has been reported that Mukul Roy, the former Railway minister, averaged only about four days a month in his office in nearly five months on the job.

The sordid saga of Pawan Kumar Bansal has to be seen in this context. In a country where, in spite of the railway network being the transport lifeline for millions of Indians, the entire institution is close to collapse, we have the disgusting spectacle of people at the helm busy greasing the palms of touts to get a posting to run lucrative departments. The tragedy is that certain departments are favoured not because they allow a person to contribute to the maximum, but because they are the best avenues for illicit money. And the quantum of money is not small. It beggars the imagination that a technocrat of the highest seniority will pay as much as ten crores and more to get a specific job. One can only imagine how much more he will make for himself and his masters, once he gets it. The tragedy is also that this money will be made entirely for personal greed. The much-needed reform of the railways will remain a completely irrelevant factor.

The episode also raises the question of who to trust. I have known Pawan Kumar Bansal for many years. It was my genuine belief that he was an honest politician. To now find out that he was running a highly questionable parallel business empire by taking advantage of his ministerial posts, and that his nephew was the tout who was collecting huge sums of money for posts at the highest echelon under the minister's direct watch, has come as a real shock. Many details of this gravy train are already in the public realm. More details will emerge as the CBI completes its enquiry, especially now that the Supreme Court has put the searchlight for the agency to carry out its mandate without taking orders from those it is investigating.

The progress made by the railways in China is an eye-opener of what can be achieved when systems work. There is corruption of considerable magnitude in China too, and I have always had reservations about the authoritarian structure of its polity, and believe that democracy is a slower but far more enduring basis in the long run for a country's success. However, I am compelled to conclude that if corruption cannot be completely excluded in any country, those countries where it does not become an absolute barrier to deliverables for the people are better than those which are corrupt *and* inefficient. When corruption is rampant and pervasive, and the functioning of the system is, at the same time, flabby and inefficient, it is a deadly combination. Countries where this happens are described as a basket case. It is time that we face the sobering truth that if immediate steps are not taken for systemic change, India is on the verge of becoming a basket case. Perhaps the only hope is that the people of India, whose interests are constantly sacrificed, will say enough is enough.

(This piece was originally published on 12 May 2013)

INDIA'S MEMBERSHIP OF THE NSG

Since the Op-Ed page of *The Asian Age* allows for democratic dialogue, I thought I would pen a rejoinder to Padma Rao Sunderji's piece on the Nuclear Supplier Group or NSG.

The making of foreign policy is a continuum. It should not, normally, be the subject of a partisan political divide where acrimony substitutes reasoned discussion, and name-calling replaces rational debate. But, democratic nations can—and must—analyse the direction and substance of foreign policy, and provide more that one perspective to any initiative.

Should India attempt to become a member of the NSG? The answer, to my mind, is a conditional 'yes'. Was India's recent bid to become a member the right way to pursue this goal? The answer, in my view, is a categorical 'no'.

Why do I say so? If membership of the NSG was likely to come India's way on the basis of an objective assessment preceded by hard-nosed backroom diplomacy, the prime minister's frenetic trip around the world pleading at the Chancelleries of countries like Ireland, Mexico and Switzerland would have been worth the effort. But if such an outcome was ab initio substantially in doubt, what compelled our prime minister to act as though NSG membership was at this juncture a matter of utmost national prestige? After all, the waiver provided by the NSG to India in 2008 following the signing of the Civil Nuclear Agreement with the USA allows us to participate in trade in civilian nuclear technology and equipment even though all our nuclear facilities are not under nuclear safeguards. A hurriedly planned bid, where success was far from ensured, has another flip side: endangering the benefits already obtained under the earlier waiver by pushing NSG countries to revisit the criteria adopted to make this exception to India in 2008.

On how we went about the NSG merry-go-round, I have serious reservations on the timing, the assumptions, and the methodology. The timing was wrong because nothing indicated that China would play ball or sever its collusion with Pakistan. Whatever the velocity of the *jhoola* (swing) on which Narendra Modi and Chinese President Xi Jinping enjoyed a view of the Sabarmati in Ahmedabad in September 2014, our recent relations with China have been far from zingy. While Xi Jinping was still our guest in India, we witnessed one of the biggest Chinese invasions into our territory. China still persists with stapled visas for people from Arunachal Pradesh. It blocks action in the UN against dreaded terrorists like Mazhoor Asad. And, it persists with its massive investments in POK, both in infrastructure and in building the One Belt, One Road (OBOR) project through POK to the port of Gwadar. Why should we have thought then that China would accede to India's request for NSG membership when Pakistan was vociferously opposing such a move, and wanted membership for itself?

The assumption that the USA would swing the deal for us was equally flawed. During President Obama's visit to India in January 2015, Modi may have affectionately addressed him by his first name, 'Barrack', a record nineteen times during a half-an-hour interaction, but this should not have prevented our esteemed prime minister from realising that Obama was in the last few months of his presidency. There are limitations to what a 'lame duck' President can do, and certainly, it does appear that Obama's exertions in our interest were far less than that of George Bush in 2008. Goodwill apart, smart nations make a coldly clinical assessment of the potency of a country's intervention in their favour. Did Modi's exuberance about his so-called 'personal rapport' with Barrack influence our foreign office on what the US will do for us on NSG?

The assumption that China will be isolated in its opposition to us was also wrong. As many as seven (nine according to China) countries of the forty-eight-member group expressed reservations on our candidature, including countries like Switzerland that Modi had just visited. The NSG is a club. It has its rules for membership, one of which is that a country must be a signatory to the discriminatory Non-Proliferation Treaty or NPT. Since there is no question of India signing the NPT, our application required members to reexamine the criteria for membership and devise an exception for India that would keep Pakistan out. Achieving such an outcome required months of quiet backroom diplomacy. Did this precede our prime minister's last minute and hurried summitry?

From the evidence available, it would appear not. And, this brings me to the question of methodology. Judged by the number of visits he has made abroad, Modi has shown unprecedented 'activism' in foreign policy. But is mere activism a substitute for careful, calibrated strategic planning? However much the adulation our prime minister may have received abroad in NRI forums, ultimately, foreign policy cannot be an event-management exercise and has to be judged by results, not the pageantry and pomp and frequency of visits abroad. In the specific case of the NSG imbroglio, no country would normally put its prime minister forward before ensuring that the outcome is commensurate with this exposure.

I do not believe that India needs to kowtow before China. Other countries respect those countries that respect themselves, and if China resents our growing closeness to the USA and to Japan and calls us the 'spoilt, smug golden boy of the west', so be it. But if India wants to look China in the eye (*aankh mein aankh dal kar baat karna*, as Modi put it in his first interview to a TV channel recently), then let us do it with better strategic planning and anticipation. At present, far from isolating China, we have isolated ourselves. More worryingly, we may have just opened up the way for Pakistan's entry into the NSG. This was a risk we need not have invited since there was no immediate hurry for this unprepared bid for our own membership. And, finally, as former Foreign Secretary Shyam Saran has warned, I do hope that what we have done now does not prompt the NSG to revisit the terms and conditions of the India-specific 2008 waiver.

(This piece was originally published on 3 July 2016)

STRATEGIC RESPONSE TO CHINA

*M*ore than two millennia ago, in the fourth century BCE, Chanakya deposed a tyrannical king, helped to repel the Greeks, united a fractious territory, groomed a king and put him on the throne of Magadha, and made the Maurya kingdom, extending from Afghanistan to Bengal and southern India, the first ever empire in India's history. He wrote the *Arthashastra*, perhaps the world's first comprehensive treatise on statecraft, some 1,800 years before Machiavelli wrote *The Prince*.

The *Arthashastra* contains an important chapter on the conduct of foreign policy. Circumstances may have changed dramatically since then, but the need for strategic clarity—which was Chanakya's strength—is as relevant now as it was then. Such clarity is at test in the serious faceoff between India and China in Doklam, near the tri-junction between India, China and Bhutan.

It is wise that India's reaction, against blatant Chinese provocation, has been measured, and has kept open the option of diplomatic resolution. Sama, or reconciliation, was the first dictum of Chanakya's famous formula of sama, dama (incentives), danda (punishment) and bheda (sowing discord). Most people don't know that Chanakya also spoke about a fifth stratagem—asana—

the strategic art of deliberately *not* taking a decision and sitting on the fence.

However, not responding in like manner to increasingly aggressive Chinese rhetoric does not mean that we should be confused about our giant neighbour's tactic or intention. China has a clear-cut policy towards India: engagement with containment. This policy sees India as a competitor that must be engaged but kept in place. The timing and nature of Chinese aggression in the Doklam plateau are entirely in keeping with this policy. Only recently, India, in a good strategic move, held naval exercises with Japan and the USA off the Malabar coast. China sees this as a hostile act, aimed at what it believes it is destined to be—the Middle Kingdom around which the globe must revolve.

If we retain clarity on what China's 'psychic apparatus', in terms of its foreign policy objectives, it will become easier to interpret the consistency with which it has acted against Indian interests. The list of its hostile actions, not necessarily in chronological order, is long: the demand for stapled visas for our citizens in Arunachal Pradesh; the blocking of our membership in the NSG; investments of billions of dollars in the POK; the building of OBOR through territory that we claim as ours; the attempt to encircle India by calibrated interactions and investments with our neighbours; unfounded objections to our exploration of oil in the South China Sea; carefully timed intrusions into our territory along the several thousand kilometres long LAC, including, amazingly enough, in Chumar, when Chinese President Xi Jin Ping was on a state visit to India; deliberate indifference to the yawning trade imbalance between both countries, with China 'dumping' its goods on us, and raising invisible tariff barriers against our exports; and, blocking the naming of dreaded terrorist Masood Azhar by the UN.

The last point, in particular, highlights China's open and defiant collusion with Pakistan against India. There can be no other reason why China, which is itself not impervious to terrorist threats by fanatical Islamic groups, should back Pakistan in this matter. The aim is crystal clear: Pakistan must be cultivated as an all-weather ally in order to keep India encircled. The strategic takeaway for us is that we must be ready to face two neighbours in open collusion against us.

If so much is obvious, we need to be absolutely clear about our strategic imperatives. Above all, there is no need to display unwarranted docility to Chinese aggression. In this context, our decision not to attend the recent OBOR multilateral conference convened by China was entirely correct. In fact, I believe that we should, in addition, have sent a protest note to all the countries that did attend, stating clearly that the proposed road passes through territory that belongs to India. One can only imagine how China would have reacted if India convened a conference for the building of a road that would go through territory claimed by China! Even now, China routinely sends a strong protest note to any country that the Dalai Lama travels to, and recently, when His Holiness visited Arunachal Pradesh, the threatening nature of the Chinese response was emphatically offensive.

I have said this earlier, countries respect countries that respect themselves. For too long now, China has come to assume that its aggressive psychological warfare against India gets only the predictable 'measured' response.

India is an emerging superpower herself. Even in defence terms, it is not a walkover for any hostile power. The Chinese have better and bigger defence prowess, but 2017 is not 1962. Yet, as once again Chanakya emphasised, countries must never neglect their defence preparedness. We have full faith in our armed forces, but we need to do everything possible to ensure that they are well equipped and battle-ready. A serious overhaul of our indigenous public-sector defence production is urgently required. Equally important is to improve the infrastructure on our side of the border. China has a motorised road going right up to Doklam. It can move thirty divisions with 15,000 soldiers each to the Line of Actual Control within a month.

The face-off at Doklam should be the turning point to change our usual response to China's threats. The plateau has far too great a strategic importance for us to yield. Nor can we let our time-tested friend Bhutan down. If sama, which in this case implies the conciliatory reach of diplomacy, works, well and good. But, if it doesn't, India must convey to China that, frankly, enough is enough.

(This piece was originally published on 13 August 2017)

THE WORLD IS WATCHING INDIA

I just returned from a trip to France to co-chair the annual Indo-French literary salon. The occasion gave me an opportunity to interact with a large number of people, both in literature and outside. There is considerable interest in this European capital on what is happening in India, and surprisingly, people are quite well informed on even the minutiae of the fast-moving political developments back home. Those who spoke to me were not necessarily from the official establishment, but people from different walks of life, including old India lovers, academics, and young entrepreneurs watching carefully what India has to offer.

I have isolated two issues, not only for their frequent reiteration but because of their importance. Firstly, the French are watching carefully the rise of Narendra Modi and the actions of the new government led by him. This interest is not without admiration but is also laced with a great deal of curiosity. What does the new dispensation mean for India? What kind of a man is Modi? What does this mean for the development of the Indian economy and the new opportunities for foreign investors?

But there is also concern. Several of my interlocutors wanted to know what will happen to the social consensus that has been one of the foundations of the Indian Republic. Will the delicately woven, centuries-old plural tapestry of India unravel? Are tensions between people of different faiths likely to exacerbate? Will the BJP insensitively pursue its Hindutva agenda, and what would be the consequences if it does? How will the BJP deal with some of the more rabid communal elements in the sangh parivar? What is the reality of the campaign of 'love jihad?' Will the 'moral' brigade of the sangh parivar run riot? Will Hindi be imposed across India? Will Sanskrit now be made compulsory, and how will Indians respond to this evangelical fiat? There were even trite questions on whether meat will be banned.

In responding to these questions, I was guided by the cardinal principle that internal political differences are best voiced within India. For instance, to several questions on what the creation of a separate ministerial responsibility for the propagation of yoga means, I ventured to say that yoga was a great civilisational asset for India, and any focused attempt to popularise it within India, including in schools abroad, was a good step. At the same time, I added that I remain confident that yoga will not be seen within a narrow religious prism, nor will it be used to push a communal agenda.

My central takeaway was that to a great many people abroad who are watching us carefully, India does not merely represent the sum of its immediate political developments or the aggregate of its current economic policies. It is seen as a civilisation, with myriad strands and vibrant diversities, a crucible of over a billion people, whose viability is both a cause of admiration and a test for composite democratic societies everywhere. Any attempt to tinker with this remarkably syncretic entity will cause foreboding, including among hard-nosed political scientists and economists and corporate players. When, at the recent World Hindu Congress, Ashok Singhal, president of the Vishwa Hindu Parishad (VHP) said that after 800 years, Hindu rule is back in India; his statement is likely to create consternation not only in India but also abroad.

A second issue in the minds of people was the rise of China, and collaterally, the state of India–China relations. Of course, China is a bigger power than India, both territorially and in terms of GDP and military hardware. It is today the world's largest manufacturer, the largest exporter, and by the end of this year will overtake the USA in purchasing power parity terms, as the world's largest economy. China and India are both seen as the new stars, not only in Asia but on the global stage. The fact that they have an unresolved territorial dispute and frequent skirmishes along the border was seen partly as proof of the continuing rivalry between the two Asian giants.

Europe, as part of its own history, tends, I think, to see the rise of nations in hostility or rivalry terms. But, Europe has also succeeded in forging the largest and most powerful collective in the world, transcending political and economic boundaries, in the form of the European Union. Will China and India contribute to global stability, or will their jostling for primacy be a cause of instability in the world, was the subtext of the questions in this area. China was seen as the more aggressive and ascendant power, but India's strengths, including most overtly in being a democracy, was mentioned.

In India, we often become completely absorbed in our insular politics. We forget that the world is watching India too, and with renewed interest every passing year. That observation has percolated to the layperson as well. This ceaseless evaluation must require us to pause and to evaluate our own actions beyond merely the prism of immediate political machinations. There is more at stake than just the transient highs and lows of internal politics. On the front line is the image and substance of what India is and what it stands for. The communications revolution has put us on stage as never before.

And, occasionally, transcending our presumptions about ourselves, it is good to expose ourselves to the hopes and concerns about us beyond our borders.

(This piece was originally published on 23 November 2014)